G000067019

The fisherman's guide to

# Coarse Fishing

Published by Marshall Cavendish Books Limited
58 Old Compton Street
London W1V 5PA



This material was first published by Marshall Cavendish Limited in the publication *Fisherman's Handbook*

First Printed in 1979

Printed in Hong Kong

ISBN 0 85685 644 4

# Introduction

Fishing means many different things to many different people. To the young angler, it offers the possibility of connecting with a large fish that will test his strength and skill. To the adult fisherman with commitments at home and at work, it will offer the opportunity to escape to the comparative solitude of the river bank where he can pit his wits against natural adversaries in their wild state.

In *The Fisherman's Guide to Coarse Fishing* we have attempted to include something for everyone. The book is divided into four sections. The initial part is concerned with the freshwater species most commonly encountered explaining their characteristics, habitat and the baits which may be offered in order to catch them. The second deals with fishing tackle and includes step-by-step information enabling some of the simpler items of equipment such as floats and plugs to be made at home simply and cheaply. This should appeal to the younger enthusiast with a limited budget. Bait has a section of its own beginning with the ubiquitous maggot and caster and progressing to the less commonly known baits such as silkweed and wasp grub. Methods of collection or breeding are considered where they become relevant. The techniques sections remains the heart of the book and here each style of fishing is dealt with in turn, with reference to bait, tackle and species sought.

*The Fisherman's Guide to Coarse Fishing* approaches its subject in an interesting way: it provides not only the information the less experienced angler needs to know before he goes fishing but also items to extend the interest of the more experienced enthusiast.

# Contents

# Coarse Fishing

# Roach

You will rarely hear an angler speak of the roach in terms of fishy 'battles' or 'rod-benders'. He cannot stretch his arms apart to describe this fish. The average mature roach is between 8in and 10in long, and the vast majority of fish are considerably smaller.

It is very difficult for the non-angler to appreciate what impels anglers to rise at four in the morning in search of this humble and extremely common fish. Yet any Saturday or Sunday morning will find thousands of them deserting their beds in a passion of anticipation for a 10in fish which is quite inedible.

**Fish that casts a spell**

Few anglers could explain such enthusiasm. It is an act of faith, almost a religion. Those who tried would probably describe the spell the roach casts in terms of variety—variety of shape, colour and size, variety of waters to fish, variety of baits and methods, and the ever-changing and endless variety of landscapes and environments to which the angler is led in his quest for excellent roach fishing. More than any other species, the roach shows that fishing is not just about catching fish.

Roach are not much to look at, but their variety does begin with colour and shape. There are two extreme forms of coloration in mature fish. Most anglers are familiar with the bronze-flanked roach found in the Kennet or Hampshire Avon, as well as with the more common silver-flanked fish found in most waters. Both varieties are nevertheless found side by side in many waters. The body shape of mature fish varies in that most roach are slim and streamlined, reminiscent of the dace, while, also found, but less common, is the full-bodied, deep-bellied fish that is often found among the angler's specimens.

**General factors**

It is tempting to suppose that the slimmer fish are found in swift streamy waters such as Thames, Avon or Stour, where their streamlining would be advantageous. You might also fairly expect that the fuller-bodied variety would inhabit the sluggish rivers, lakes and other stillwaters. Nothing could be further from the truth for both shapes are found not only in the same rivers or lakes, but also in the same shoals. Clearly,

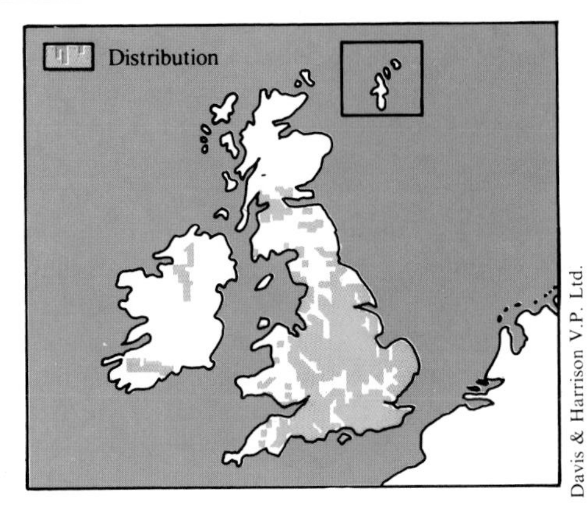


Davis & Harrison V.P. Ltd.

### Habitat

*The roach,* Rutilus rutilus, *is common in all English freshwaters which support weeds, insects, snails and algae that form its natural diet.*

### Bait

*All freshwater baits, float-fished or on ledger rig, catch the roach.*

*(Below) The slow-flowing rivers of East Anglia are ideal for the roach fisherman.*

Rod Sutterby

England Scene

these variations of colour and shape are due to genetic and not environmental factors, the characteristics being transmitted from parents to offspring.

The roach (*Rutilus rutilus*) is found commonly in southern, central, and northern England as well as in southern Scotland and eastern Wales. It is less common in the North and West, and not found in the extreme West of England and Wales, nor north of Loch Lomond.

**Where 'roach' are rudd**

Roach are not indigenous to Ireland, but coinciding with the coarse angling boom in Southern Ireland over the past two decades they appeared and are now established in the Foyle river system, and in Fairey Water and other places. No doubt further introductions will occur. The rudd, which is common there, has always traditionally been called 'roach' by the Irish. Anglers fishing in Southern Ireland would therefore be wise to bear this in mind, and treat the local use of the term 'roach' with some reserve.

A roach of a pound is a good fish in any water. Over this it is excellent. Two pounders are not common, and specimens above this size are, for most anglers, the fish of a lifetime.

Anyone examining a roach for the first time would probably notice the lack of teeth, which would at least establish that the species is non-predatory. A closer examination, by dissection, reveals that like all fishes of the carp family (to which roach belong) the roach has pharyngeal teeth set at the back of the throat. These, bearing on the upper hard palate, enable the fish to grind up food before swallowing it.

Dissection also reveals that the roach has no stomach, the gullet extending from the throat, thickening, and then folding upon itself to pass directly to the vent where wastes are expelled. The digestive processes are carried out by enzymes and bacteria lining this gullet. As with most non-predators, the diet is mixed and, while over half the roach's

Peter Stone

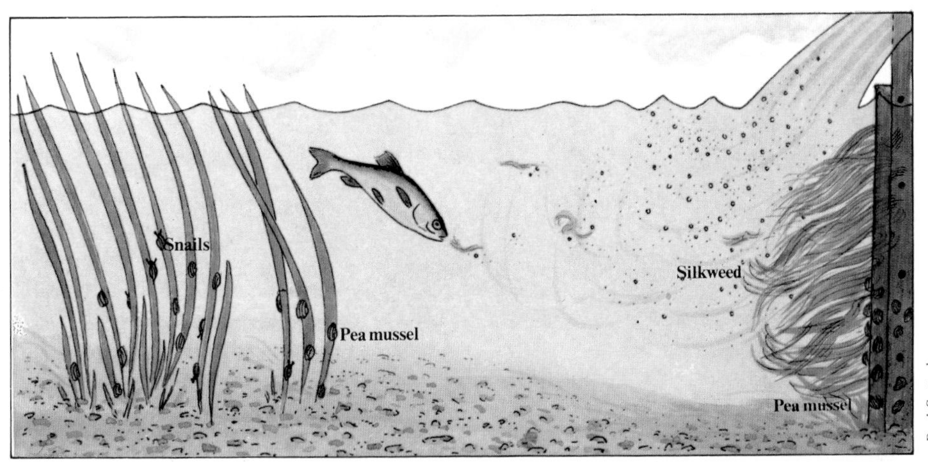


Rod Sutterby

Bill Howes

*(Above and right) Roach and other mid-water fishes are attracted to the well-aerated water in the vicinity of weirs, feeding on snails, silkweed and the pea-mussel. Punts make ideal fishing platforms at weirs. (Left and below) In slower stretches, such as the Dorset Stour in our photograph, the roach feed on snails on the waterplants, the freshwater shrimp, and bottom-living creatures such as the caddis larva.*

food consists of plants and such algae as silkweed, it also eats insects, crustaceans, molluscs and diatoms.

The haunts of roach are as variable as their shape and colour. However, they prefer gravel, rock or hard bottoms and will settle over hard clay or mixed sand rather than silt or soft mud. Often they have little choice as the waters in which they are found vary from the swiftest chalk streams to the most sluggish and coloured lowland streams and small ponds. To survive, shoals must locate good feeding. For this they turn to the weed beds, not only for their plant food but for insects and other creatures. Roach, therefore, often shoal within easy reach of such natural larders, which also offer them protection from predators.

In rivers the current forms an endless conveyor belt bringing food along to waiting shoals. Roach will sample almost any suitably sized morsel brought down by the stream. They can sample and reject incredibly swiftly any item which arouses their suspicions, as anglers well know.

**Testing Food**

In this kind of habitat the shoals lie below the overhanging weed beds reaching up to the surface, often on the edge of a run between the weed. From this vantage point they regularly sally into the clear runs to take other foods.

*(Above) Roach eggs are left attached to water-weed stems and small stones.*
*(Left) Male roach develop 'nuptial tubercles' in the spawning season.*

Eric Birch

As the need arises, fish will cruise from one weed-bed to another. From time to time they must cross open water, cruising on to the bottom, hugging the deeps, probing the mud or gravel for molluscs and larvae. Adventurous fish on the fringes of such shoals patrol the outer cruising area, occasionally rising to a surface morsel.

In stillwaters the absence of a stream means fish will be found in or hovering over weeds, or cruising. They cover the marginal waters at depths between 5ft and 15ft, foraging into marginal reed fringes and weed. Here, the angler hopes his groundbait will allay their natural suspicions, hold them in the vicinity, and get them to take his hookbait.

**Reproduction**

During the closed season roach move into the gravelly shallows, seeking a compromise between the gravel they love and the silt and mud inevitable in weedy fringes and shallow margins. Between March and June—later or earlier according to the severity or mildness of the season—the concentrations of fish build up until spawning occurs. Individual fish dart in and out of the dense mass, jostling and splashing. Prior to spawning, the male fish develop temporary warty growths or 'tubercles' on the scales of the head and shoulder. These enable fish to distinguish the sex of their neighbours and no doubt play a part in courtship preliminaries. Spawning is communal, often as if at a given signal. Then the quivering mass of fish discharges eggs and milt into the water in large clouds. The eggs are fertilized in the water, sinking slowly to adhere to reed and weed stems until hatching later in the season.

Such indiscriminate spawning gives rise to hybridism with other species. There is always considerable competition for suitable spawning places on the shallows, and it is not unusual for shoals of bream, rudd, dace or chub or even bleak, to be spawning in close proximity to the roach shoals. Fish on the edges of the shoals sometimes intermingle, and eggs from one species are then fertilized by milt from another. The result is hybrids, usually with characteristics intermediate between parents. These give rise to occasional problems of identification for the angler.

**Recognizing a hybrid**

Every year the current roach record is assailed by claims for fish which, upon examination, prove to be hybrids. The bream/roach hybrid is usually the culprit. Such fish should be recognised immediately by any angler of experience but, regrettably, they are not. The angler should be suspicious when he takes a good fish which seems to be slimier than usual. Its identity can be established by counting the number of

*(Right) Roach-bream hybrid. An intermediate form between the species.*

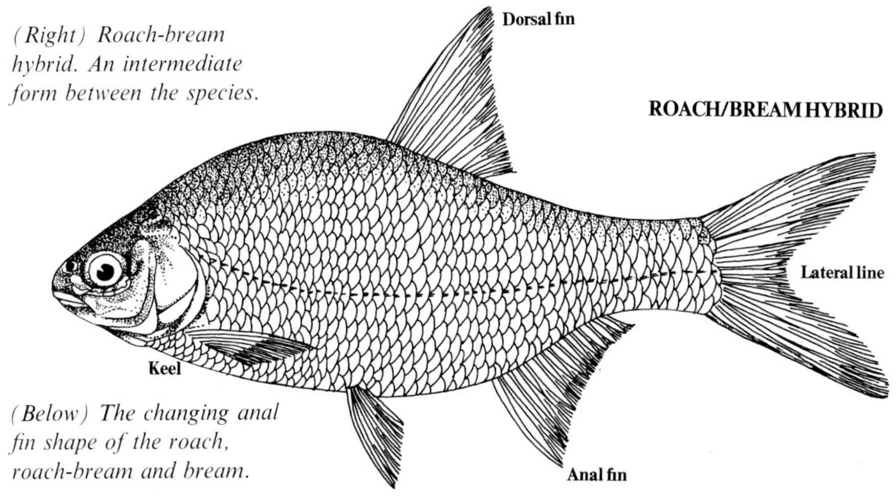


*(Below) The changing anal fin shape of the roach, roach-bream and bream.*

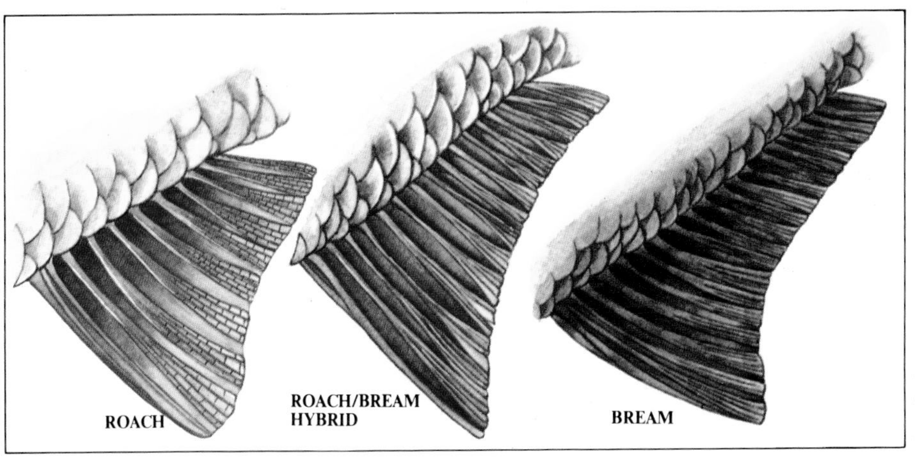


Lyn Cawley

branched rays in the anal fin. Roach have 9-12, bream 23-29, while the hybrid is intermediate with 14-19..If the specimen has more than 12 such rays it cannot be a roach.

By mid-June, when the fishing season opens, the roach shoals have forsaken the shallows for the streamy runs, weirpools and swifter reaches, where the well-oxygenated water restores their lost condition within a week or a month according to locality and the kind of year. By July or August they have moved into deeper waters, lying in the swift current between and under weed beds. In lakes, they will be farther from the margins. Now they must make the most of high summer and plentiful food.

By October, the onset of colder weather and shorter days cause roach to settle in the depths. In shallow lakes their choice is restricted, and in very deep ones they seldom penetrate below 20ft or so as food supplies below this depth are limited. A lessening of activity coincides with the fall of leaves into the water.

In winter stillwater roach only become active during mild spells, when they temporarily resume feeding. By now the best of lake fishing is over. In rivers, there is a resumption of activity after autumn when rain arrives and the river is flushed. When flooding occurs the shoals will often follow the levels over the banks to flooded meadows

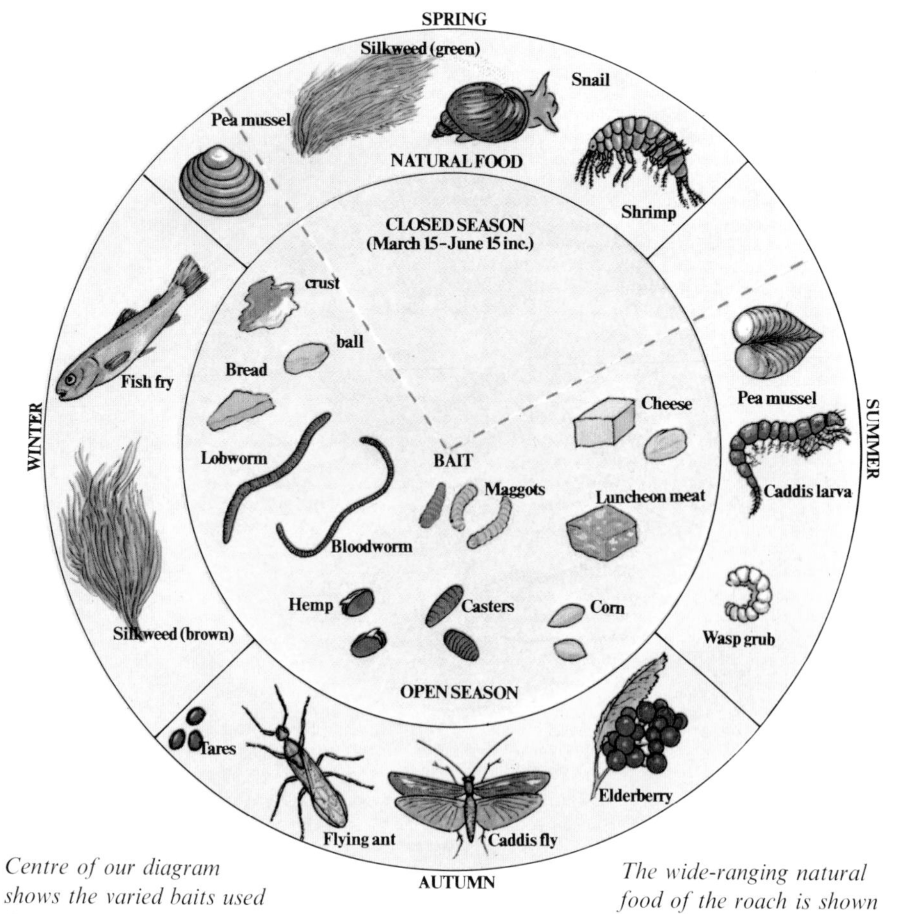


*Centre of our diagram shows the varied baits used for roach fishing.*

*The wide-ranging natural food of the roach is shown on the outside ring.*

Rod Sutterby

where food is replenished by the new pastures, and where lay-bys are favourite places to take refuge, or rest from the force of the river in spate. When levels fall again, the fish instinctively seek deeper water to avoid being left stranded. Throughout winter they cruise in the deep and feed as they can to attain a superb condition. In spring the cycle starts again.

This varying pattern of feeding and movement dictates the range of methods that the skilled roach angler must be able to command. In the early season he must often use fine tackle to tempt fish from their weedy strongholds in gin-clear water. Silkweed is a good bait then, and he must wield this light tackle with precision and finesse to present the bait in a natural manner, and so produce a take. He needs swift reflexes to hook this flighty fish, and angling skill to keep it from the weed in order to land it.

By the end of the year, with vastly different conditions, he must use heavily-shotted tackle to cope with the river in spate. He will cast accurately and surely to the shoals, or perhaps fish lay-bys or eddies with ledgered tackle. Between the extremes he must practise a wide variety of methods at different times of year and in differing waters.

The angler must also relate his baits to his knowledge of the natural feeding habits of the fish. Fortunately, the maggot is similar to many underwater larval forms, and the worm, which resembles other water creatures, is also found by roach grubbing on the bottom. Wheat, barley, hemp, tares, corn and other cereal baits are familiar to fish in their natural form at harvest time, during high winds, and in flood conditions. The enterprising angler will always find suitable baits. Caddis fly, bloodworm, freshwater snail and shrimp, mussel and woodlice are all effective alternatives to the more usual baits. Silkweed too can usually be had at the fishing place. Bread baits such as paste, flake and crust, are all proven and easily obtained. The prime consideration is that all baits must be presented in the right place at the right time.

**Where roach are found**

You can confidently expect good roach from any major river system within the areas where roach are found. Specimens of 3lb are recorded from Hampshire's Test and Avon, and the Dorset Stour. In the Home Counties they come from the Thames, Medway, Kennet and Essex Stour. In the Midlands and North, the Trent, Colne and Great Ouse produce big fish, while the Norfolk Bure, Waveney and Broadland lakes offer excellent prospects. Many reservoirs and gravel pits, to be found all over the country, also produce good fish.

The angler may fish in silent reed-fringed fenland dykes with a very fine line and a matchstick float to take a good bag. He may stret-peg the Thames, Kennet, Ouse or Trent, or shot-ledger in gravel pits and ponds. Long-trotting in quiet streams bordered by the Dales or rolling a ledger on the northern border rivers will take roach too. He can take his pick of silent shallow marshy meres or inland lakes; southern chalk streams or lowland canals. All provide good roach, and each favours its own local styles of fishing.

*A superb catch of well-conditioned roach up to 2lb from the River Kennet at Newbury. There is one small perch among them.*

P. H. Ward, Natural Science Photos

# Chub

Predominantly a river fish, the chub (*Leuciscus cephalus*) is found where currents flow fast over gravel or stony beds. It is a fish of clean, unpolluted water where both oxygen and food exist in plenty. The species provides fishing of quality for the angler prepared to stalk this cautious and stealthy prey with great care and skill. The chub is shy in habit—a thick-bodied ghost that fades into the depths at sight or sound of man or beast. Yet the chub is renowned for the dogged resistance it displays to the efforts of angler and rod.

**Chub in Ireland?**

While the chub is found throughout most of England, it is absent from West Wales and from Scotland above the Forth-Clyde valley. Until recently the species was not thought to exist in Ireland but reports indicate the possibility that the fish has been introduced into the Blackwater river system, possibly as livebait by pike fishermen.

We think of the chub as a pure river fish but it has been successfully introduced to stillwaters, where it thrives and can grow larger than its river counterpart. Where rivers are diverted, notably by the construction of motorways, stillwaters are formed which are populated by chub, barbel and dace.

The chub is one of Britain's bigger coarse fish but even so it rarely reaches 6lb (although specimens of nearly 10lb have been taken from salmon rivers in the Scottish Borders). The present record fish weighed 7lb 6oz and fell to Bill Warren while fishing the Royalty in 1957.

The chub belongs to the carp family, though it does not resemble the carp in appearance. The mature fish is solidly built, with a blunt head, large mouth, and thick, pale lips. The back is greenish brown and the belly a yellowy white. The fins, which are well-defined and powerful, can range from colourless to a rich red. It is easy to identify by its large scales, which have a slight black edging, and can only be confused with other fish when young, when it is often mistaken

Rod Sutterby

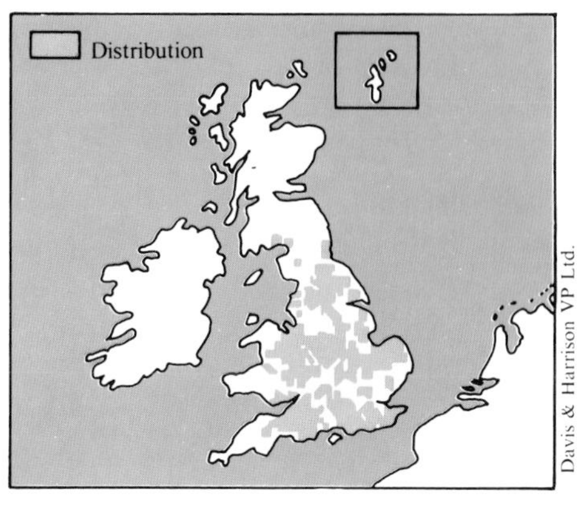


Davis & Harrison VP Ltd.

**Baits**

*The chub can be caught on all the freshwater angler's baits, including plugs and spinners.*

**Habitat**

*Although a river fish, it is also found in small streams and rivers. (Below) The Avon at Ibsley is a beautiful example of a typical chub river, with weed-channels and plenty of bankside cover where trees overhang the water.*

Robin Fletcher

for a dace. The distinction between the two should be clear, however, for the chub has large fins with rounded, convex rear edges, especially noticeable on the anal fin, and has 44-46 scales along the lateral line, while the dace's fins have concave rear edges and its lateral line averages 47-54 scales. The dace is a much slighter fish and is about 12ox when fully grown.

**Spawning**

Like other coarse fish, the chub spawns in the spring. Different water and weather conditions affect breeding times but this usually occurs between April and early June. The eggs are small—the female will release over 100,000 which stick to plants and river debris. After about 8-10 days hatching takes place in the shallow water of the gravelly runs favoured by the species. After cleaning itself in the fast water of the shallows, the fish will slowly head for deeper waters, where it has both security and space.

The chub is more solitary than other river species and tends to establish a definite territory. Old fish, particularly, will seek out a hole and lie up for long periods. All rivers have known chub holes, which the seasoned angler can point out to the newcomer, but it is unlikely that more than one or two chub can be caught from the swim. Younger chub do shoal and form mixed shoals with dace and roach in areas that can provide the necessary abundance of food.

Hybridization occurs as a result of this mixed shoaling and cross-breeding between the chub and the bream, roach, rudd or dace is quite common. This can lead to identification problems, especially for the claimant to a record for a species.

**Trespassing chub**

Chub often inhabit stretches of river set aside for trout fishing. Anglers are sometimes encouraged to fish for them during the trout close season and to remove their catch to conserve the game fishing.

Chub are famed for their wide-ranging

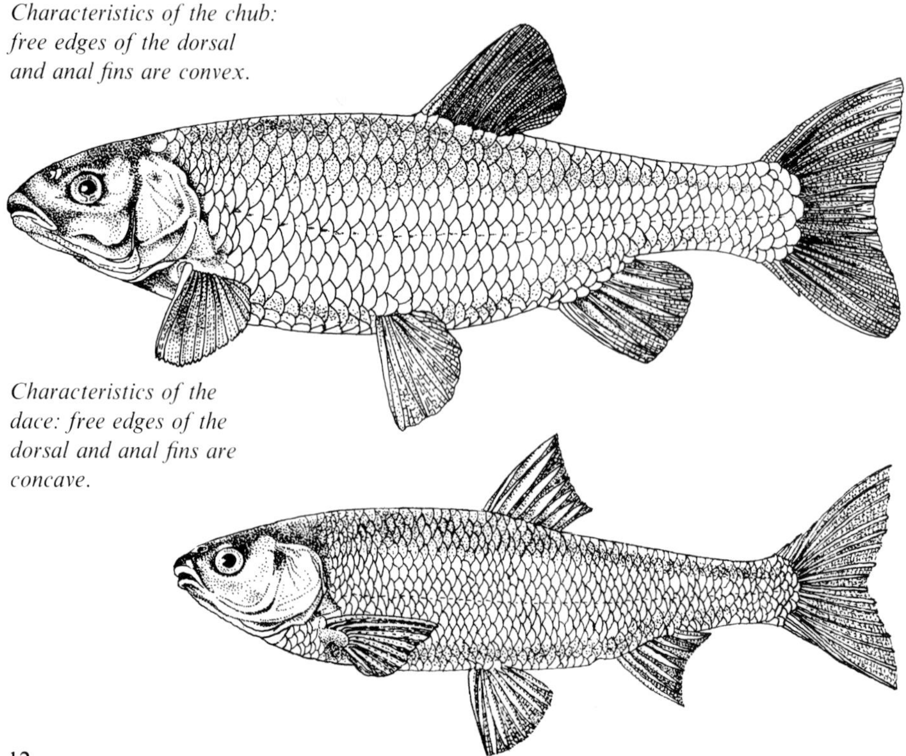


*Characteristics of the chub: free edges of the dorsal and anal fins are convex.*

*Characteristics of the dace: free edges of the dorsal and anal fins are concave.*

P. H. Ward, Natural Science Photos

*The merest flicker of an eyelid will be enough to send these wary chub back into the depths.*

*Peter Ward demonstrates the correct way to hold fish for photographing. The chub is being supported properly, with wet hands, and there is little pressure on its body or gills.*

Robin Fletcher

*The kingdom of the chub. This tiny pool on the River Itchen at Ovington, Hampshire, has all the signs of chub territory—even though the Itchen is a chalkstream carefully maintained and preserved as an exclusive trout fishery and coarse fish are not encouraged. Learn to read the water: that dark hole beneath the gnarled willow, a tangle of vegetation on the left, the stand of reeds in mid-stream. All these must hold fish. Why? Insects, berries and food particles will drop from the tree's over-hanging branches and the bushes, and in these calcium-rich waters the reeds always harbour aquatic life of many sorts—nymphs, larvae, snails, shrimps, crayfish, so fish will feed there.*

appetites and can be taken on a variety of baits. Try float-fishing with cheese, ripe-fruits, especially berries, bread, worms, silkweed, dried blood, slugs, or maggots. Natural and artificial flies can also be used, as can other insects and grubs. The smaller members of a shoal will feed on aquatic insects and bottom-dwelling invertebrates, while the older fish will add a substantial amount of vegetable matter to their diet and will chase and eat the fry of many species, including their own. Livebaiting with minnows and small fish gives good results.

**Anything edible . . .**

The chub rises, trout-like, from deep water to take a small fish, fly or anything edible that disturbs the surface. A rapid rise in air or water temperature will encourage the fish to lie, head to current, just beneath the surface, watching for anything the current brings along above it.

Remember that fruits fall constantly into rivers and that the chub expects to feed on them. Baits such as elderberries may not be an obvious choice, but they produce results, especially after high winds or other disturbances have swept a lot of fruit or berries into the water.

Other baits available at the water's edge

include crayfish, which can be gathered by scraping the undercut banks below the water level, and swan mussels, which are used as a bait for other large species as well.

The chub's carnivorous inclinations mean that it can occasionally be taken on a small blade spinner intended for trout. This often happens when the fish is in shallow water after spawning,—when its large appetite will overcome its usual caution.

**The all-rounder**

The chub's taste for many types of bait and the fact that it can be caught at any time of year, if the right technique is used, make it something of an all-rounder for the angler. It can be relied on to give good sport and to repay the concentration and patience with which it must be hunted. The chub can also provide a fine bonus to a day spent fishing for other species for it sometimes quite unexpectedly and impulsively takes a bait such as a lobworm float-fished along the far bank, which it may have been ignoring for hour after hour.

Such a fish will probably not shatter any records. Nevertheless we can confidently expect the capture of a fish to at least match the 10lb 8oz chub taken from the Annan by Dr J. A. Cameron in 1955. This specimen has since had its record status withdrawn but the once-awesome 10lb barrier has proved breakable.

P. H. Ward. Natural Science Photos

*(Above) Peter Wood playing a 4lb chub to the net from a classic fishing position on the River Kennet in Berkshire. This stretch holds many fine specimen chub, but being narrow it demands a very cautious approach by the angler. (Left) The bait that tempted the chub being played by Peter Wood in our photograph above. It is luncheon meat and one of the favoured and successful chub baits.*

P. H. Ward, Natural Science Photos

*In 1653, Izaak Walton recommended the large black slug as a bait for the chub, this 'fearfullest of fishes'. The fish has not changed since then—it still falls to a fat slug impaled through its body on a No. 4 or 6 hook (right) offered to it.*

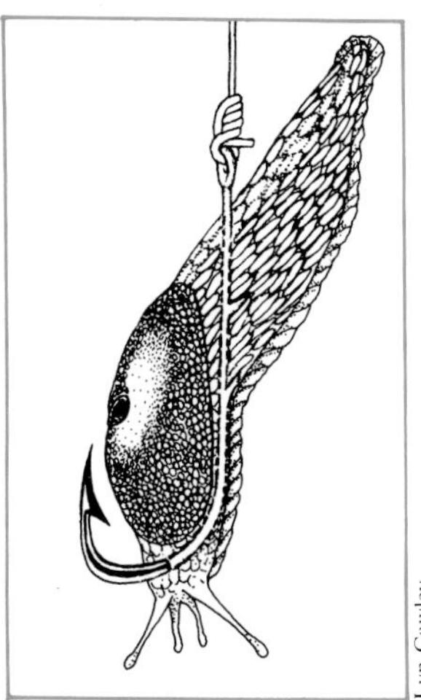

Lyn Cawley

# Common bream

The freshwater bream, *Abramis brama,* has a dark green or brown back, but in older fish it may take on a slate grey hue. The flanks of the bream are olive-bronze and their white or creamy underside is often marked with scarlet streaks. The body is heavily covered with a thick layer of slime, which sometimes gives the fish a blue appearance. The bream is deep-bellied and full-backed. The tail is unsymmetrical, the lower lobe being rounded and the upper lobe pointed. A long anal fin extends almost from the middle of the belly to the tail.

**Habitat**

The body-shape of the bream gives some clue to its habits. Not only is the shape suited to bottom living, but also enables the fish to swim easily through the closely-spaced stems of reeds and sedges common in sluggish and stillwaters. This increases the potential feeding grounds for the fish as well as providing ready shelter from predators.

Normally bream are bottom feeders, and as shoals may contain as many as 50 fish they

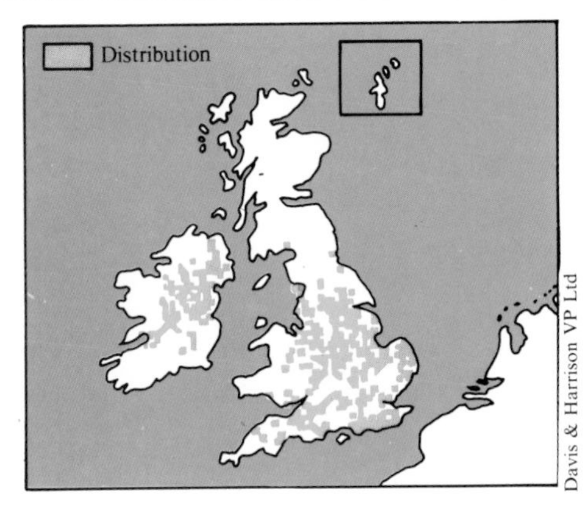


Davis & Harrison VP Ltd

Rod Sutterby

**Habitat**

*The Common Bream,* Abramis abrama, *naturally occurs in the rivers of Eastern England, but is also found in many enclosed waters. The Silver Bream is localized.*

**Bait**

*Bream can be taken on bread, maggots, sweet corn and worms.*

*(Below) Farnborough Lakes, Hants, where bream and other species may be caught.*

Bill Howes

Irish Tourist Board

*(Above) Some of the best fishing in the British Isles is found in Ireland. This angler is about to net a bream from Grove Lake, Tulla, County Clare.*
*(Right) With its wide-ranging feeding habits the bream falls to many baits.*
*(Below) This Fenland dyke, or drain, is typical of many waters in the Eastern Counties. They hold bream shoals.*

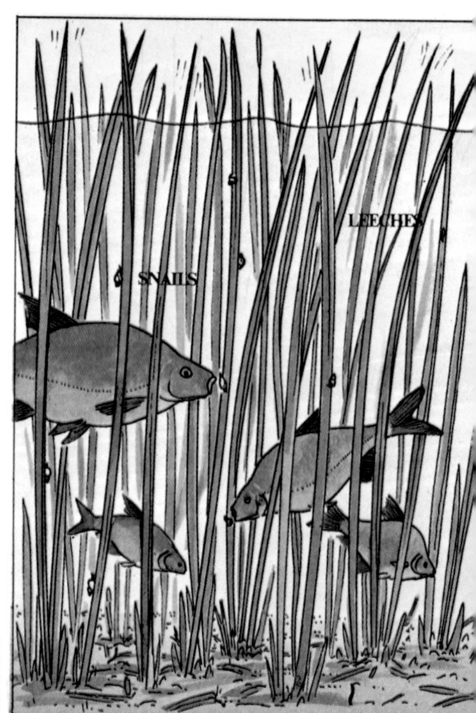

Bob Church

must cruise continuously to find food. They feed extensively on algae, plankton, insect larvae, crustaceans and molluscs, also grubbing among the bottom debris for the many micro-organisms which live there.

Once feeding the shoals move slowly along the bottom, rather like a flock of sheep working its way across the meadow when grazing. The comparison is apt because the fish soon denude the bottom of food, like sheep cropping grass. Fortunately, when the bream have passed, other small bottom-living creatures will soon take up residence.

When feeding in earnest a large shoal will stir up a great deal of mud. Gases are released which carry the colour of the mud quickly to the surface, even in quite deep waters. Anglers seeking bream should be aware of this, and keep an eye open for both the bubbles and the muddy colouring. In stillwaters this is invaluable in locating feeding fish. In rivers some judgement is required to decide how far the current has washed the colour from the feeding place, and whether or not to fish up or downstream. Fortunately bream also like to roll about, playing on or near the surface prior to feeding.

Twilight and dusk are good times to seek bream, which take advantage of the failing light to enter the shallower marginal waters in search of food. Sometimes they give themselves away by gently moving the marginal reeds, and a bait on the edge of the margins will often take fish.

Spawning occurs in May or June. After a severe winter anglers will sometimes take bream spawning as late as the end of June and even after the season has opened. The males can be recognised by the tubercles on the head and shoulder, typical of cyprinoids during spawning. The fish usually seek wide reedy bays and margins, and sometimes enter the tangles of waterside tree roots which extend below undercut banks. Once spawned they move into deeper water, remaining there throughout the summer, cruising when feeding, or lying motionless.

Rod Sutterby

Bill Howes

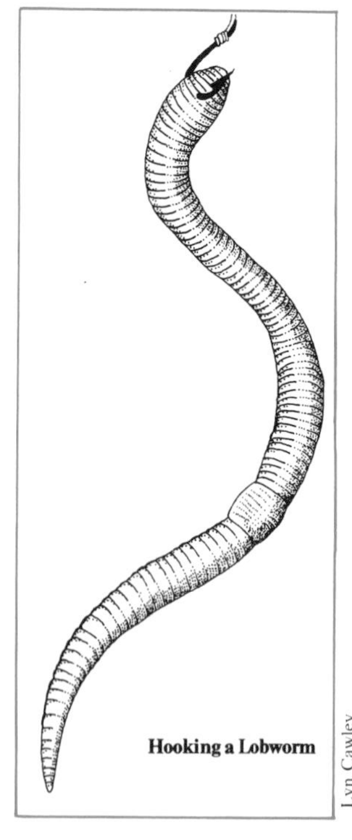

Lyn Cawley

*(Above) Peter Stone's own preferred method of hooking worms for bream fishing. (Left) Unhooking this good bream over the keepnet is a wise safety measure in case the fish jumps loose.*

When frost sets in they seek out the deeper gullies and holes in the bottom, moving out at intervals to feed, and remaining quite active, especially at night when the water is warmer than the air, or by day during bright sunny spells. In stillwaters bream tend to become comatose during winter, moving only when tempted out of their sleepiness by warmer weather.

**Bream growth**

The freshwater bream generally attains a length of 3-4in during the first year. During the second year it will probably double its length, and weigh up to 20oz. This is the angler's typical 'tinplate bream'. In the third year the body fills out and the fish attains 9in by the time it is 12in long it is four to five years old. A specimen of 7lb is probably 10 years old, and fish in the record class of approximately 12lb may be between 12 and 15 years old. In Britain this is probably close to the maximum life span.

The search for big bream has continued for many years. Before the war the British Record Fish lists noted many fish over 12lb, and during the war a 13lb 8oz record was set by Mr E. Costin fishing at Chiddington Castle lake. These older records were abandoned when the new British Record (rod-caught) Committee was set up. The current record is a 12lb 14oz common bream taken from the Suffolk Stour, in 1972. Ten pounders are listed from both the Thames and the Lea.

The freshwater bream is common in most parts of England except the western extremities. It is also plentiful in Ireland, where the average run of fish is larger than elsewhere. It is less common in Southern Scotland, and absent north of Loch Lomond; is found throughout Europe north of the Alps and the Pyrenees, except in the west and north of Scandinavia, and in the south and west of the Balkans. Anglers on holiday in Europe have a chance of good bream fishing.

Throughout their range, bream are as much at home in lakes as in rivers. They prefer sluggish waters and in swift large rivers tend to be found in the slower reaches. They attain the best sizes in stillwaters, but fight better when taken in such faster waters as the Thames, Trent, or Great Ouse, where they turn their broad flanks to the current when hooked. Some of the best bream waters are in the Norfolk Broads waterways, and in the Lincolnshire and Fenland drain systems. Traditionally, too, the Arun, Nene, Welland and Witham are noted for bream. Some of the best specimens in the last few decades, however, have been taken from the reservoirs of Walthamstow, Tring, Staines and Marsworth.

**Confusion with rudd**

Bream are not easily confused with roach, but may be mistaken for large rudd. The short anal fin of the rudd should separate them. Unfortunately, bream spawn in similar places to those sought by roach and rudd, and the species occasionally interbreed accidentally when fish on the edge of shoals intermingle. Eggs from one shoal are sometimes fertilized by milt from the other, and the resulting hybrids are fairly common. In England the common roach x bream hybrid was once believed to be a separate species, and called 'Pomeranian bream'. It even warranted its own specific title, *Abramis buggenhagii,* which is still found in older text books on fish. Now it is known to be a hybrid

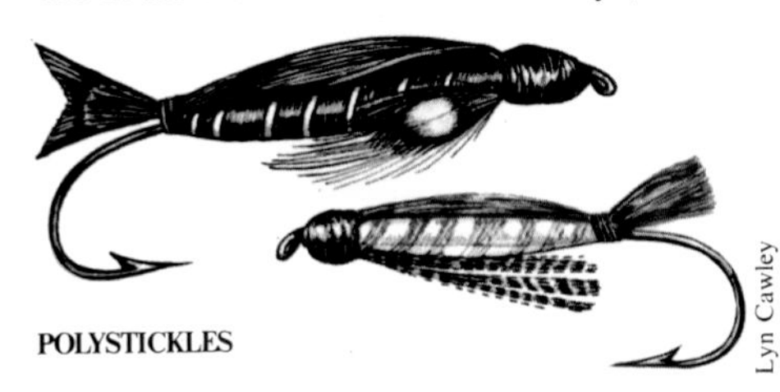


*(Left) Polystickle, imitations of the tiny stickleback. Bream are known to eat them. (Below) While bream can be caught on all the usual roach baits—bread, maggots, worms, and so on. Their habit of taking small fish suggests bleak, which bream have been seen to attack.*

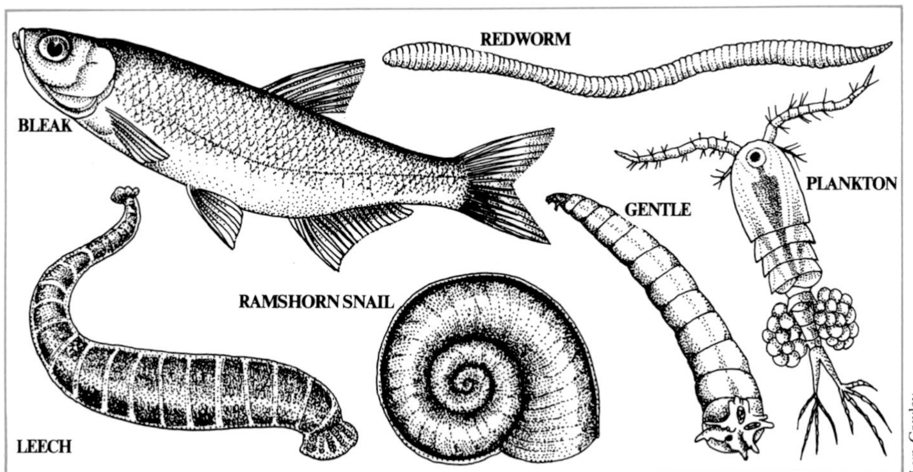


Lyn Cawley

P. H. Ward/Natural Science Photos

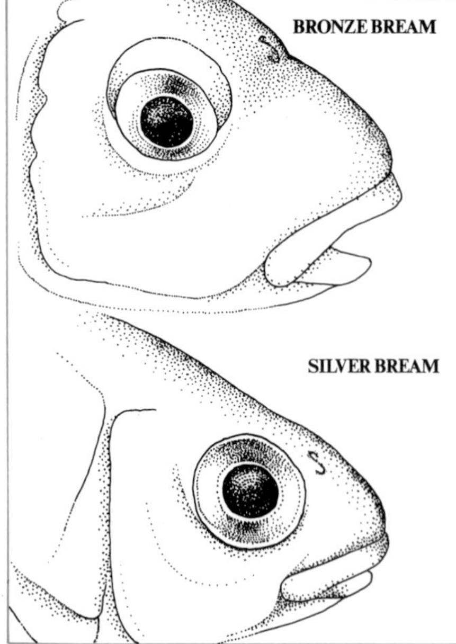


Lyn Cawley

*(Above) Top is the silver bream and beneath it the common.*
*(Left) Eye position is an identification point between the two species.*

which is nevertheless popular with anglers. Sharing the characteristics of its parents it sometimes attains good weights. When it exceeds three or four pounds there is a danger of wishful thinking, and the fish is put up as a record roach, or at least as a specimen. No angler should make such a mistake because the anal fin of each fish is distinctive, bearing a specific number of branched rays. True roach have 9-12, true bream 23-29, and the hybrid 15-19. This is a very simple count to make and if the branched rays are counted at the outside edge of the fin they cannot easily be confused with the unbranched rays at the fore-edge.

The rudd x bream hybrid is not often

found in England, but is common in Ireland, where, to complicate matters further, the native true rudd has traditionally been called 'roach'. Such hybrids are fortunately easy to recognise if the anal fin ray count is carried out. True rudd have 10-13 branched rays and the hybrid has 15-18. If your specimen has more than 13 branched rays in its anal fin it cannot be a rudd. If more than 12, it cannot be a roach.

Almost all roach baits will take bream, but usually bream like a good mouthful. The bait must therefore be bigger and presented on hooks up to size No. 8 or No. 6. Good baits are bread derivatives, sweet corn, worms, swan mussels and gentles. A bunch of gentles will often work, and a large lobworm will often take the better fish. When fish are coy a maggot or a brandling may tempt them.

**White bream**

The white or silver bream, *Blicca bjoerkna,* is only found in a few slow-flowing rivers and stillwaters in the East of England. It is similar in shape and colour to the common freshwater bream but the pale flanks have a silvery sheen. Other distinguishing features are the two rows of pharyngeal teeth and a'V'-shape under the abdomen where the scales lie back to back along the ridge.

White bream are similar to the common bream in habitat and diet, but tend to be more selective in their feeding and are less confirmed bottom-feeders. Bream caught in midwater are always worthy of a close scrutiny. White bream are small reaching a maximum length of 9½in and the current British Record (rod-caught) is open at 1lb 8oz, and will perhaps be surpassed by the first angler who can correctly recognize the species.

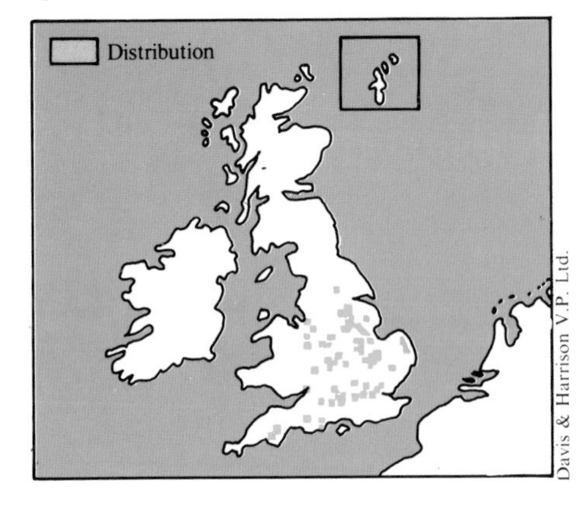


*(Above) Distribution map of the silver bream shows it is not as wide-spread as the common species.*
*(Below) Smaller of the two freshwater bream the silver record is open at 1lb 8oz.*

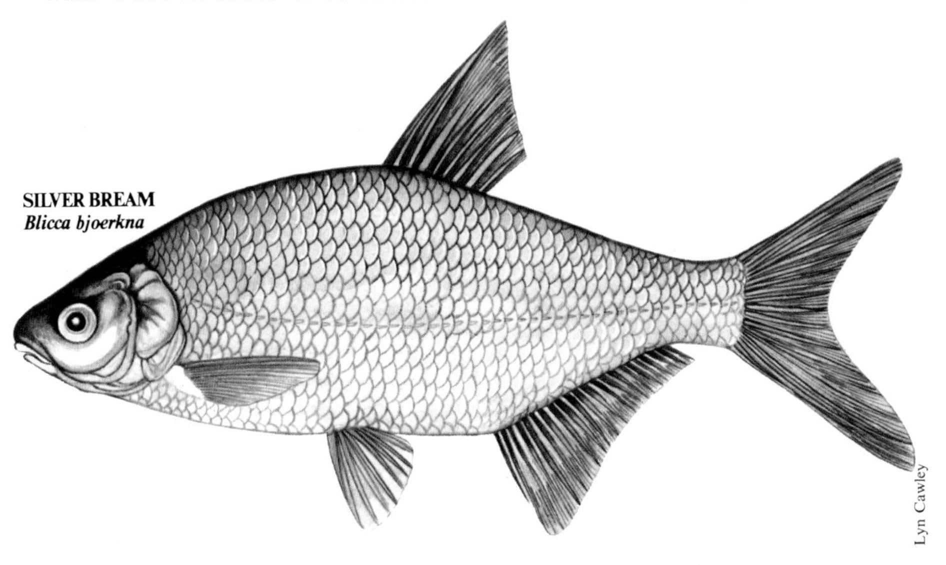

# Wild carp

In evolutionary terms a relatively young freshwater fish, unlike the pike, for instance, the carp originated in Central Asia, around the area of the watershed of the Black Sea and the Caspian Sea, during the last post-glacial period. There followed a natural spread east into China and the surrounding regions, and west, as far as the Danube.

The carp, *Cyprinus carpio,* has always been one of the most important to mankind of freshwater fish. Carp breeding is the oldest form of fish culture, and has been practised for at least 2,400 years in China and 1,900 years in Japan, while in Europe the Romans transferred wild carp from the Danube to Italy during the first to fourth centuries AD. After the collapse of the Roman Empire, and with the advent of Christianity, further western introductions took place, the carp gradually spreading throughout Europe. The earliest reference to carp in England dates from 1462, and so it appears that the species was introduced at least some little time before.

The wild carp is among the most majestic and beautiful of our freshwater fish, and for no little reason was it referred to by Izaak Walton as 'the queen of rivers'. Furthermore, its natural attributes make it almost certainly the most difficult to catch. It grows to a large size where there is an ample food supply, to become an extremely strong and tenacious fighter, and a fish with a cunning second to none.

**Introduction of King carp**

Unfortunately, the wild carp is slowly becoming less widespread, not only in Britain, but throughout the world. One reason suggested for this is that the introduction of the 'King' carp strain into many habitats has caused interbreeding, thus losing forever the purity of the wild carp stock. However, there is evidence to suggest that with adequate spawning facilities, the true wild carp and the selectively bred 'King' carp will not spawn together.

Probably, the most significant reasons for the drop in numbers have been, with the

Rod Sutterby

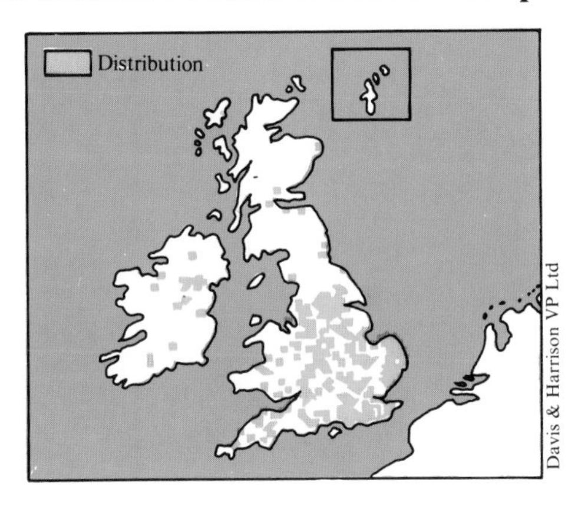


Davis & Harrison VP Ltd

**Habitat**

*The wild carp,* Cyprinus carpio, *introduced into Britain hundreds of years ago, is found now in slow-moving rivers, ponds and shallow lakes. Typical is Brooklands Lake, Dartford (below), a popular carp fishery.*

**Baits**

*Although naturally a herbivore, the carp is caught on maggot and worm, as well as bread, meat, potato and cereal baits.*

N. J. Fickling

P. H. Ward/Natural Science Photos

enormous increase in popularity of carp fishing since the 1950s, the detrimental changes which have taken place in their particular habitats, and because the species has been overshadowed to some extent by the faster-growing 'King' carp.

The wild carp has a much more slender body, similar in some respects to that of the chub, than the cultivated species, which is often hump-backed and much deeper. In Britain the wild carp seldom exceeds 10lb in weight, although a few over 15lb have been captured, and the maximum, under favourable conditions, is probably about 25lb.

**Carp coloration**

Coloration is variable, depending mainly on the environment. Usually, the top of the head and body are dark brownish-blue, the sides bright golden, and the underside off-white near the head, changing to a yellowish near the tail. The dorsal fin has the same colour as the top of the body, as does the upper portion of the tail, while the lower part of the tail often has a reddish-orange tinge. The pectoral, ventral and anal fins vary between slate-grey and pale reddish-orange. Variations in colour in individual fish can take place throughout the year, and are especially noticeable during spawning.

**Carp variety identification**

There exist discrepancies in the literature regarding identification of the carp. A notable example is that for the number of scales along the lateral line, Wheeler (1969) quotes a figure of 35-40, while Sigler (1958) gives 32-38, Muus and Dahlstrom (1967) quote 33-40, and Dick Walker, in a letter to an angling magazine, states that all carp he had examined had 37 such scales. The present author found that in several carp there were between 37 and 39 scales in the lateral line.

Wild carp usually mature at about 2-4 years, the male often reaching maturity earlier than the female. The time taken appears to depend to a large extent upon temperature, for under artificially controlled conditions carp have reached maturity after only 4-8 months.

The wild carp is an adaptable fish, surviving and flourishing in a wide variety of habitats in Britain. Generally, however, it favours shallow lakes and ponds, rich in aquatic vegetation, and still, sluggish, or

Bill Howes

*(Above) The lean lines of this carp caught by Bill Rushmer make it plain that the fish is a wildie.*
*(Left) Thicker in the body, a 19lb 8oz common carp taken by Peter Ward.*
*(Right) The sun goes down over Bill Chillingworth's Woolpack Fishery. Time for the carp to begin their nightly patrols.*

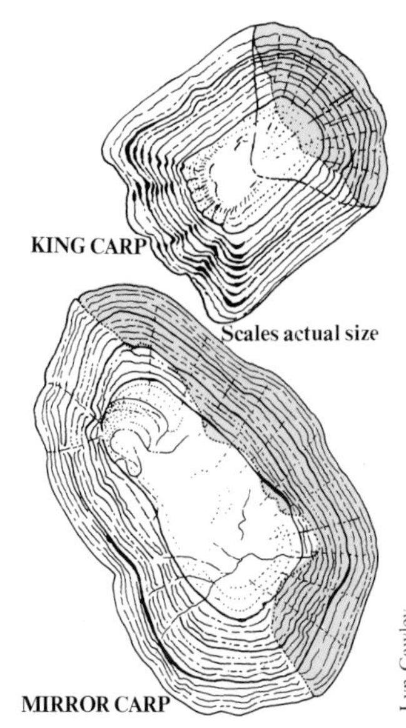


Lyn Cawley

P. H. Ward/Natural Science Photos

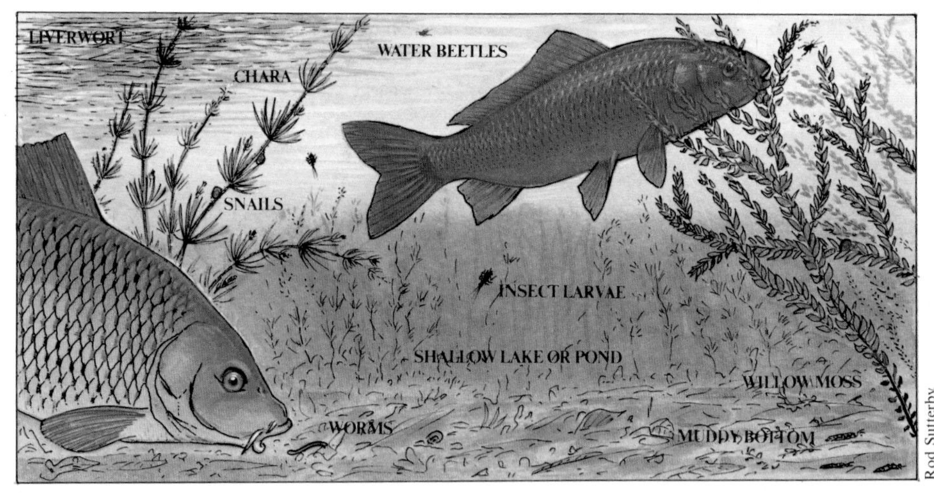


Rod Sutterby

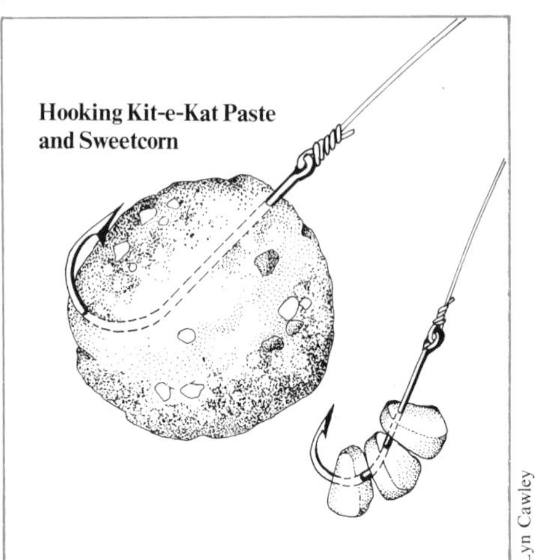


Lyn Cawley

*(Above) The carp's habitat: shallow lakes, slow rivers, with plenty of weed and cover. (Left) Among the many carp baits are sweet corn and certain branded cat-foods. (Below) A sunny summer's day at Essex Carp Fisheries, South Ockendon. (Below right) The carp's natural food.*

slow-moving rivers and canals. Since Britain is at the northernmost limit of the area in which carp reproduce, it follows that, in general, the distribution and occurrence of the species are greater in the south of these islands than in the north. The most northerly wild carp fisheries the author knows of are Bayton pond, near Aspatria in Cumbria, and Danskine Loch, in Scotland.

Spawning generally takes place between early May and late July, and is primarily dependent upon water temperature. Usually, this needs to be in excess of 17°C (62.6°F) to stimulate the wild carp into spawning. There is strong evidence to suggest that spawning is often prolonged over a period of several days, or even weeks, although whether different fish are involved, or the same fish makes repeated efforts, is not apparent.

The eggs are usually shed in shallow water, on soft aquatic vegetation. In deep ponds and lakes, with no shallows, the carp have been known to come close to the margins to spawn on overhanging vegetation, and even on fibrous roots and branches. The female is generally accompanied by two or more males, and the actual spawning is carried out very energetically so that the splashing and slapping of the fish near the surface may be audible over considerable distances.

**Carp eggs**

The small, translucent-grey eggs, 1mm in diameter, swell and are sticky on contact with water, and then become attached singly to whatever medium the carp are spawning over. The amount of eggs carried by the female is directly related to her size, but may also vary according to environmental factors. The proportion by weight of eggs in a female wild carp, just prior to spawning, is less than in the cultivated 'King' carp variety, amounting to approximately 10-20% of body weight, while the roe of a female 'King' carp can represent up to one third.

**Development**

The eggs hatch in 4-8 days, depending on the temperature, the newly hatched larvae having a yolk-sac on which to feed initially. The larvae are able to attach themselves to plants, or will lie on the bottom, before floating to the surface after two or three days to fill their swimbladders with air. They then become free-swimming, and feed on microscopic algae, rotifers and water fleas. Growth is variable and depends mainly on the amount of food available and water temperature, but other factors, such as the oxygen content, also have an effect.

Adult wild carp typically inhabit warmer environments, such as shallow areas of ponds and lakes, or slack eddies in rivers, usually where there is aquatic vegetation. On

Bill Howes

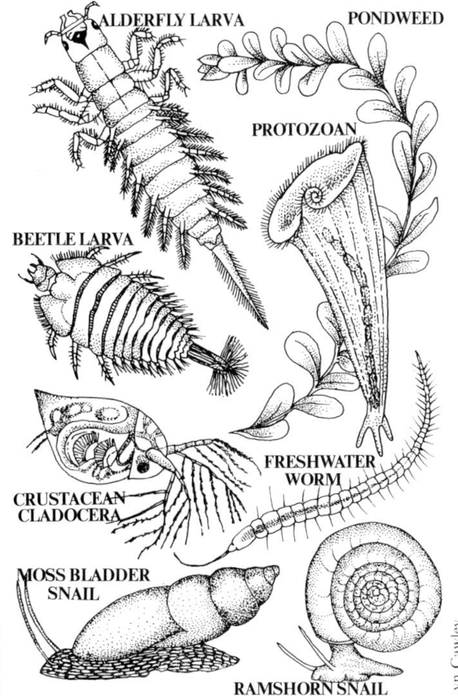


Lyn Cawley

rare occasions, they have been noted in swift, mountainous trout streams, and netted to depths of nearly 100ft.

**Browsing carp**

The adult fish slowly browse on food from the bottom of ponds and lakes, using their well-developed senses of sight, smell and taste. Sometimes, they feed at mid-water and on the surface, especially when the water temperature is very high. Their natural food consists mainly of crustaceans, worms, insect larvae, protozoans, small molluscs, and vegetable matter such as the various algae and the seeds of water plants.

It has been suggested that water fleas such as daphnia and cyclops also form a substantial part of the adult wild carp's diet, but the author has found that when other, larger items of food are available, water fleas are eaten only by carp of up to about 2-3lb. There are also reports of small fish found in the stomachs of carp, but it is generally assumed that these were dead at the time of the carp's swallowing them.

Wild carp grow, according to the environment, for about 12-18 years, but can live considerably longer, and certainly, under favourable conditions, can attain 40 years.

A myth perpetuated among carp anglers in the past, and indeed which was recently put to the author in no uncertain terms by the Secretary of a well-known carp angling organization, is that there is no biological difference between the wild carp and the domesticated 'King' carp. In fact there are many differences. For example, the wild carp has 18-19% more red blood corpuscles and haemoglobin than the 'King' carp. Its blood sugar and serum are 16-26% higher, and it has much less water in the liver and muscles. Furthermore, the wild carp has a higher concentration of fat in individual organs, glycogen in the liver, and Vitamin A in the eyes, liver and entrails.

Although often scorned by many of today's 'ultra-cult' carp anglers because it does not grow to the same massive size as the domesticated variety, the wild carp, because of these differences, is not only a much stronger fighter, but is also equipped to battle for longer periods. Moreover, as has been demonstrated in recent experiments by Beukema, in Holland, the wild carp, not having the 'King' carp's 'in-built' desire to feed intensively, is a more difficult fish to catch under similar conditions.

**Wildie is supreme**

There can be little doubt among those who have given this beautiful freshwater fish a fair chance to show its qualities, that the capture of a large 'wildie' is a supreme achievement.

*(Left) Both* Cyprinus carpio, *but the leather is almost scaleless, while the mirror has groups or rows of very large scales.*
*(Right) Smiling John Wilson with a 16½lb leather carp he is about to return to a syndicate water in Norfolk.*
*(Below) A fine specimen of a young mirror carp. The large scales along the lateral line show up well on the photograph.*

John Wilson

Bill Howes

# Pike

Ask any freshwater angler which fish he fears most and with certainty he will say, 'The pike', Why the pike (*Esox lucius*) should be feared is debatable. The fish is by no means the only fresh-water predator—the perch and the brown trout also eat other species. Indeed, the trout kills more immature shoal fish than either the pike or the perch.

**The solitary pike**

Streamlined, powerful but graceful, the pike is the supreme predator in our rivers and streams because of the enormous size it can grow to. It leads a solitary life, lying in ambush tp dart out and feed on smaller shoal fish—species such as roach, rudd and bream. The pike is built for speed, but only over short distances. It prefers to wait until an unwary fish comes within striking distance, then, in a burst of energy launches its body forward to grasp its prey.

As the pike gets older and slower it becomes a scavenger, seeking out ailing fish and searching the bottom of the lake or river for dead fish. In this way the pike contributes to the balance of Nature, regulating the numbers of fish that any water is able to support. At the same time, by removing sickly or stunted fish, the feeding habits of the pike ensure the long-term health of other species.

The pike is widely distributed throughout the British Isles. It is found in both flowing and stillwaters. Lakes, especially those containing vast shoals of fodder fish, will hold the larger pike. An absence of current is a further attraction to the pike as energy, otherwise spent on battling currents, can be diverted to the kill.

**Maturity and spawning**

The female pike will always grow larger than the male, which rarely exceeds 10 lb in body weight. During spawning, which can occur at various times, depending on geographical location and temperature, a number of male fish will accompany each egg-laden female. Often these male fish are only a pound or so in weight. They become sexually mature after the third year of life, whereas female

Rod Sutterby.

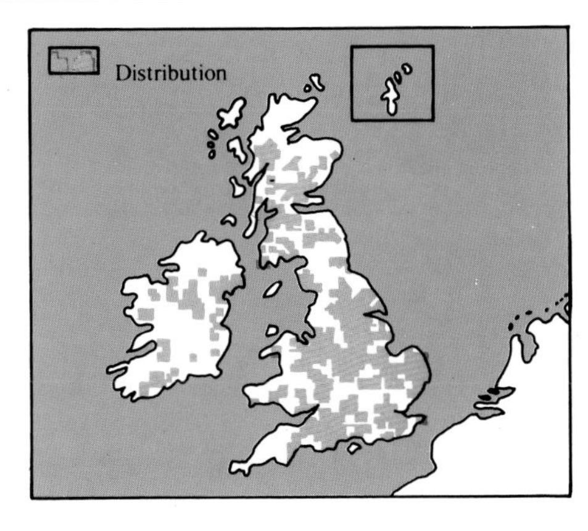


### *Habitat*

*The natural habitat of the pike (Esox lucius) is river, lake, reservoir or pond.*

### *Bait*

*It is caught by livebaiting with most coarse fish, including its own species; by deadbaiting with these or with herring, sprats or mackerel; and on all types of spinners and plugs.*

*Silvergrove Lough in County Clare, Ireland – an example of the pike's ideal habitat.*

Mike Prichard

**Pike Growth Diagram**

At this stage the eyes are prominent, but the mouth and gills are not yet formed.

Actual size

Clinging to reeds and stones by its sucker-pad, the larva hangs head-down to absorb nutrient in the yolk-sac.

Adhesive gland

Actual size

The fins begin to take shape, allowing proper feeding to take place on plankton.

Caudal fin

Anal fin

Actual size

Now all the fins are formed. The pike can eat fish nearly its own size.

Actual size

Approaching maturity.

Actual size

The fully mature pike.

Not to scale

Lyn Cawley

fish mature slightly later—between the third and fifth year. Spawning begins in March but may extend to June in northerly areas. Pike seek out shallow parts of a lake or stream and have a liking for flooded grassland around the perimeters of stillwater and for the water meadows that border some of our rivers. The slightly sticky eggs are released haphazardly to adhere to grass stems and waterweed.

If the temperature is right—about 11°C—the eggs will hatch in 10-15 days. The tiny pike will remain attached to the plant stems for a few days until they absorb the yolk sac. An adhesive pad on the head prevents their being swept away by currents. When the sac has been absorbed and the mouth fully formed, the larvae become free-swimming, moving to the surface to feed on minute water life. If the water is warm enough, the larvae grows fast over the first few months, attaining 3-7 in in a year, but many of them will be eaten by other predatory fish. Over a period of two or three weeks a female pike of

*(Above) During its life, the pike grows from half an inch to possible lengths of 4 or 5ft.*

*(Below) Even at a few weeks, the pike is an active predator, even on its own species. Here a hungry hunter swallows a fish of its own size.*

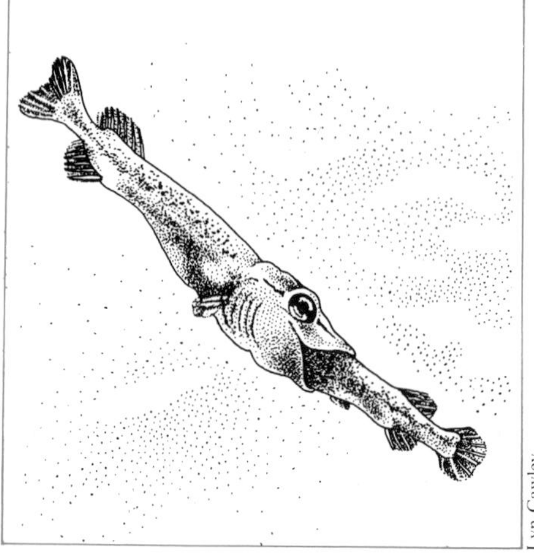

Lyn Cawley

14 lb probably spawns around 100,000 eggs, of which only a few will make a year's growth, with even fewer growing to the size of the female parent.

**Record pike**

The present record pike weighed 40 lb when taken from Horsey Mere, Norfolk, by Peter Hancock in February 1967, but numerous specimens of over 40 lb, and one of 53 lb have been taken from Irish and Scottish water. A 43 lb pike was caught in this country in 1974 but following a spurious claim the fish was never credited to its true captor whose name did not enter the record fish lists. There is some evidence for the existence of pike of up to 70 lb in British waters. Certainly, if you wish to join the record-breakers, it is advisable to fish in the early part of the season when female fish are heavy with spawn. But conservation-minded anglers may object to this.

To locate the pike, inspect the likely lying-up places for signs of activity. A sudden wild splashing from a rudd as it leaps clear of the water is a possible indication of a pike's presence. The movement of fish on the surface may also indicate an urgent desire to escape the attentions of a predator.

Learning to 'read' the water is something all angers should do. It involves studying the area and deciding where fish are likely to be found. And to do this an understanding of the pike's habits and needs is invaluable. Pike often lie in holes in the undercut banks of rivers and streams. Where a tree has fallen into the water it diverts the flow and sets up an eddy, which produces a drastic slowdown in the current. This creates a natural lie for a predator. On stillwaters the pike will pounce from the edge of beds of reedmace and rushes, coming out from gaps between the stalks, where it has cover.

But finding pike on large lakes and reservoirs can be more difficult. Stillwater lacks the identifying features which aid the angler's search. Underwater contours assume importance in this situation. Natural fall-offs in the slope of the lake bed, ledges and underwater obstructions are the places to find pike. But as these places are invisible to the angler he must locate them by plumbing.

**MONA'S LENGTH/ WEIGHT PIKE SCALE**

| in | lb | in | lb |
|---|---|---|---|
| 20 | 2·500 | 41 | 21·537 |
| 21 | 2·894 | 42 | 23·152 |
| 22 | 2·327 | 43 | 24·845 |
| 23 | 3·802 | 44 | 26·602 |
| 24 | 4·300 | 45 | 28·476 |
| 25 | 4·882 | 46 | 30·457 |
| 26 | 5·492 | 47 | 32·444 |
| 27 | 6·150 | 48 | 34·585 |
| 28 | 6·860 | 49 | 36·774 |
| 29 | 7·621 | 50 | 39·062 |
| 30 | 8·437 | 51 | 41·453 |
| 31 | 9·309 | 52 | 43·940 |
| 32 | 10·240 | 53 | 46·524 |
| 33 | 11·230 | 54 | 49·207 |
| 34 | 12·282 | 55 | 51·992 |
| 35 | 13·398 | 56 | 54·880 |
| 36 | 14·580 | 57 | 57·872 |
| 37 | 15·829 | 58 | 60·972 |
| 38 | 17·147 | 59 | 64·180 |
| 39 | 18·537 | 60 | 67·500 |
| 40 | 20·000 | | |

Pike can be made to come to the angler in just the same way as smaller fish are lured. Groundbait, though not of the cereal type, can attract pike. Mashed fish offal with pilchard oil added and mixed into a stiff paste may be dropped into likely spots. The pike's acute senses allow it to detect food at some distance.

Pike can be caught by a variety of methods. Because of the fish's voracious appetite, it will attack both live and deadbaits. Fish, for example, can be presented either live, swimming in mid-water, or as deadbait, lying on the bottom. Practically any species can be used as a live-bait—even small pike are an attractive lure for the larger ones. The most important thing is to use a lively bait that will work well, swimming strongly in order to arouse the attention of a pike. However many anglers consider the use of one fish to catch another as being cruel. Indeed, the use of livebaits has been banned recently in Ireland, although the Irish authorities were not concerned with cruelty so much as with the transfer of shoal fish species from one water to another.

Artificial lures play an important part in pike fishing. Spinning is both a pleasurable and successful method. Almost any material can be employed in the manufacture of lures but metal is most often used. Essentially, this is because metal can be worked and bent to the required shape to provide the spinner or spoon with an attractive action when pulled through the water. Obviously metal has its own weight so there is little need to add lead to the end tackle in order to cast it. There is much controversy about the type of action that a spinner should have to make it attractive to the pike and other fish. Trout and perch will dash after a minute blade spinner that represents a small, lively fish. On the other hand, pike, especially the big ones, are only prepared to surge after a lure over short distances.

**It pays to experiment**

The spoon should be larger for pike and incorporate good-quality treble hooks. Bright colours seem to attract pike. A copper spoon with one side painted red will give alternating flashes that simulate the appearance of an escaping rudd, while a silver

*(Above) Pike tend to keep to constant depths when patrolling for food. They also hang around protruding ledges and the spot marked 'X' on our diagram would be a good place from which to fish. (Right) The mottled green and brown flanks of the pike, speckled with lighter spots, help the fish to blend into the bed of similarly coloured reeds.*

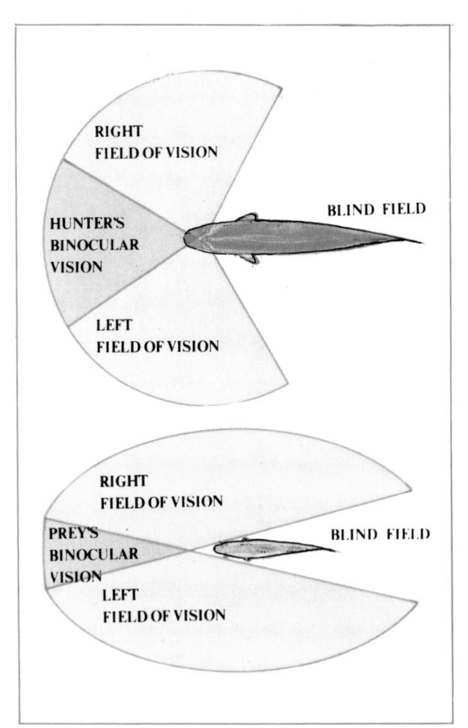


spoon with red stripes resembles a roach. The colour combinations are never-ending and should be exerimented with. Quite often a black-painted spinner is the only type that induces pike to attack. It could be that the pike see the lure as a moving silhouette, which annoys it. An attack (that cannot be called a 'feeding response') is often made on an artificial lure. Is the pike responding to an invasion of its territory when it strikes to kill or drive away?

Plugs came to us from America, where they are used successfully to catch a wide variety of species. Made of wood or plastic, they do not really resemble anything found in Nature. Anglers rely on the action built

*(Left) A predator needs a good field of binocular vision to attack and grasp its food. But its prey only needs monocular vision. (Below) After attacking and grasping its prey the pike turns away and moves off for a few yards before swallowing the fish head first.*

Rod Sutterby.

*(Right) Distinctive pores on the gills and head of a young pike act as sensors for the predator. (Below) The pike's skull showing the complex bone structure. Age can be assessed by the circular growth markings on the gill covers. Evidence of the pike's predatory nature are the huge teeth.*

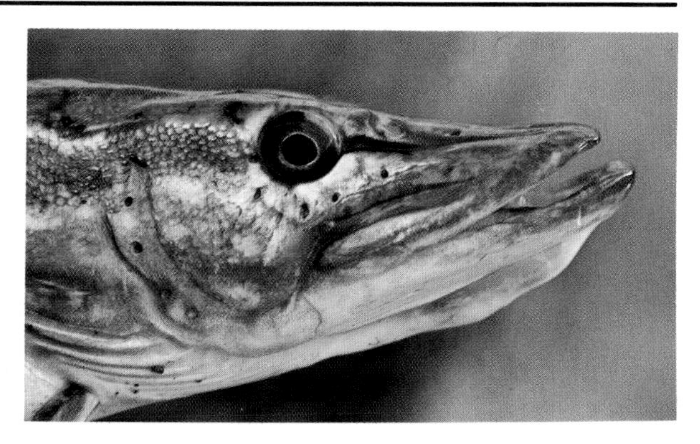

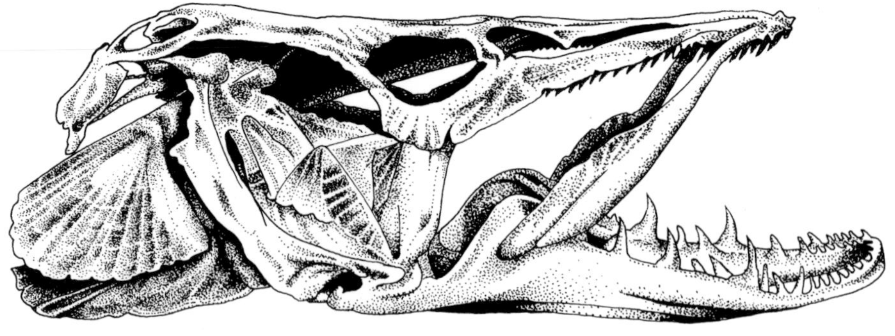

Lyn Cawley

Bill Howes

into the plug to attract fish. The shape of the plug, position of the diving-vane and treble hooks all serve to give the plug a motion that urges pike to attack. There are plugs, and the colour patterns range from the sensible to quite outrageous combinations—but they all catch fish.

One can vary pike-fishing methods by setting out to accurately simulate what pike might eat in the course of a feeding session. Lures simulating mice and voles can be made from fur and leather strips. Plastic frogs and fish are already available but their value to the pike fisherman is doubtful. This type of artificial lure rarely has the natural appearance and movement necessary to

*Unhooking a pike taken on deadbait. The fish is held behind the gills to stop the head turning, while forceps are used to extract the hook. The mouth is kept open by a gag, used sparingly to avoid tearing. (Right) Using a large net to boat a pike. Note the unusual use of a fly rod.*

simulate the living creature's movement.

Where the pike fisherman can score is in extending the sport of fly fishing to the species. All that is needed is to tie large flies from materials that will look like a small fish. These have been used with encouraging results on the Irish pike loughs.

With its beautiful marbling of green and brown, the pike is superbly camouflaged. The supreme hunter in our rivers and lakes, this species needs to be stalked with care by the angler, and when caught deserves to be treated with respect. Put the fish back into its environment for it is as important to preserve the species as it is to safeguard the future of our pike fishing.

Bill Howes

*Here a young angler carefully returns a fine 28lb pike to the water. Note the way in which the fish is firmly supported and held close to the body so that it is not dropped and cannot turn its head to bite.*

Mike Prichard

# Float rods

Bill Howes

*(Left) Ian Bryant, of Langley, Bucks, netting a fish from one of a group of lakes belonging to the Leisure Sport A.C. at Yateley, near Sandhurst, Surrey. The long match rod and fine tackle being used means that a landing-net is necessary even though the fish may not be in the specimen category. (Right) A selection of float rods: (Left to right) 13ft Sundridge tip-action match rod; 13ft Intrepid soft-action float rod; 10ft light carp rod by Shakespeare; 22ft collapsible roach-pole by Shakespeare. Three groups of different-type floats are illustrated, together with the caps for the bottom section of the pole which holds the others.*

Rods for float fishing should be 12-13ft long, able to handle lines of 3-5lb b.s., and have a slow action. Other types of coarse fishing rod may be used: the specimen hunter, for example, may find a light carp rod best when float fishing for tench or carp in weedy conditions and with the expectation of a big fish. The beginner will often use a glass-fibre spinning rod because it is cheap, adaptable and sturdy. But the term 'float rod' is usually applied to the longer rods used for general and match fishing.

These two uses have resulted in the development of two distinct kinds of float rod: slow-action rods, which bend along much of their length when playing a fish or casting; and fast-action rods, usually rigid to within 25 per cent of their length with the action concentrated in the tip.

General-purpose float rods are slower in action than match rods and have stronger tips, usually made of glass-fibre and 2½-3mm in diameter. The tip of a match rod is nearer 2½mm in diameter to allow their use with lines of 1½-2lb b.s. In addition, the match rod is usually stiffer in the butt to give quicker striking. Fish control, however, is more difficult with a stiffer rod, but as a rule, matchmen are not pursuing large fish. There are exceptions to this, such as on the Severn where matches are won with good-sized chub and barbel. These fish demand a stronger rod than that used by the average match fisherman.

**Match rod development**

Due to the changing demands of match fishing, the match rod is constantly being developed. Different areas of fishing call for

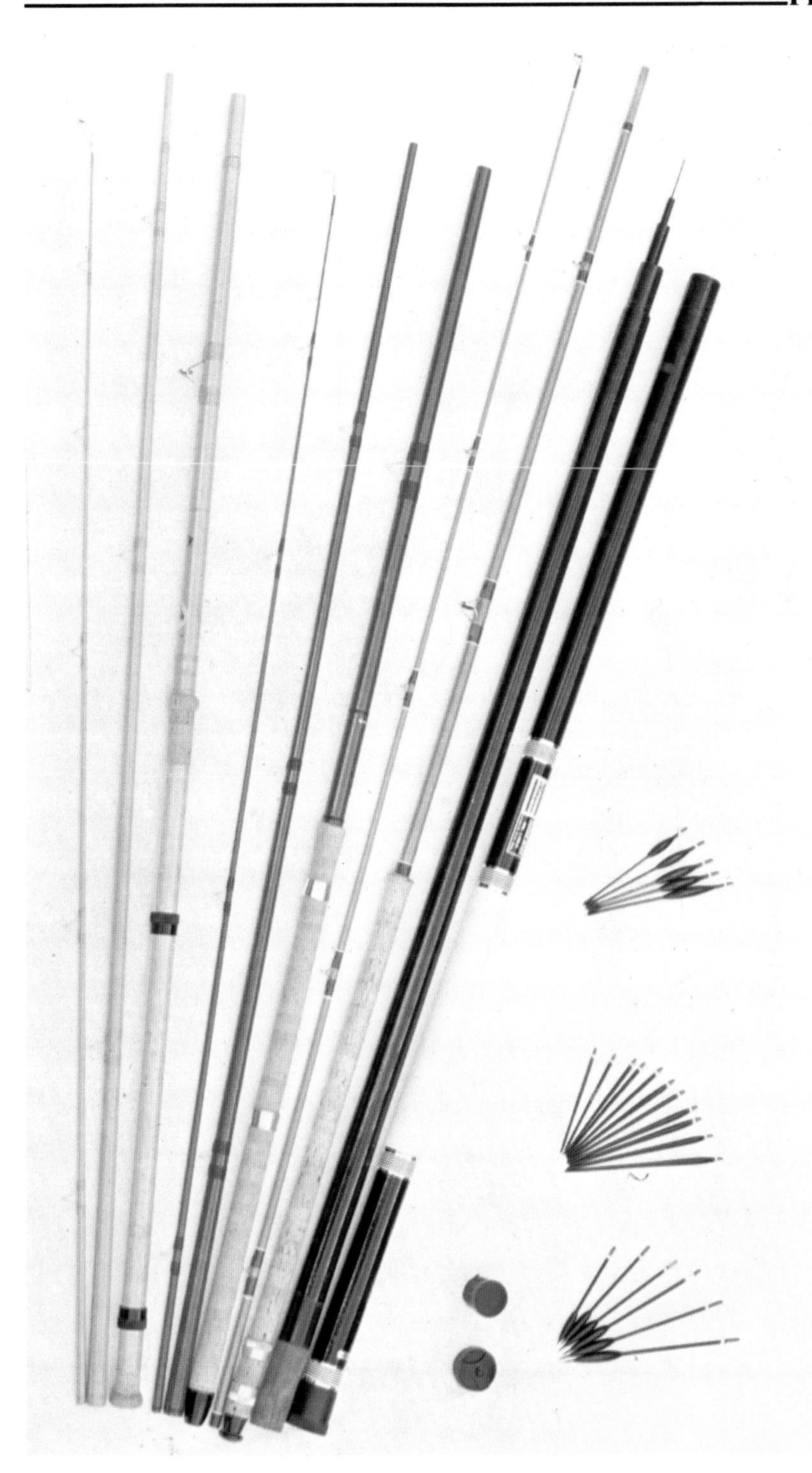

P. H. Ward/Tackle Carrier, Watford

S. L. Ward/Tackle Carrier, Watford

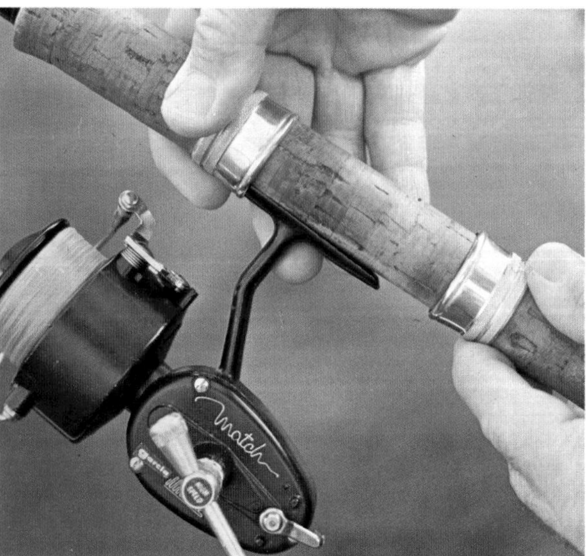


P. H. Ward/Natural Science Photos

*(Above) Here, Peter Ward demonstrates two types of float rod. In his right hand he holds a 13ft tip-action match rod, and in the left a 13ft soft-action float rod.*
*(Left) This is the correct way to attach a reel to a match rod.*
*(Right, top) Swing or quiver tips are attached to rod tips by being screwed into specially designed tip rings.*
*(Right, lower) Roach-pole tip showing the method of attaching the alloy crook and the elastic shock-absorber.*

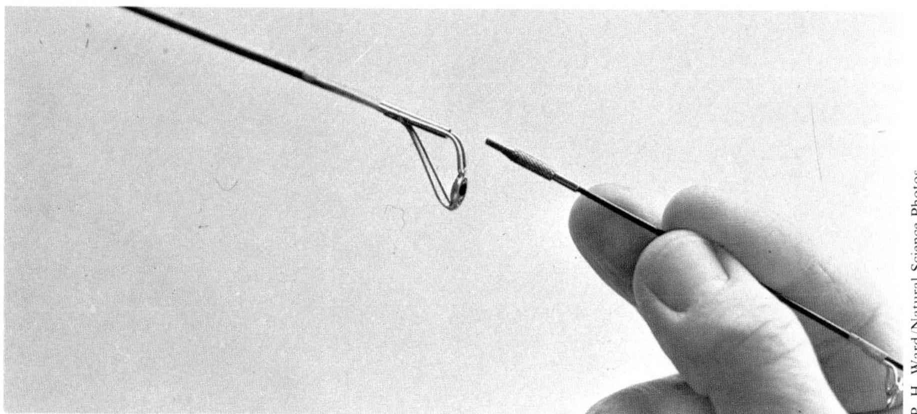

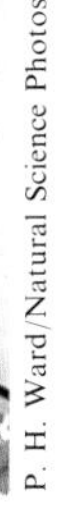
P. H. Ward/Natural Science Photos

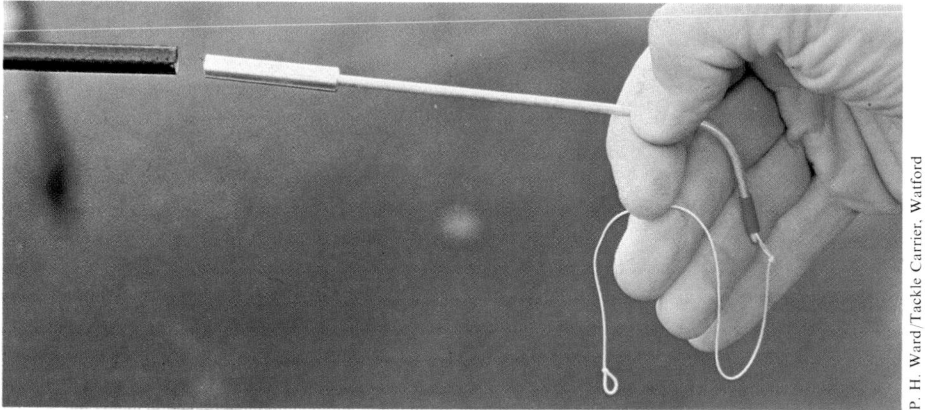
P. H. Ward/Tackle Carrier, Watford

different actions so there are variations in the type of rod in use.

Most float rods today are made of tubular glass-fibre, though carbon-fibre rods, still in their infancy, are increasingly popular.

Float rods are usually equipped with cork handles fitted with sliding rings for holding the reel. This keeps the weight to a minimum.

With a threaded tip ring fitted, the float rod may be used with various screw attachments, such as a swing tip for ledgering. Care should be taken, however, to ensure that the tip of the rod will stand up to the casting weight or the use of a swimfeeder.

A rod of this description is also suited to long-trotting, when float tackle is allowed to trot down with the current of a river or stream and the fish are hooked and played some way downstream from the angler.

Specimen hunters tend to use the longer, lighter ledgering rods—those designed by Peter Stone, for example—since they are capable of casting tackle long distances and controlling heavy fish.

**The ideal match rod**

Match rods, too, have a specific job to perform. They must be light and well-balanced enough to be held comfortably for the duration of a contest. They must be capable of casting float tackle with precision and sometimes over a considerable distance, and they must be able to strike into fish both close-to and at a distance.

This has resulted in the use of a fast-action rod with a soft top which helps to overcome line breakage by acting as a shock absorber. Commonly made of glass-fibre, match rods are now available with a proportion of their

construction in carbon-fibre. While retaining a glass-fibre top, the carbon-fibre butt and middle of the rod have added stiffness where it is needed—but such power can prove too strong for use with fine lines.

The most popular lengths for match rods are between 12 and 13ft as these appear to provide the best compromise between length and ease of handling. Shorter rods cannot control fish as well, while longer rods are difficult to manage. Further development of carbon-fibre rods, may well change this.

**Pole fishing**

Pole fishing has recently become very popular in this country. With this style of sport, a rod in the region of 20-28ft long is used and the line is fixed direct to the end of the rod without the niceties of reel or rod rings. The float tackle—often very small and

*Roach-pole fishing is now coming back into fashion with a vengeance. It is a very sensitive method of taking small coarse fish and demands a particular expertise. Here, Peter Ward is attaching a section of a Shakespeare roach-pole before fishing.*

sensitive—is fished extremely close to the top of the rod. This makes it easier for the angler to strike at very small bite indications, since he is in almost direct contact with the bait. Because of the stiffness of the pole, a shock absorber of fine elastic may be fitted between the rod and line so that, on striking, the line does not snap. This type of fishing is becoming more popular, particularly where bleak are the quarry, as the pole can be used to strike quickly and place the bait accurately.

# Ledger rods

Ray Forsberg

The term ledgering is applied to the style of fishing where the bait is allowed to rest on the bed of the river or lake and a float is not used for bite indication. Rods specially designed for ledgering are comparative newcomers to the angling scene.

Until comparatively recently, the art of ledgering was undeveloped and a fairly heavy rod was commonly used. Probably the earliest rod which was used for ledgering was the traditional Avon-type rod used for fishing the Hampshire Avon and other fast flowing rivers. It has a length of 11ft, is in three pieces with a built-cane middle section and top with a tonkin cane butt. It was followed by the built cane MK IV Avon and MK IV Carp designs by Richard Walker.

The carp rod was obviously designed for carp fishing but found ready acceptance by the specimen barbel hunters. The lighter MK IV Avon was a scaled-down version suitable for general fishing for tench, chub, barbel and perch in flowing or stillwaters. Both were very successful designs from which have evolved today's range of specialist ledger rods.

*(Above) Two-rod ledgering for barbel on the Swale at Thornton Bridge.*
*(Right) An angler deep in concentration and water while ledgering for bream. He is using a swing-tip.*

**Types of rod**

Today these rods are manufactured mainly of tubular fibreglass, although a few rods in built-cane of the MK IV type are still made and no doubt carbon-fibre rods will be further developed.

Present-day ledger rods vary from 9ft to 11½ft, the longer rods being used more by the specimen hunter and the shorter kinds usually by the competition angler. They are also used with various types of bite indicators, although some rods have a built-in bite indicator called a quiver tip, which consists of a finely tapered piece of solid glass which, because of its small diameter, is very sensitive. This type, known as a quiver tip rod, is usually 9½-10ft long.

Rods of 9ft to 10ft long are usually employed by match anglers for ledgering in conjunction with a swimfeeder. This is a weighted, perforated container used for holding ground bait of some form, which gradually disperses in the water to attract fish into the swim. Because of the weight of the swimfeeder, rods of this type are usually fairly stiff to aid casting. This necessitates some form of bite indicator to show the takes of the feeding fish.

The longer type of ledgering rod is more used by specimen hunters who usually rely on fine tips and bite indicators on the line to hook fish. Quiver tip rods are used for shy-biting fish such as roach, while the longer rods are used to cast to and to strike at fish at long range. A rod with a test curve of approximately 1 to 1¼lb is necessary due to the drag and stretch of the line but with steep-taper rods the test curve can be less to give better bite indication, while the relatively strong butt and middle will pick up a line rapidly.

**The best length**

For general purposes a rod of this type of 10-11ft is suitable for swimfeeding or match ledgering. A stiff rod of 9½ft is the best all-round length. The rod should be fitted with graduated stand-off rings with a screw-in tip ring which will accommodate any one of the various attachments for bite indication—swing tip, quiver tip, spring tip and others. With this type of rod, lines of 3-6lb b.s. are normally used, while the larger rods used by specimen hunters can require the use of lines up to 10lb b.s.

Many of the lighter carp rods made today can make excellent ledgering rods, as they are primarily designed for fishing on the bottom of the lake or gravel pit for carp, unlike specially designed ledgering rods. The tips are rarely used, however, for bite indication, and this should be considered when selecting a rod.

For some aspects of ledgering, where dead fish are used as ledgered baits for eels and

Bill Howes

pike, stepped-up versions of ledgering rods are made. These are capable of casting heavy baits up to 3oz and coupled with lines of breaking strains 12-15lb have sufficient power to fight large pike and eels.

**Float ledgering rods**

Many float rods today have screw-in tip rings to take a bite indicator, which enables the rod to be used for ledgering. Usually, however, if they have fine tops for float fishing, they should not be used for heavy ledgering with swimfeeders, which may damage the rod.

Rods used for float ledgering are usually standard float rods. These use the float as a bite indicator, which means the float is usually well under the rod top. Here, a fairly long rod is required.

When choosing a ledgering rod, the main points to be considered are: weight to be cast, whether it be a lead of some sort on a loaded swimfeeder; breaking strain of lines to be used and rod length required. For instance, the match angler, due to the limitations of his swim by the match rules, would not cover the same area of water in casting as a specimen hunter. The ability to cast 30 yards and strike fish at this range is probably all the matchman needs to do. But the specimen hunter may need to cast and strike fish up to 70 yards, calling for a much longer rod to have the necessary control.

*The 9ft hollow-glass Hardy Touch Ledger, designed by Fred Taylor. A longer pike rod lies next to the Touch Ledger.*

Hardy's

# Spinning rods

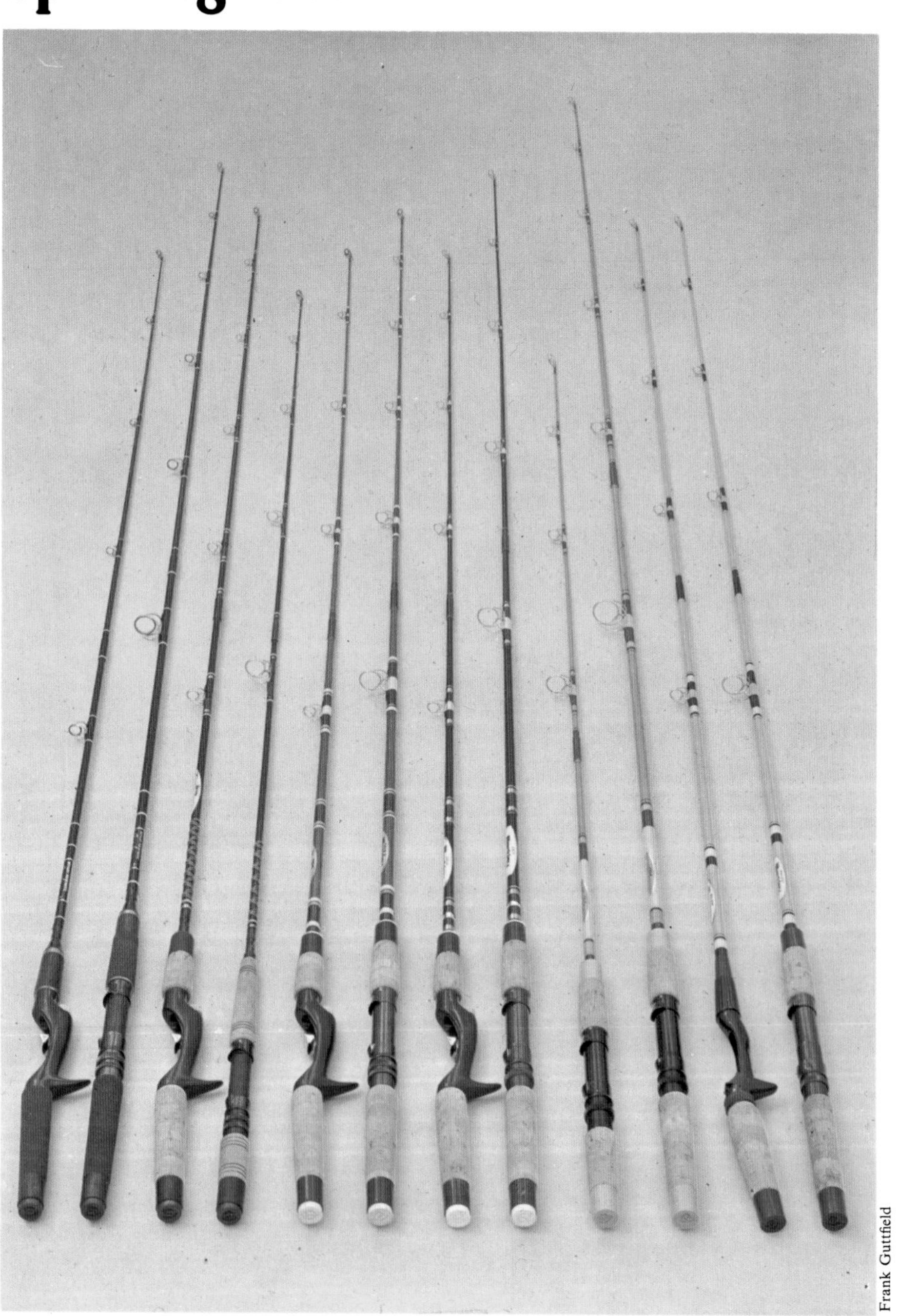

Frank Guttfield

Spinning rods may usually be classified by the weights they can cast and the line strengths the rod can handle, their basic function being to cast a lure and control a hooked fish.

As a general rule, the lighter the lure or spinner to be cast, the lighter and shorter the rod. In general also, the lighter the lure, the finer will be the line used with it. This is because the heavier and thicker the line the more weight is required in the lure to overcome the drag of the line, which is to be avoided when long casts are needed.

Most rods designed for use with the lighter spinning lures (up to ½oz) are 6–8ft long and are teamed with fixed-spool reels and relatively light lines of 4–8lb b.s. Rods for the heavier lures are more often 8–10½ft long and may be used with fixed-spool or multiplier reels loaded with lines up to 20lb b.s. These heavier spinning rods are very often used with two hands when casting and so are naturally referred to as 'double-handed'.

In addition to the standard patterns of spinning rods, there is a special type which originated in the US and is known as a 'bait casting' rod. This rod, designed to be used in conjunction with a multiplier, features a pistol-grip, cranked handle to allow the fisherman to cast and control the reel using one hand. It is made with a one-piece top 5–6ft long, and the reel is mounted on top of the rod. This arrangement enables accurate casting but has the disadvantage that long-distance casts are not possible.

**Baitcasting rods**

These outfits are used extensively in America for freshwater black bass fishing, but are not popular in Britain as they are best used with plug baits which, by contrast with spinners, spoons, Devon minnows and similar lures, have not yet gained wide acceptance here. Baitcasting rods also require a fairly heavy plug or lure to cast well

*(Left) A selection of spinning and bait-casting rods. The pistol-grip baitcasters are an American innovation, not yet fully accepted by anglers in this country.*

*(Below) Heavy-duty spinning rods are long and may need two hands for casting. Such rods, some of which are up to 10ft 6in long, are designed to cast weights up to 2¼oz.*

Rod Sutterby

and it is still more usual in Britain to use longer rods in this situation.

For light spinning for trout, sea trout, perch and pike, a rod of 7–8ft long, capable of casting up to $\frac{3}{4}$oz, makes a good all-round tool when coupled with a small-to-medium fixed-spool reel carrying line of 4–8lb b.s. depending on the type of fishing. This pattern of rod is usually made of hollow glass-fibre, with cheaper rods in solid glass.

A cork handle about 18in long, fitted with a screw winch-fitting to hold the reel securely is the basis of all spinning rods. The size of rod rings should be graduated to aid casting

*(Above) Heavy-duty spinning rod with a multiplier mounted on top.*
*(Right) Spinning rod with fixed-spool reel.*

S. L. Ward/Natural Science Photos

by ensuring smooth line flow from the spool.

A rod suitable for heavier types of lures in the $\frac{1}{2}$–1oz range should be $8\frac{1}{2}$–$9\frac{1}{2}$ft long. The handle should be about 24in long, with a screw winch-fitting about 14in from the bottom of the handle when used with a fixed-spool reel, and 2–3in higher with a multiplier. This subsitution of lines of 9–15lb b.s. makes the outfit suitable for the heavier types of freshwater spinning—salmon and pike—and for lighter saltwater spinning for bass, pollack, mackerel and other species.

**Heavy-duty spinning rods**
The heaviest patterns of rod are required for spinning with deadbaits for salmon and large pike in very unfavourable water conditions. The deadbaits can weigh up to 2oz, and lines up to 20lb b.s. are needed.

A rod capable of handling heavy lures and leads should be $9\frac{1}{2}$–10ft long and fairly strong, with a test curve of $1\frac{1}{2}$–$2\frac{1}{4}$lb. This type of rod is very often used with a multiplier, for heavy spinning. The handles are usually 24–28in long.

**Greenheart rods**
The design of spinning rods has altered considerably over the past 50 years. The original rods were heavy and long, and made for salmon spinning. They were usually of greenheart (a special type of hardwood), or built cane. The centrepin reel used with these rods required them to be slow in action to assist the revolving drum to accelerate evenly and allow line to flow off without jamming.

With the introduction of the fixed-spool reel, rod action could be improved. They could be faster in action, as well as lighter. The fixed-spool reel could cast lighter baits and, because the spool of the reel did not revolve, the line did not jam or overrun, making casting much easier.

The multiplier became popular at about the same time, and was an improvement over the centrepin so far as casting was concerned. However, it is only in the last 10 years or so that the multiplier's braking systems for casting have been developed enough to allow rod-makers to match them with the lighter, faster-actioned rods now favoured. The latest material to be used in spinning rods is carbon-fibre. These rods are expensive, but perform well.

Prices for the various types of spinning rod vary considerably, depending on the quality of the materials and workmanship. A good tubular glass rod by a reputable maker costs from £20–£30, while imported rods may be bought for as little as £5.

# Centrepin reels

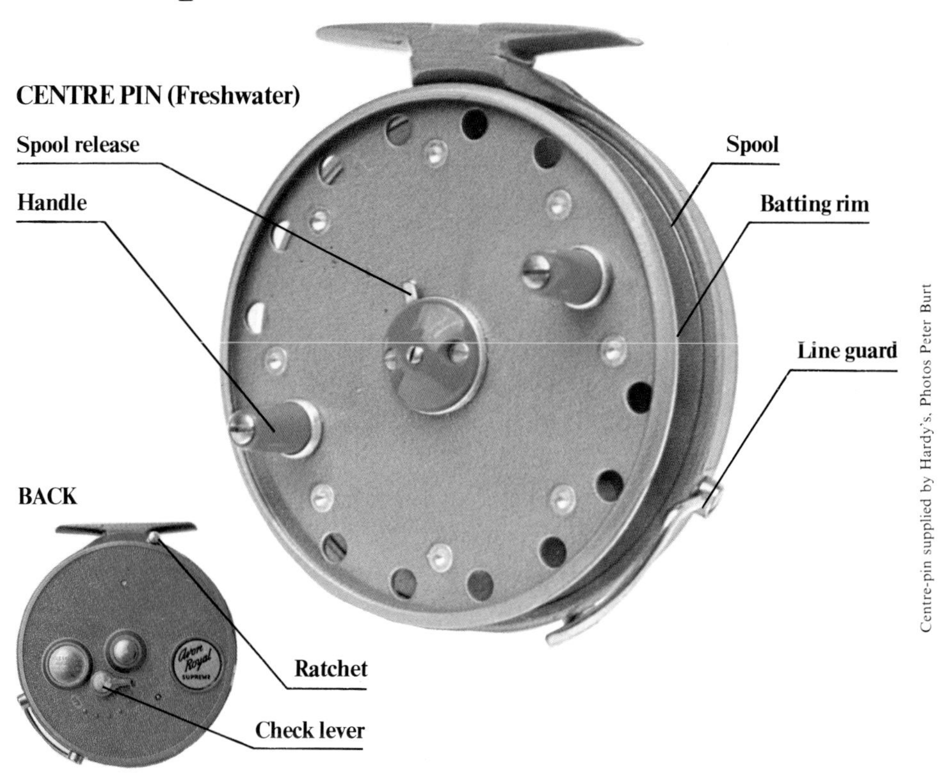


Centre-pin supplied by Hardy's. Photos Peter Burt

**The centrepin reel**
A centrepin is a reel acting as a line reservoir with its axis at right angles to the rod. Good centrepins consist of a flanged drum, machined to very fine tolerances, which revolves freely on a precision-engineered steel axle. Many models have appeared over the years, ranging from the cheap and simple kind in Bakelite to the comparatively expensive models manufactured from stainless steel or enamelled metal. Wooden models have also been produced, but are now not so common. The centrepin is simple in construction, and—by virtue of this—reliable, as well as being easy to operate and to maintain. It is important as a beginner's reel because it helps develop basic casting skills. Once the use of the centrepin is mastered many anglers prefer it to the fixed spool to be discussed in a later feature.

The centrepin is used, preferably in conjunction with an Avon-type rod, which has an all-through action, mainly for 'trotting'—allowing the river's current to carry float-tackle smoothly down-stream, allowing the bait to cover long stretches of water at one cast. It is with this method that the free-running centrepin drum is put to best advantage. To recover line quickly, the experienced user will give the drum a series of taps with all four fingers in a practice called 'batting'.

The diameter of the reel can vary, but most are between 3½in and 4½in. The drum's diameter will be almost as large, and the larger the drum the more rapid will be the

Bill Howes

line recovery. Most centrepins have a line-guard and optional ratchet, while some also have a drag mechanism. An exposed smooth rim, which allows finger-pressure to be applied to control the line when casting or playing a fish, is a valuable feature of some varieties. Many of the older centrepin reels are now very much in demand for their fine, free action.

**Centrepin's comeback**

Although the centrepin is still widely used—and indeed has made a come-back in recent years—its popularity suffered greatly when the fixed-spool reel was introduced 40 years ago. This reel permits almost effortless long casting, because the drum is at right-angles to the rod. To achieve similar distances with a centre-pin is a satisfying accomplishment.

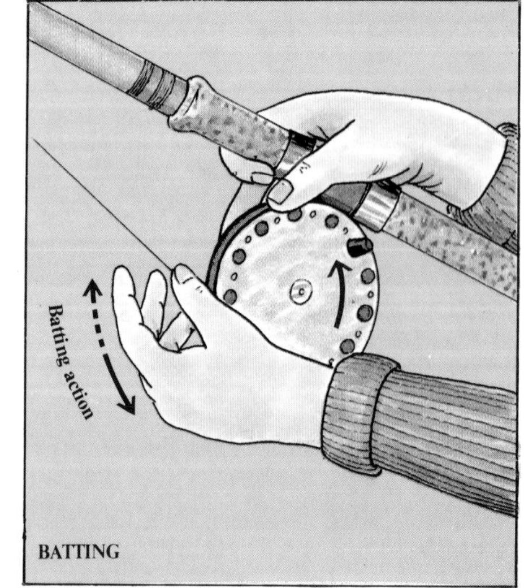


BATTING

Rod Sutterby

# Multiplier reels

In 1977 a centrepin reel for fly fishing, made entirely of carbon fibre, made its appearance. This, the 'Line-Shooter', is a big reel with a wide drum and exposed rim, allowing rapid line recovery by winding or 'batting'. It is also the lightest centrepin reel ever made, weighing only 5oz. The ratchet is optional and, by contrast with many other models, is reasonably quiet. It also incorporates an extremely sensitive drag control. Although built as a fly reel it has found favour with coarse fishermen, who use it for trotting. For this, the drag should be set so that the reel revolves with the current's pull. For 'laying-on' (float fishing but with about 18in of line on the bottom, which gives a clear bite indication) or 'stret-pegging' (again setting the float higher than the depth of the water and casting the tackle into a groundbaited area) the setting should not allow the line to pay out too freely and so tangle.

**The multiplier reel**

The multiplier is essentially a reel with a small-diameter drum geared to a ratio of 3 or 4:1 so that line is retrieved rapidly by winding. Models with automatic gears are available, but are far more expensive. These have ratios of about $2\frac{1}{2}$ and $4\frac{1}{2}$:1. As with the fixed-spool reel, there is a wide variety.

To the beginner the multiplier may appear complicated. But you should become familiar with its star-drag, brake and other parts before going fishing with it. Most multipliers are right-handed and cannot be adapted for left-handers.

## MULTIPLIER (Freshwater)

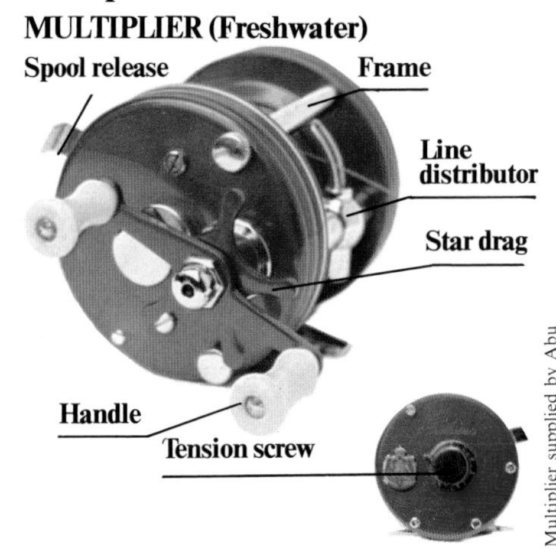


Multiplier supplied by Abu

*This precision-made freshwater reel is a multiplier, the Ambassador 5000. It is ideal for baitcasting and spinning with weights between ½oz and 1oz. A level-wind line distributor ensures the line is rewound evenly. This reel, with a gear-ratio of 1:3½, has a line retrieve of 15½in per single turn of the handle on a full spool.*

The main problem with the multiplier reel is that of the line over-running and tangling into 'bird's nests'. To reduce the possibility of this, whether when lowering the bait over the side of a boat and down to the sea-bed or casting up to 100 yards from the shore, the thumb must rest gently on the line as it pays out. Various devices have been incorporated by manufacturers in some of their models to overcome this difficulty. These include spool tensioners, centrifugal governors, oil 'drag' retarders and 'lift' and 'brake' gadgets, but bird's nests can be avoided by the angler if he learns how to use his reel properly.

The more expensive multipliers have ball bearings set in both end-plates. Leading from one spindle is a governing mechanism, usually consisting of fibre blocks, which are thrown out of centrifugal motion, thus acting as a brake when the bait hits the water. To keep the spool revolving with the weight while casting, a manual brake in the form of a drag is employed. Another feature of superior reels is a 'line-spreader', which ensures the even distribution of line on recovery.

The mechanism of the freshwater multiplier is extremely delicate, and sand, dust, and, worse still, saltwater, are to be avoided at all costs. The heavier saltwater models still need keeping clean and oiled, but they are usually rust-proof. Unlike other reels, which are fixed to the underside of the rod handle, the multiplier is used with the rod reversed and the reel uppermost.

It is essential after each outing to rinse the reel thoroughly in freshwater and, after drying it, to apply a recommended lubricant, especially if the reel is not to be used again for some time. Periodical inspection is also advisable, for sand or grit in the gears can wreak havoc and a jammed reel while playing a strong fish is an event no angler wants to experience.

The multiplier used in pike fishing will, with practice, allow baits, spinners and plugs to be cast as far as with a fixed-spool model. As a bonus, playing fish on a drum reel, which demands special skills, can be a real delight.

*Line retrieve. The centrepin (1:1) compared with the multiplier (1:3½). Amount of line on the spool is an added factor.*

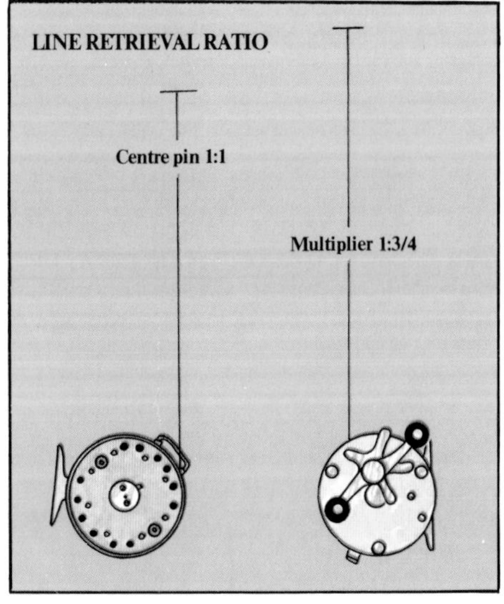


Rod Sutterby

# Fixed spool reels

The modern fixed-spool reel is a masterpiece of engineering design. It has banished one of the angler's oldest problems, that of casting to the required spot, and has doubled, or even trebled the distances over which the average angler can hope to cast accurately. At the same time, it has reduced the problem of tangled line to a minimum.

Anglers have become so accustomed to these benefits that they take them for granted nowadays, much as they do their wife's washing machine. Yet anyone who grew up with nothing more than a wooden centrepin reel can recall the constant practice needed to learn to cast direct from the reel, and the inevitable tangles and 'bird's nests' which resulted all too often.

Despite this, we still occasionally hear the reel's critics bemoaning the fact that it has taken the skill out of casting. Even if this were wholly true, it would be no more a cause for regret than the fact that the washing machine has taken the drudgery out of washing day.

The first fixed-spool reel was patented by Alfred Illingworth in 1905. It incorporated all the basic principles of the modern reel, which still hold good today. The line spool was fixed with its axis at right angles to the direction of casting. When line was released, as long as the tackle provided the necessary inertia to pull it off, it simply spilled over the edge of the spool, with practically no unnecessary friction, and without requiring the spool to revolve. Hence the modern name—fixed-spool.

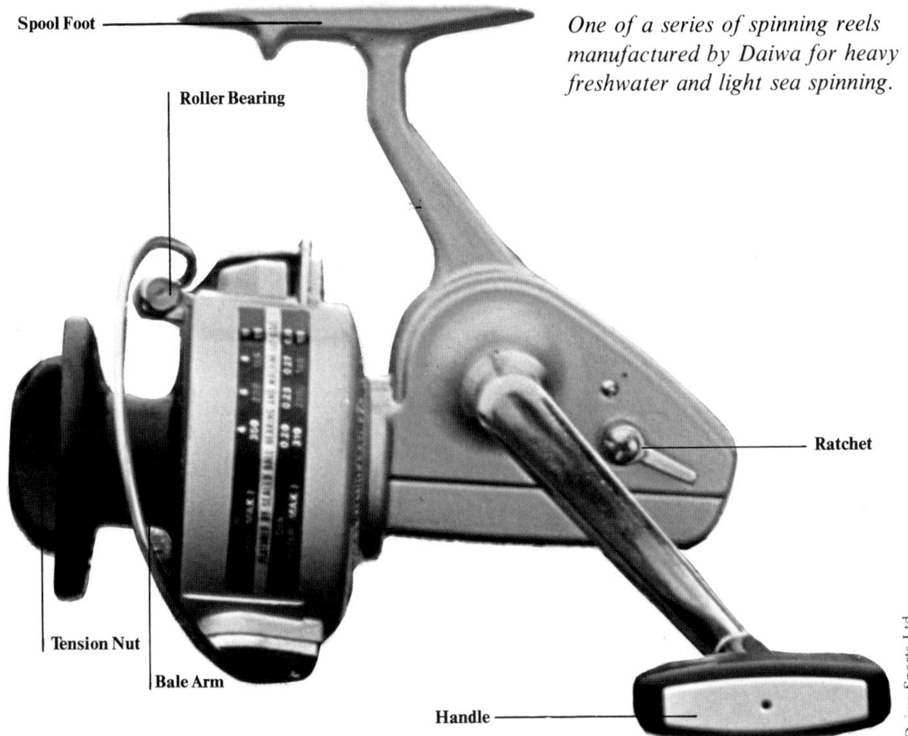


*One of a series of spinning reels manufactured by Daiwa for heavy freshwater and light sea spinning.*

Daiwa Sports Ltd.

Line was retrieved simply by hooking it onto a primitive bale-arm, which revolved around the fixed-spool, laying line back when the reel handle was turned.

**Slipping clutches and crosswind reels**

To provide the faster retrieval desired for spinning, Illingworth geared the reel handle to the bale-arm to provide a retrieval ratio of approximately 3:1. The fixed-spool reel has come a long way since those days, and, not long after Illingworth's first reel, slipping clutches and crosswind reels were developed, although these only entered the market in the early Thirties, not really coming into common usage until after the war.

Now it is possible to buy such reels with a wide variety of retrieval ratios suitable for every possible kind of fishing. All have adjustable clutch mechanisms, a reciprocating reel movement which provides even laying of line, and a crosswind action to prevent the reel jamming.

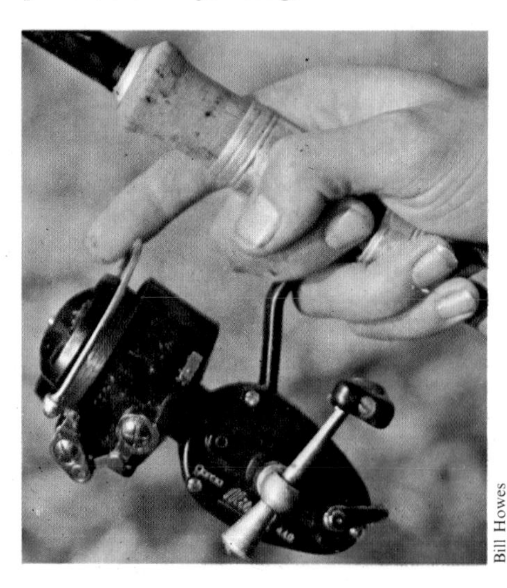

Bill Howes

*(Above) When the bale-arm is closed, the line can be held back by a finger.*

To be effective, such a reel must be properly used. Most manufacturers' instructions today refer to the loading capacity of the various spools, which varies with the b.s. of the line required. Many manufacturers provide a spare spool, and since most spools are quickly detachable the angler can change spool and line in a moment to suit his needs.

**Loading the spool**

When loading the spool it must be borne in mind that the rotary action of the bale-arm around the spool imparts twist to the line, and that over a hundred yards of line this becomes considerable, especially when medium-weight lines, which are fairly springy, are employed.

This twist in the line is largely responsible for the manner in which the monofilament lines often tend to spring off the spool. To prevent twist it is recommended that the line be pulled off the manufacturer's spool not by letting it turn on a pencil as you wind, but over the flange of the manufacturer's spool in much the same way as the line spills over the edge of the fixed-spool itself. Since pulling line off and laying it on both impart twist to the line, the tactic is to impart opposite twist as the bale-arm lays the line on the spool.

**Pumping a fish**

When the slipping clutch is set, this must be done so that if a dangerous strain is put on your line, the clutch will slip before the line breaks. This also implies that you must select a line b.s. suitable for the rod you intend to use. If, for example, your line is of 20lb b.s. and you set the clutch at, say, 18lb, you have a margin of safety of roughly 2lb. However, if you are using a rod of a ½lb test curve there is considerable danger that you will already have strained or damaged, or even broken your rod before the clutch will start to slip. To allow this to happen is clearly absurd, and so lines must be selected to suit the rod. If you must use heavy lines on a light rod you would be better to set the clutch to give when the rod is entering the test curve position, or somewhat before.

Once the clutch is properly set you can safely expect that the line will not break, but a safety margin should be allowed to give you complete control. When a heavy fish takes and you make a successful strike, the fish can run, taking line off the spool as the clutch slips. All you can do is to hold the winding handle steady. On no account should you attempt to wind in line by turning it, for this will only twist the line as the fish continues to run against the clutch.

When you judge that the fish has tired a little you can exert pressure by extending your index finger so that it rests against the revolving spool, so making the fish fight harder for line, and eventually halting it. To retrieve line, retain the finger control and raise the rod tip gently, then lower it as you turn the handle to retrieve line until the rod is more or less horizontal.

This pumping process can be repeated to bring the fish under control. If necessary, let the fish have its head when it surges in between pumps. You will find that by applying side strain and finger pressure, with a bit of pumping in between, you can subdue most fish after some practice. The fixed-spool reel leads you to replace the skills of casting with the greater skills involved in playing your fish with finesse and judgement, and until these are acquired your reel will not assist you in landing many big fish.

**Long trotting**

Long trotting is a fishing method for which many anglers prefer an ordinary centrepin reel, but this does not mean that they cannot practice it perfectly well with a fixed-spool reel. The technique is to take up slack after casting, and then open the bale-arm so that as the float drifts down through the swim it pulls line off the spool freely. If line is running out too freely, the extended finger comes into play, not on the spool, but close by it so that as line slips off it brushes

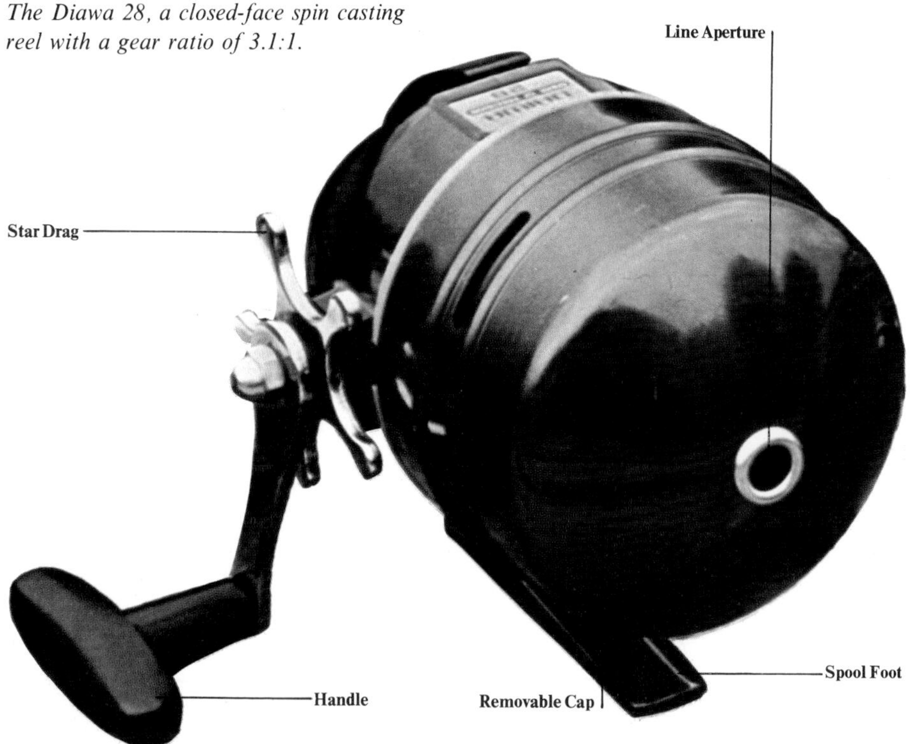


*The Diawa 28, a closed-face spin casting reel with a gear ratio of 3.1:1.*

Daiwa Sports Ltd.

against the finger, the friction slowing the rate of flow. When the float disappears, the finger is clamped hard on the reel spool, stopping the line flow at the same time as the rod is raised swiftly to strike.

One of the minor problems of the fixed-spool reel is that line occasionally springs off the spool without warning. Sometimes this is due to the wind, sometimes to twisted line, and sometimes to overloading. Whatever the cause, this has been the subject of criticism by anglers fishing with fine tackle over long distances. Others complain that for long trotting it does not give the instant control which is required.

**Closed-face reel**

The closed-face reel was designed to overcome these problems and to provide easier reel control.

This kind of reel is closely related to the fixed-spool and works on the same principle in that the drum itself is stationary.

Bill Howes

*(Above) This is the correct grip to be used when fishing with a closed-face reel. Pressure on the reel face releases the line; a turn of the handle engages the spool for retrieval.*

The same problems of casting light weights are involved, and as the line spirals off the drum and out through the vent of the reel face the friction is slightly greater.

Most closed-face reels are sold with line of about 6lb b.s. already wound on. The optimum b.s. for these reels should be 15lb of monofilament. Do not use braided line. It tends to bunch and pile up inside the reel facing, wasting line and fishing time.

**Fixed-spool v. closed-face**

Opinions differ as to whether this reel is better than the fixed-spool, but many anglers prefer the closed-face reel's simpler mechanism. Instead of a bale-arm, a rotating metal cap fits over the spool. This carries a retractable metal stud against which line is trapped. A second metal case over the stud prevents line slipping over the top of it. The inner case revolves when the reel handle is turned and the stud acts exactly like the bale-arm, laying line evenly on the reciprocating inner spool. The stud is linked to a release catch. Pressure on this retracts the stud, allowing the line to run out freely.

**Closed-face casting**

The casting action is very similar to that of the fixed-spool reel. However, instead of having to hold the line across a crooked finger and manually releasing it, the thumb button or front-plate catch is pressed at the appropriate moment to free line.

Like the fixed-spool reel, the closed-face model has an adjustable clutch mechanism, although in most cases this operates on the winding handle rather than the spool itself. The result is much the same. It also has an anti-reverse button, like the fixed-spool reel.

So, fixed-spool or closed face, this style of reel has certainly solved many of the purely mechanical casting problems once faced by anglers. It will not cure clumsy casting, and it will not help catch fish if the angler casts to the wrong places. Nevertheless, used properly and in conjunction with watercraft and other basic angling skills, investment in one of the reels, or both types, is certainly worthwhile. Careful handling of the reel will be repaid by years of use.

# Nylon line

Fishing line is one of the most sophisticated and important items of tackle. For many years anglers had to use lines of such materials as braided flax or silk, with a hook link of gut made from the stretched silk-glands of the silkworm. No other material suitable for a hook line could be made in sufficient lengths for use as a continuous line, and no material which was made in lengths of over about 15 yards was fine or strong enough. The invention of nylon in the 1930s and its subsequent development mean that anglers now have a tool suited to the job.

**Artificial silk**

An angler writing in 1949, having tried the 'new' line for the first time, said that the monofilament he had bought had increased his casting distances amazingly. It had enabled him to catch 34 perch up to 2lb using spinners tied to 5½lb b.s. nylon.

Nylon was first developed as an artificial silk, copying its molecular structure, but capable of manufacture in much greater quantities than could be produced by the silkworm. This was achieved by joining simple molecules into long 'chains'. The addition of other elements can be used to change the structure of the nylon, so producing different physical properties.

**Monofilament line**

Nylon monofilament line, the kind used by most anglers, is manufactured by first drawing the nylon into a thread while in a semi-molten state and then straightening out the molecular chains by drawing it out a second time. Its value to the angler lies in its great strength, fineness, and resistance to kinking. All these qualities are supplemented by nylon's natural elasticity.

Nylon line has the property of absorbing between 3 and 13 per cent of its own weight of water. This has the effect of reducing the breaking strain, in some cases by 10 per cent.

Figures issued by one nylon manufacturer showed that a line of 3.2lb b.s. out of water would absorb sufficient liquid to reduce its breaking strain to 2.2lb.

Another advantage is that it deteriorates, very slowly, if at all, even with frequent use. There used to be a suspicion that if not stored in the dark nylon tended to weaken quickly because of the ultra-violet rays in daylight. Certainly the lower breaking strains of line, up to about 3lb, were likely to snap very easily after a season's fishing. But it is debatable whether this was due to continued strain or to ultra-violet light. Another boon to anglers is that nylon line does not need stripping off the reel and drying after use, a chore users of silk had to reckon with.

It should be mentioned that the elasticity which aids strength also has a definite disadvantage in that a strike is softened by the line stretching, especially if it is of low breaking strain. This must be borne in mind and a strike over long distance made correspondingly forceful if the fish is not to be missed. Braided nylon, which stretches less, is sometimes used in sea fishing to overcome this difficulty.

**Camouflage**

Manufacturers claim that their clear nylon lines are virtually invisible in water, but even so camouflaged varieties in blue, green or brown can be bought. Some enthusiasts even dye their lines themselves to match water conditions.

Spools of nylon monofilament come in lengths of up to 100 yards, but when they are received from the suppliers the spools are not separated. This enables the angler to buy total lengths in multiples of 100 yards.

When nylon is retrieved onto the spool under pressure, as when playing a large fish the drag created by the weight on the line can cause it to wind back on the reel tightly, this is especially the case with a multiplier reel. After fishing, the line should be wound at normal speed onto another reel, for if left on the first it can distort the spool and ruin the reel. It is also worthwhile to wind off your line occasionally and then wind it back onto the spool, making sure that it is distributed evenly. When tying hooks

*(Right) A sight too often seen. This bird died when an unthinking angler left some unwanted nylon about. Always take it home and burn it.*

Peter Burt

A. J. Deane Bruce Coleman Ltd

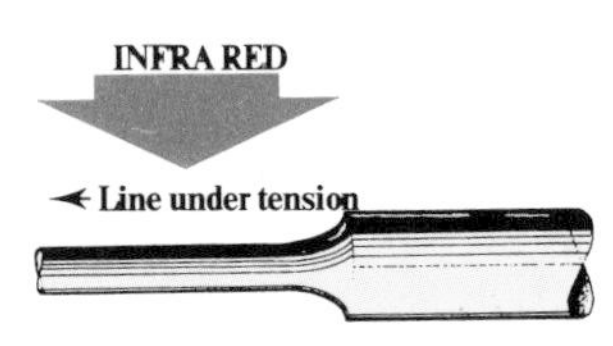


*(Above) Nylon receives its strength when it is extruded and, under tension and heat, its molecules bond together. (Below) The transparent nylon monofilament and its strong braided form.*

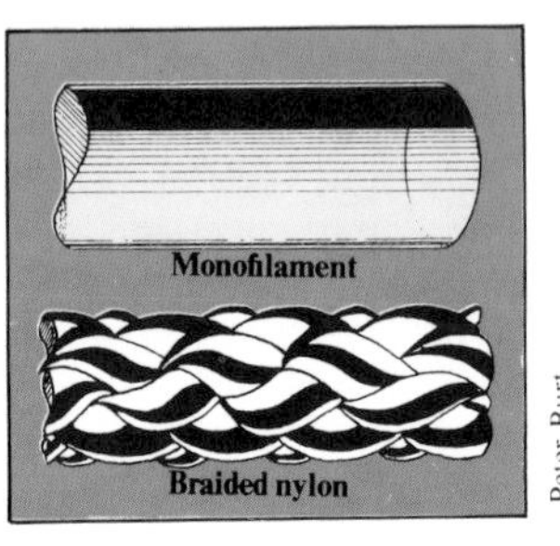


directly to your nylon, be careful to remember that one of the properties of nylon is that the old-fashioned 'granny-knot' will not hold. The best knot for tying hooks to nylon is the half-blood.

**Discarded line**

As with nylon line's elasticity, its resistance to decay has a serious drawback. Hook lengths, 'bird's nests' and odd lengths of unwanted line are frequently thrown away or left at the waterside after fishing. These coils and loops can easily become entagled in birds' feet, especially as they will often investigate the remnants of bait that anglers also leave nearby. Birds are even hooked occasionally on discarded tackle. The consequences of careless jettisoning of line are all too often fatal for birds and so it should be taken home and disposed of, or burnt at the waterside.

It is always advisable to fill your spool with line, especially if the reel is of the fixed-spool variety, for this will mean that line flows off more easily when casting and will be more rapidly retrieved on account of the increased diameter of the loaded spool. While freshwater fish tend to make shorter runs than saltwater types, it is advisable to have a good reserve of line on the spool in case a fish should make a long run, taking a good proportion of your line. A fish can easily be lost through lack of line on which the angler can play it. Backing lines are available from tackle dealers and are used to pad out the spool, which, on a fixed-spool reel, should be filled to within $\frac{1}{8}$in of the rim.

# Freshwater hooks

Hooks are the most important items of an angler's tackle and yet, all too often, they are not chosen with enough care. Admittedly the range of hooks available is bewildering to the beginner, but in order to enjoy consistent success a reliable hook is indispensable.

**Categories of hooks**

Freshwater hooks fall into three categories: eyed, spade-end and ready tied to nylon. The first are tied to the line by the angler, who can use a variety of knots. The important thing is to be sure the knot holds, as this can easily be the weak point in your tackle which will fail when most needed. Spade-end hooks, as the name suggests, are flattened at the top end and are whipped to nylon or gut using the method illustrated or some other reliable method. Ready tied hooks are bought already whipped to a short length of line, nowadays usually nylon.

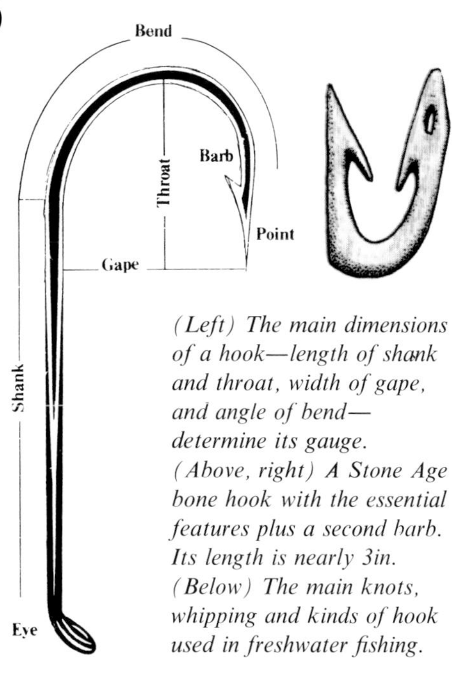


*(Left) The main dimensions of a hook—length of shank and throat, width of gape, and angle of bend—determine its gauge. (Above, right) A Stone Age bone hook with the essential features plus a second barb. Its length is nearly 3in. (Below) The main knots, whipping and kinds of hook used in freshwater fishing.*

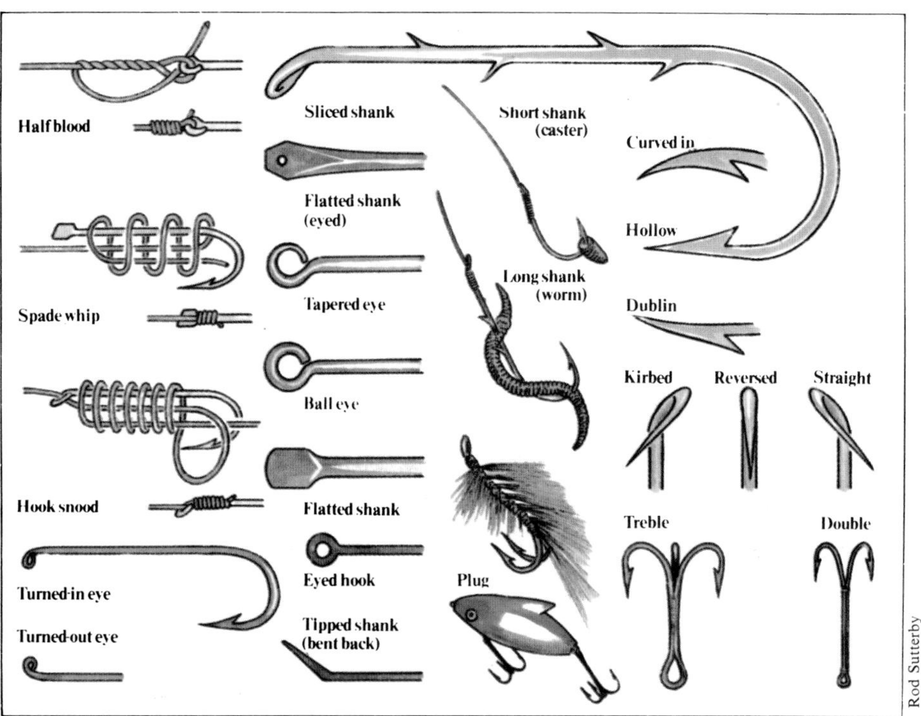


Rod Sutterby

## Freshwater hooks

There are many variations as to bend, length of shank and so on, but these are mainly variations on the three main kinds of hook. Double and treble hooks are mounted on lures and spinners for pike, perch, chub and trout. Stewart hooks comprise two single hooks set a couple of inches apart.

**The basic requirements**

The essential requirements of a hook are the same for all kinds. It should be well-tempered and thin in the body (or 'wire'); the point and barb should be sharp; the barb should be set close to the point and not stand out at too great an angle from the body.

The thickness of the 'wire' is very important. The weight of a thick hook can cause a bait, especially a light one such as maggot or caster, to sink too quickly when 'freelining'—using no float but allowing the bait to sink naturally down to the fish. An additional disadvantage of a hook that is too thick is that it can puncture a bait instead of entering it cleanly.

Before using a hook, test the temper of the wire. Under pressure it should bend but not remain bent, and it certainly should not snap. To test it, hold the hook by the shank and pull just above the point with pliers.

The barb is most often the trouble-spot in a hook. Most are cut too deep (stand out too far from the body), which causes weakness at that point. This, coupled with the common

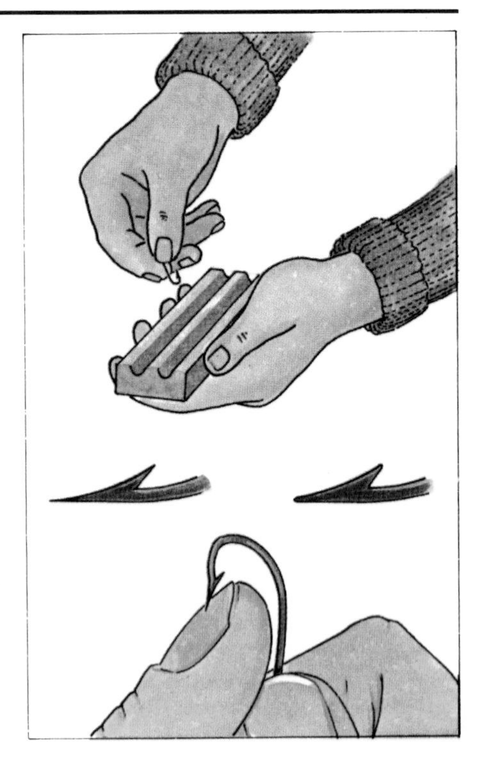

*(Above) Test a hook's temper by pulling it against a thumb-nail. This also tests its sharpness. It should resemble the point seen above, left. A blunt point (above, right) can be sharpened on a carborundum stone (top), which every angler should carry. (Below) A selection of freshwater hooks.*

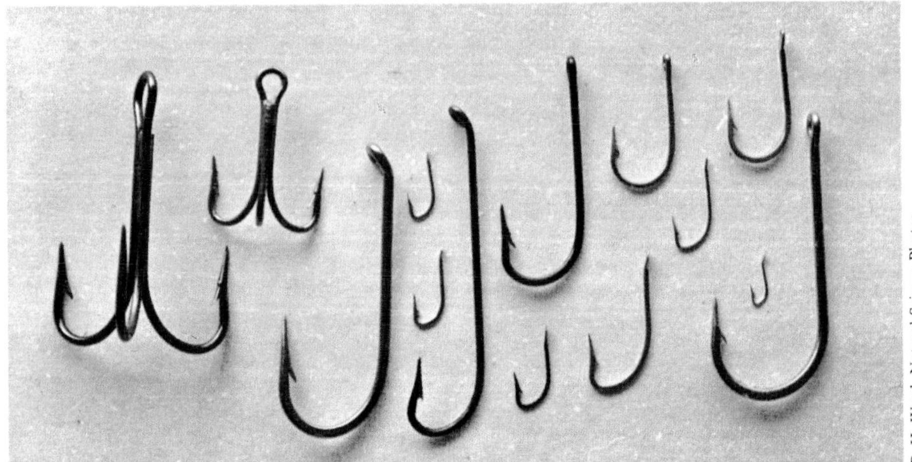

R. H. Ward Natural Science Photos

*(A) A correctly whipped hook lies straight. (B) Faulty whipping causes it to dangle. (C) A deeply cut barb weakens the hook. (D) Line will slip through an overlarge eye-gap (Below) Anglers sometimes remove the barb.*

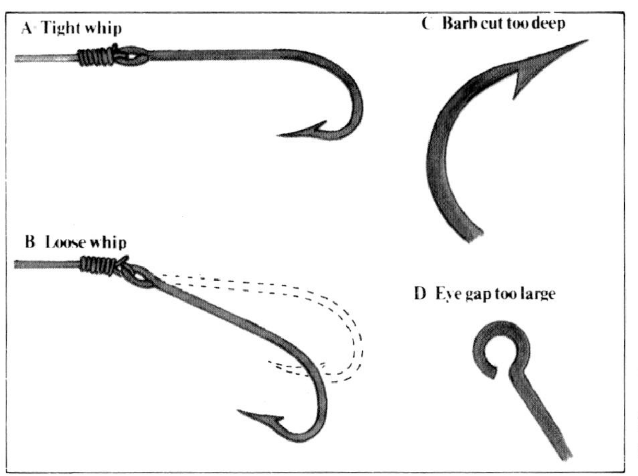


Rod Sutterby

fault of the barb being set too far from the point, means that undue force is required to drive home both point and barb, sometimes causing the line to break. If the strike is less forceful, a hook of this sort will not fully penetrate the fish's skin, particularly if it is a hard-boned and tough-skinned species like the pike, perch or barbel. A big, deeply-cut barb may look effective but is not.

The eyes on eyed hooks should be examined. The size of the eye will depend on the gauge of the hook but always try to pick one which will just take the thickness of the line you intend to use—there is no point in having a gaping, obtrusive eye which causes the hook to hang at an odd angle.

The length of the shank is important where some baits are concerned. For crust, paste, lobworms and sweetcorn a long shank is best; for maggots a short one. For casters, the variety with a long shank, known as a 'caster hook', is essential. It should be remembered, however, that the longer the shank relative to the eye, the smaller will be the angle of penetration. This means that the hook will penetrate more easily but to a lesser depth. With short-shanked hooks it takes a stronger strike but the hook will drive home deeper.

Hooks to nylon should always be treated with caution. First, see whether the whipping reaches the top of the shank. On some hooks it is too short, thus causing the hook to turn over when making contact with a fish and preventing proper penetration. Make sure that there is sufficient varnish on the whipping, for there are many with too little, which fall apart after taking a few fish, especially if a disgorger has been used. Examine the loop at the end of the nylon trace. If the loop is not straight it has been tied badly and may be unreliable.

**Sizes and patterns**

The size of hooks is indicated by even numbers on a scale from 2 to 24; the lower the number the larger the hook. A number 2 is about $\frac{3}{4}$in long, a 12 is $\frac{3}{8}$in and a 20 is $\frac{1}{8}$in. Hook sizes, unfortunately, are not yet standardized. The 'Goldstrike', to illustrate this, is one size bigger than most other brands.

The angler will sometimes use a different pattern of hook to suit particular circumstances. The 'Crystal' is a combination of curved and angular, which requires little force to drive home but which, because of its sharp bend, is weakened and not recommended for strong, fighting fish such as carp or tench. The 'Round Bend' has a curve with plenty of 'gape', and is preferred for use with lobworms by many anglers.

The 'Model Perfect' is an old-established hook patented by Allcocks. The point, which is off-set, has wonderful holding power and has accounted for a great number of big carp.

# Shot and shotting

Shot or split-shot: what does it mean to the average angler? Probably not very much. But these humble pieces of lead are so many things: they help in casting, and presenting the bait correctly, they carry the main responsibility for bite-detection and on many occasions act as a substitute for a float.

Let us first consider the shot itself: what you need, how to care for it and its basic uses. Many years ago, shot was kept in sacks behind tackle-shop counters. Anglers bought it by the ounce or pound. Nowadays it comes pre-packed in a variety of containers and dispensers. The author's preference is for the plastic tray with slide-on lid, moulded to provide compartments for eight different sizes of shot. Apart from a pack of micro-dust, this holds all the sizes of shot that is likely to be needed for an average day's fishing—Nos. 8 (commonly known as 'Dust'), 5, 4, 3, 1, BB, AAA and the largest, swan-shot. There are more sizes, but they will not be considered here.

**Quality of the shot**

No matter what its size, or how packed, it is the quality of the shot that counts. The lead must be soft enough to open and close easily to make alteration of terminal tackle a quick and simple operation. Shot should be soft enough to be pinched onto the line, with emphasis on the word 'pinched'! If you have to squeeze it very hard or even bite on it with your teeth or use pliers then it is too hard. Having to force the halves together can—and very often does—damage the line as the edges of the shot are closed. Also, shot that is too hard cannot be prised open again without breaking it. Ideally it should be opened so easily that it can be moved on the line when necessary and just pinched tight again by hand in the new position.

Never slide shot in its 'pinched' state up and down the line. Sliding tight shot creates tremendous heat. Try putting, say, a swan shot on a length of 6lb b.s. line—run it up and down very quickly and you will literally feel the heat that has been generated. Remember this next time you lose a big fish because the line breaks where you have slid shot along it. Open the shot, move it and pinch it shut again.

You can improve on the basic split-shot which you buy. For example, chamfer the edges of the split to take away any sharp edges that may damage the line, and to make it easier to insert the thumb-nail to open the shot at the end of a day's fishing. Having

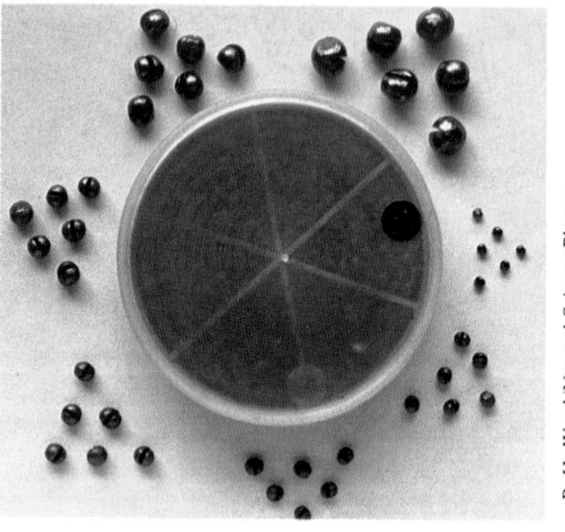

P. H. Ward/Natural Science Photos

*(Above) Plastic shot-dispensers can carry either one size in all compartments or a range of shot.*
*(Right) Shot-pliers are better than teeth, and more healthy. (Far right) Tiny shot for matchmen, called 'mouse-droppings', need special flat-sided pliers to squeeze them onto the fine line.*
*(Below) The shot range in actual size.*

| SPLIT SHOT [actual size] | SSG | AAA | BB | 1 | 3 | 4 | 5 | 6 | 7 | 8 |
|---|---|---|---|---|---|---|---|---|---|---|
| Number per ounce | 15 | 35 | 70 | 100 | 140 | 170 | 220 | 270 | 340 | 450 |

gone to this trouble, anglers do not want to waste the time and effort put into perfecting an item of tackle. They are not being mean when, instead of throwing away their shot at the end of a session, they carefully take it off the line and store it for another day. If you are lucky enough to get a good batch of soft split-shot you may not want to go to so much trouble, but it is worthwhile taking care of it.

Shotting patterns vary with methods, and this feature is designed to show how the proper use of shot can help your fishing. At a match in Northern Ireland the author was using a pole float which carried three No. 4 shot. That was too light for the existing conditions, so another float was chosen and a cork 'collar' mounted on it, converting it to a three-AA-carrying float. With the three No. 4 shot the bait was probably taking six seconds to reach the feeding level of the fish, while with three-AAA shot it was taking perhaps three seconds to reach the bottom. Not very important you may say? Wrong! That shotting change resulted in 800 fish being caught to make a world match record.

**The full value of shot**

Allowing for the fact that fish were not caught on every cast, it can be said that there was a saving of two seconds per fish. That works out at a total saving of 1,600 seconds, or 26½ minutes. No one can afford to lose 26½ minutes in a match, yet thousands of anglers must do so every week by not realizing the full value of a lead shot.

To drop on to a shoal of fish at such an event is a once-in-a-lifetime experience, but it illustrates the value of not being frightened to put plenty of lead on the 'business end' of the tackle. If the shotting is too light it just cannot do the vital job of emphasizing bites. Irish anglers fishing the Newry Canal and using sliding-floats with dust shot as a 'tell-tale' were getting their baits mangled without seeing the bite. The solution was not to fine down, but to use heavier shotting.

**Get the bait down quickly**

The explanation is simple: fishing in deep water requires quite a bit of lead to get the bait down reasonably quickly. This is the job of the bulk shot which, on a slider, can be anything up to three or even four swan shot. So the float has to be bulky. With a light weight the float will not react either as quickly or as positively as with a heavy one. The effect of the fish lifting that dust-shot was too small to be detectable by the Irish anglers. When they hit upon the answer to the problem they put a BB near the hook as a tell-tale. This gave obvious unmissable 'lift' bites, with the float rising as the fish takes the weight of the shot with the bait. The lesson in this is to consider carefully what function your shot or any other item of tackle is to perform and then try to make sure that it does so with maximum efficiency.

Here there will follow a contradiction—

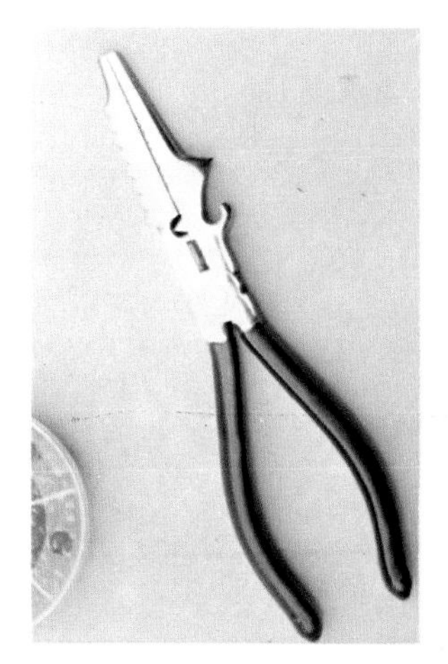

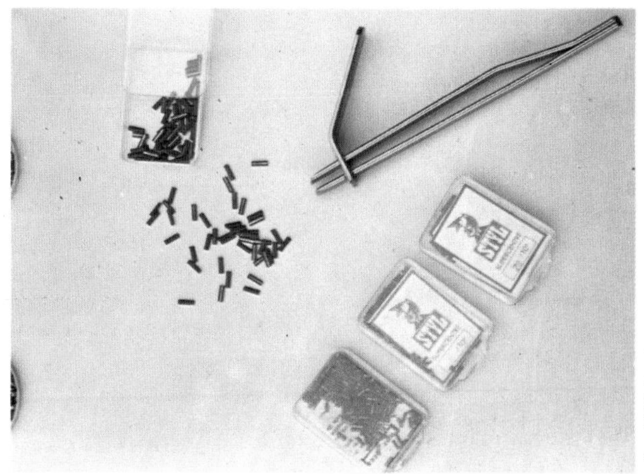

Ken Whitehead

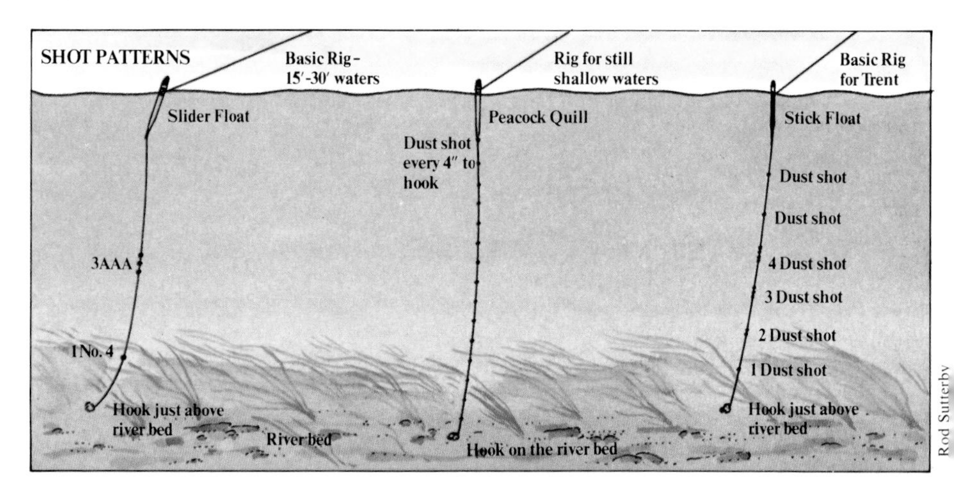


*(Above) Shot patterns—the way shot is grouped on the line below the float—can bring success or failure whether they are used in specimen hunting or matches. (Below) When it is correctly shotted, the float in the lift-method should sit well down in the water. As the fish bites the weight is lifted off the float, which shoots upwards and lays flat on the surface.*

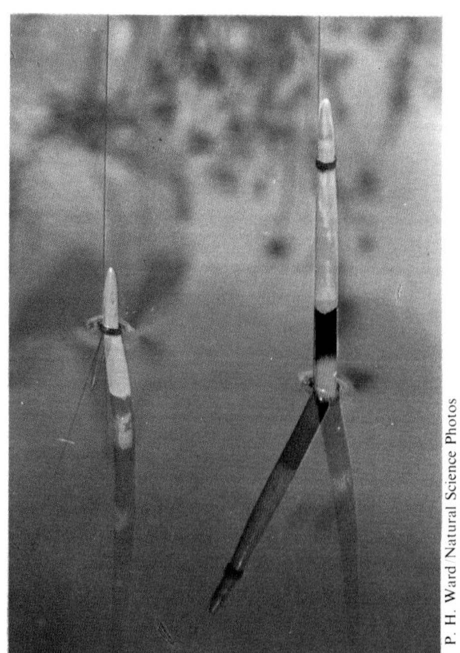


and there will be more because fishing is not a sport where hard and fast rules can be applied. Conditions are constantly changing and this requires changing styles and methods. The author does not favour Continental micro-micro shots, but there is one situation where they are invaluable—fishing the caster on the drop.

**Copy the falling rate**

Casters thrown in as feed must all be 'sinkers', that is, taken and stored soon after they cast. Those we use on the hook are the darker 'floaters'. The art is to copy, perfectly if possible, the falling rate and action of the loose-fed caster. This is something you can try out and prove in the bathroom at home. Throw in a few casters and watch them sink; now try putting a fine wire hook, size 20, in one of the sinkers. You will notice the difference in rate of descent. This is also somehow recognized by the fish. Now repeat the test with a floating caster on the hook. Again, you will see a difference, but by balancing your terminal tackle with micro-micro dust you should be able to achieve a rate of descent of your bait so similar that it will be accepted by 90 per cent of the fish: and if you catch 90 per cent of any shoal you are better than the world champion.

These are by no means all the shotting patterns available. More will be dealt with as they become relevant, it is down to the angler, finally, to use the method he thinks most suitable.

# Freshwater leads

*The basis of all ledger fishing is lead in one form or another. It ranges from split shot to the shaped coffin, spiral, Capta and bored barrel. The universal Arlesey bomb was an important design which improved ledgering technique. New leads are too shiny and should be dulled by soaking for 24 hours in vinegar.*

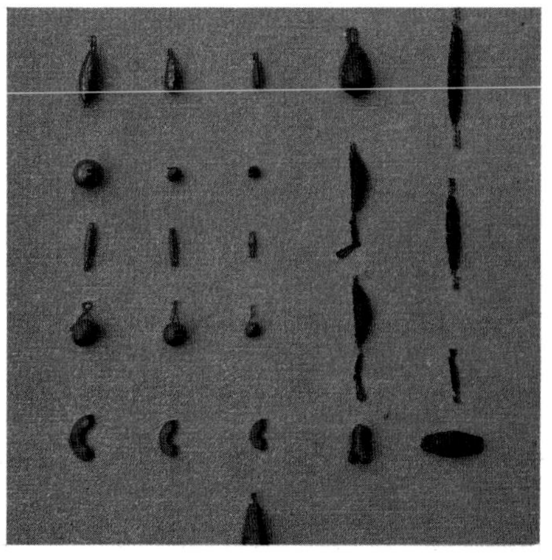

Ken Whitehead

Leads are used mainly by the float fisherman to cock the float and to give extra casting weight to his tackle. They are also widely used in ledgering.

The number of different leads on offer in any tackle shop today will surprise you. Thirty years ago the range was limited, with the most popular leads being the coffin, the bored bullet, the barleycorn and the Wye. In the Fifties Richard Walker introduced his own invention, the Arlesey bomb, and later came the pyramid-shaped Capta lead. In recent years various French-made leads have gained popularity, particularly with the match fishing fraternity.

**Split shot**

By far the most commonly used lead is the split shot. These are round, with a split across them, which is pressed shut over the line to hold the weight in place. Their use is common to float fishing and ledger fishing and they are needed by anglers ranging from the beginner to the specimen hunter. Split shot as a method of weighting line when float fishing has already been dealt with. It is, however, also used in a variety of ways for ledgering. It may be used in conjunction with heavier leads, in which case its role is to prevent the lead sliding down the hook line and concealing the bait. This method has the added advantage that the line is free to run through the lead on the take. Alternatively, shot may be used as a ledger weight in its own right.

Today, with anglers more sophisticated in their approach, both coffin leads and bored bullets have lost much of their popularity. While the latter are still used by some ledger fishermen, the majority now prefer the sliding link rig, a length of nylon with swan shots pinched on it, first publicized by the author in 1956. By using this rig and adding or removing shots, the angler is able to adjust his tackle to fine limits, the bait either rolling along the bottom or remaining stationary, to suit his purpose.

There are further advantages to this rig. First, because the shots are positioned away from the reel or main line, less resistance is felt by the biting fish. Second, when the line becomes snagged the shots will either pull off the link or this, if of lower b.s. than the reel line, will break, so avoiding the loss of hook and perhaps yards of line.

**Coffin lead**

The coffin lead was designed to hold to the bottom in fast water—a function it performs very well. Its length and shape, however, require at least 1in of line running through it and this sets up considerable resistance to the taking fish. This difficulty can be overcome by placing a swivel at one end of the lead and passing the line through it. This is by no means a perfect rig, but it does reduce resistance while also enabling the angler to keep the bait in one place in a fast current.

## Freshwater leads

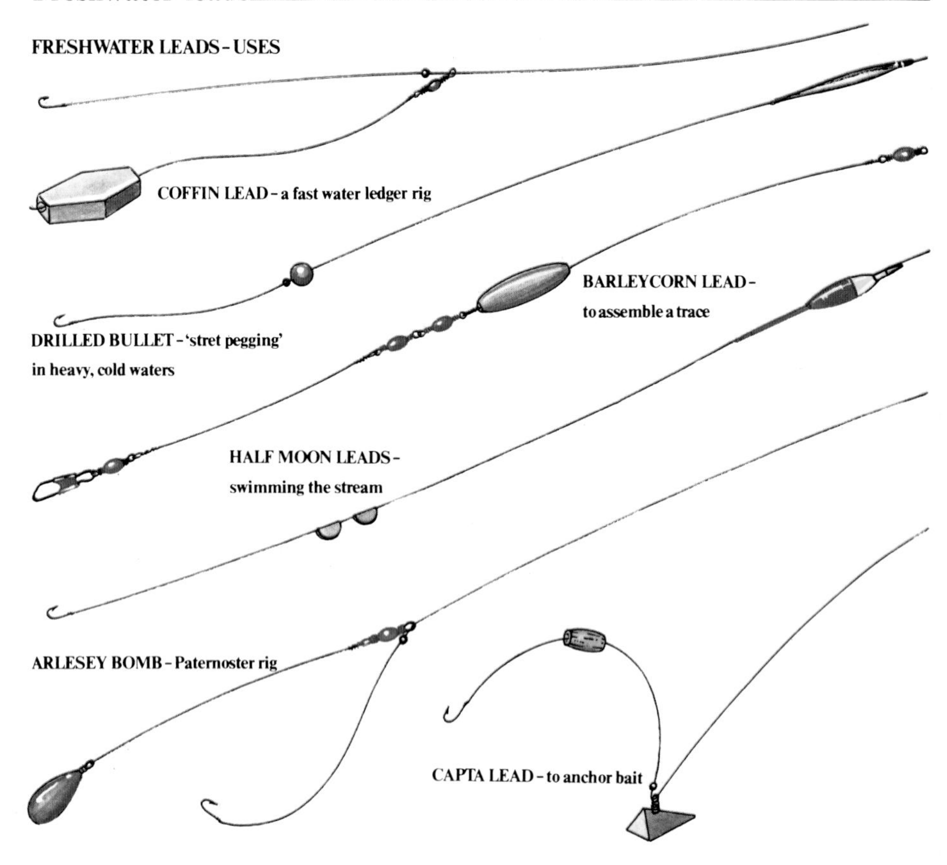


*(Above) Some of the ways in which ledger weights are used in freshwater.*
*(Right) The plummet is an important item for checking the depth of water.*

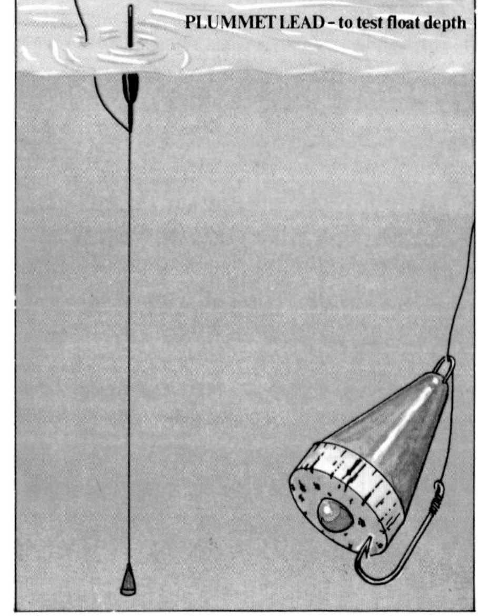


Rod Sutterby

Like the coffin lead, the once popular bored bullet is now seldom used. This, apart from the fact that the gap between each size is too great, is again because of problems of resistance in the line. However, in fast water, and where the size of the bullet allows the bait to roll along the bottom, this lead is sometimes effective. Here, when a fish picks up the bait and moves off, the pressure on the line or the weight, or both, helps shift the lead so that the fish does not feel it. Despite this, it remains a crude form of ledger weight, and has no use to the float fisherman.

In the Fifties another lead similar to the coffin, again intended for use in fast water, made its appearance. The Capta was pyramid-shaped with a swivel in the top, and came in a number of different sizes. It was rather like a cross between an Arlesey bomb and a coffin. The Capta did not last long. Although it held bottom firmly and was held away from the main line by the swivel, its shape made accurate casting difficult and set up resistance when being retrieved.

**Arlesey bomb**

By far the most successful modern lead is the Arlesey bomb. This lead was designed by Richard Walker for casting baits 50 yards into Arlesey Lake. Streamlined in shape, it is easily cast and the swivel in the top through which the main line runs creates minimum resistance. This swivel also ensures that if the tackle becomes twisted as it flies through the air the twists in the line come out as the tackle sinks. The line also runs easily through the eye of the swivel no matter what the direction of pull. The Arlesey bomb, because of its rounded shape, has the additional advantage that it does not easily snag on the bottom. It is available in five sizes: $\frac{1}{8}$oz, $\frac{1}{4}$oz, $\frac{1}{2}$oz, $\frac{3}{4}$oz and 1oz.

The barrel lead is shaped like an elongated barrel and is drilled through its length to take the line. It can be used for ledgering, but, like other types of lead, puts up more resistance than the sliding link rig and so no longer has the popularity it once enjoyed.

The fold-over or half moon lead is occasionally used in small sizes to replace split shot, but has more value as a lead which gives casting weight for spinning but which does not allow the line to become kinked by the strain this technique puts on it.

**Plummet**

The plummet is another form of lead with a particular application. It is used by the angler to discover the depth of the water in which he intends to float fish. The hook is passed through a ring at the top of the plummet and then sunk into a cork base. Its weight carries the tackle to the bottom and the float can be adjusted so that the hook and bait will rest on the bottom when the plummet has been removed.

**Barleycorn**

One very old pattern of lead which still has its uses in freshwater fishing is the barleycorn. This is mainly used for float fishing when long casts and heavy baits are necessary, as when, for example, 'trotting' the far bank with bread or meat bait for chub. The lead is streamlined and, used in conjunction with a heavy float carrying two or three SSG shots or the equivalent, smooth and accurate casts of considerable length can be made, even against a wind. The barleycorn, however, is not suitable for ledgering.

The Wye lead is spiral-shaped and has a wire spiral top and bottom. This allows the lead to be attached and detached without disconnecting the line and trace, and when slightly bent, it has a useful anti-kink effect. Employed mainly by salmon anglers, this lead is not used in coarse fishing.

**Continental leads**

In recent years, Continental styles of fishing have grown popular. This has resulted in several different Continental leads becoming available to British anglers. Styl leads are cylindrical in shape and are claimed to be the most carefully-made leads on the market. The lead is grooved and the groove is shaped so that the line is not damaged when the lead closes on it, which is important when using very fine lines.

These leads are very small—size 7 is the smallest production split shot made—and because of their shape do not attract false bites when using hemp, which has a similar appearance to the fish.

The Paquita lead is shaped like a tear-drop with a minute central hole. It is attached to the line by either squeezing the thin end or stopping it with a minute shot.

Other Continental leads include the Torpille, a lead similar to the Paquita but mounted on even finer wire and made from slightly harder lead, and 'mouse droppings', shaped as the name suggests.

All these leads are used mainly by pole fishermen in conjunction with very fine lines of 1lb b.s. or less.

# Float making-quills

Peacock quills are the 'Jack of all trades' of float-making and are used in pieces. An average peacock quill can be used to make two, three or even four floats, all for a few pence. To make a very versatile float from a length of peacock quill, all you need is a length of peacock as straight as possible and around 7 or 8in in length, a piece of welding rod or thin cane— depending upon whether you want the float partially self-cocking or not—a used ballpoint refill, a razor blade, pliers, waterproof glue and emery paper.

**First, clean the quill**

The first job is to clean up the quill, rubbing down with emery paper or fine 'wet and dry'. You will see the quill is thicker at one end; after cleaning, carefully insert the piece of cane or welding rod into this thick end—use welding rod if you want the float loaded or partially self-cocking—so that the quill and cane are as straight as possible. Then separate the cane and quill again, add glue and then place them back into position. The piece of cane or rod should protrude from the quill about $\frac{3}{4}$in.

The next job is to cut the ball-point refill into small pieces about an inch long. Slide a suitable piece onto the cane or rod and again glue it in position, leaving a quarter inch of the tubing protruding beyond the cane at the bottom. When the glue has set, heat this bottom 'overhang' and then tightly squeeze it with either pliers or a pair of forceps to flatten it, so making a tab. When the plastic has cooled and hardened, all that remains to do is to make a hole in the centre of the tab with a fine piece of wire or a needle and then to trim the tab with the razor blade.

**A simple and useful float**

Finished off with a lick of paint, this simple float is very useful on stillwaters such as ponds or canals. An added refinement, favoured by some anglers to increase sensitivity, is to insert a second, finer peacock quill or cane into the quill at the top end. But

unless the original peacock used is very thick, this is not usually worthwhile. The dimensions of the float as described can be varied, to give you a range of very useful floats.

The cane or welding rod at the bottom is essential in making the float as it gives at least one part which can be handled without damage. The ball-pen tubing, too, makes a very tough base, not liable to corrode as wire does. Simply pass the line through it and it can either be locked on with shot or used as a simple slider. The base can also be loaded with lead wire if required—again without damage to the peacock.

The versatility of these floats can be increased by using a set of float corks. Ream out the holes in the corks carefully—a round file is suitable for this—so that they just fit over the peacock and can be pushed down to the base of the quill. When this is done, the simple float is transformed into a waggler or a small zoomer for occasions when extra distance is required.

A little extra effort, to mark the bodies of your homemade floats with the amount of

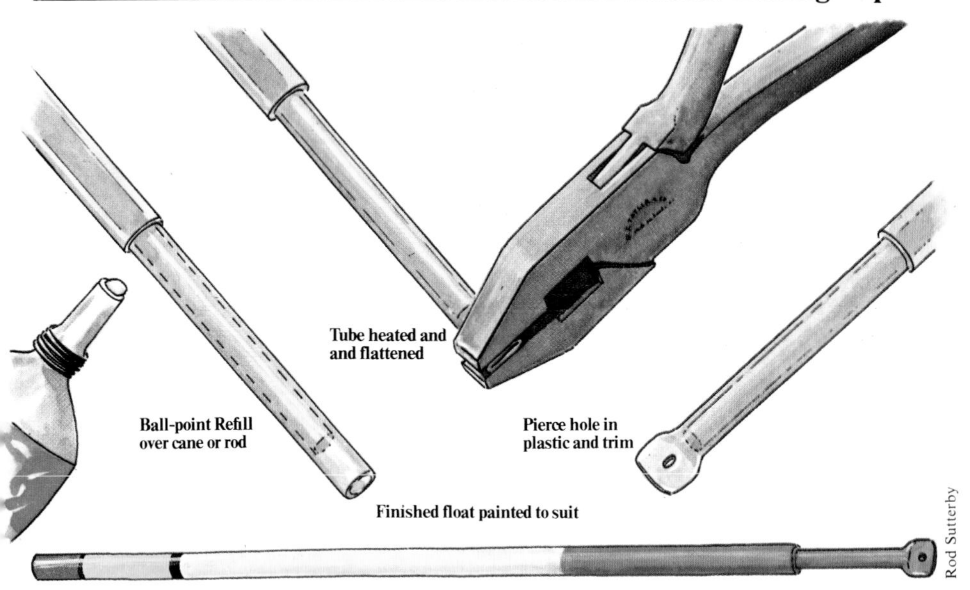


*(Above) The basic peacock quill float can be made with a few simple tools and will help the angler cut tackle costs.*

*(Below) Painting home-made quill floats is easy. They can be coloured to suit the angler's preference.*

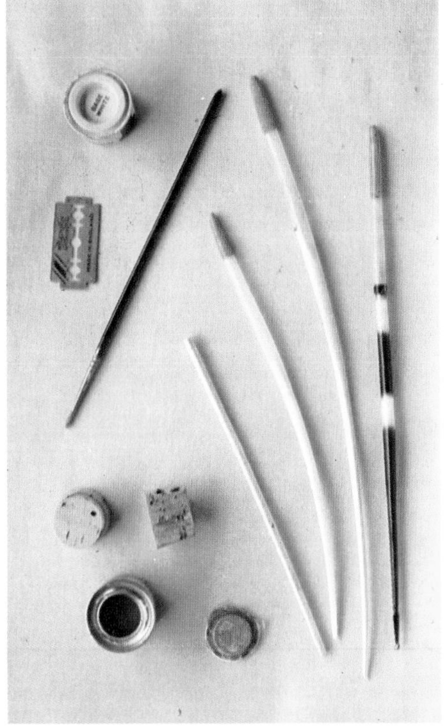


shotting they will take, is well worth the trouble. It saves a lot of time on the bank. Once more the tough base is useful here in avoiding damage to the quill when pushing on the weights.

**A goose-quill float**

The peacock quill float just described is fine for stillwaters, such as canals, but for fishing big rivers with delicate baits such as wasp grub or bread flake, a better float can be made from a combination of goose quill and balsa wood. To make it, first cut off the top inch or so of a goose quill—this is not quite so simple as it sounds for it is surprisingly tough and care is needed to make sure it is cut straight. Then obtain a 4in length of $\frac{3}{8}$in balsa wood, and taper it from one end to the other with the thick end just rubbed gently with rough sandpaper to give it a round 'shoulder' instead of a rough edge. When it is roughly shaped, give a smooth finish with 'wet and dry', and finally, glue the goose quill to the top of the 'shoulder'.

Before tapering the balsa, however, drill a small hole into the future base—the thin

Frank Guttfield

*(Above) Float-making at home can be done using the minimum of tools and without creating a mess. A board should always be used for cutting and glueing.*
*(Right) The steps in making an antenna and quill/balsa float. The shotting for the quill/balsa float is illustrated.*

end— insert a small piece of cane, about ½in long, and glue it in place. For strength the cane should be inserted as far into the balsa as it protrudes outside—like this it provides a strong place to which the line can be attached without damage. Balsa is so soft it can easily be drilled using any sharp pointed object carefully worked round and round; but if you want to save yourself trouble you can buy balsa which has been already drilled.

**Better than balsa**

Fished double rubber—that is, attached to the line at top and bottom with elastic bands— this goose quill is a superb float for such fish as chub and barbel. It gives better buoyancy at the tip than a straight balsa because, as the goose quill head is hollow, you are virtually fishing with an air bubble. One point which must be emphasized when using it, however, is that it should only be cast underhand or sidearm. Cast a float like this overarm and you are inviting tangles.

The float should take between two and three swan shot: basically a No. 4 right under the float to stop it sliding down, the bulk two-thirds up the line—bearing in mind this is a float to be fished in water not much deeper than, say, 7ft—and perhaps an AAA halfway between hook and bulk shot.

Finally, a few general hints on float making. First of all finishing. Colour is entirely up to the angler's personal taste, as is the choice of a matt or a shiny paint, but to get a good finish, care is essential. Primer, undercoat and top coat must be applied and allowed to dry properly. And they must also be rubbed down well between coats. Fluorescent paints *must* be applied over the correct white-undercoat if they are to work properly, while to get a straight edge when

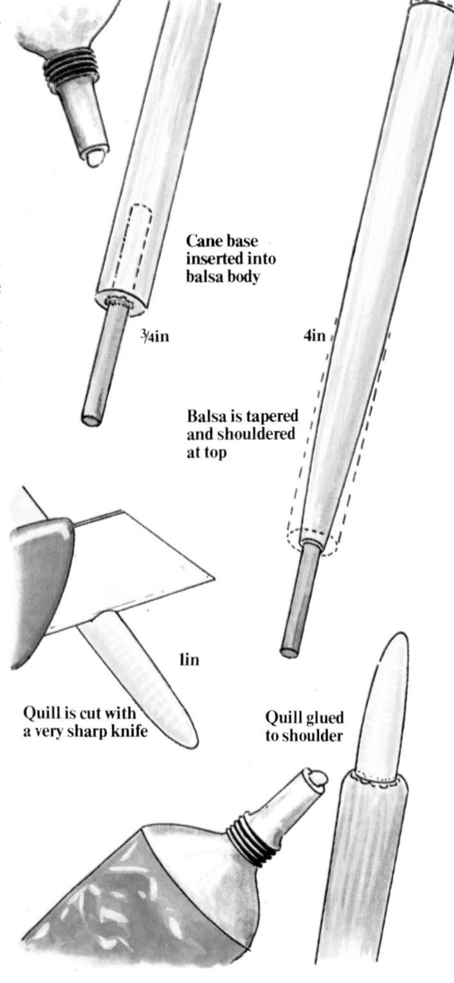

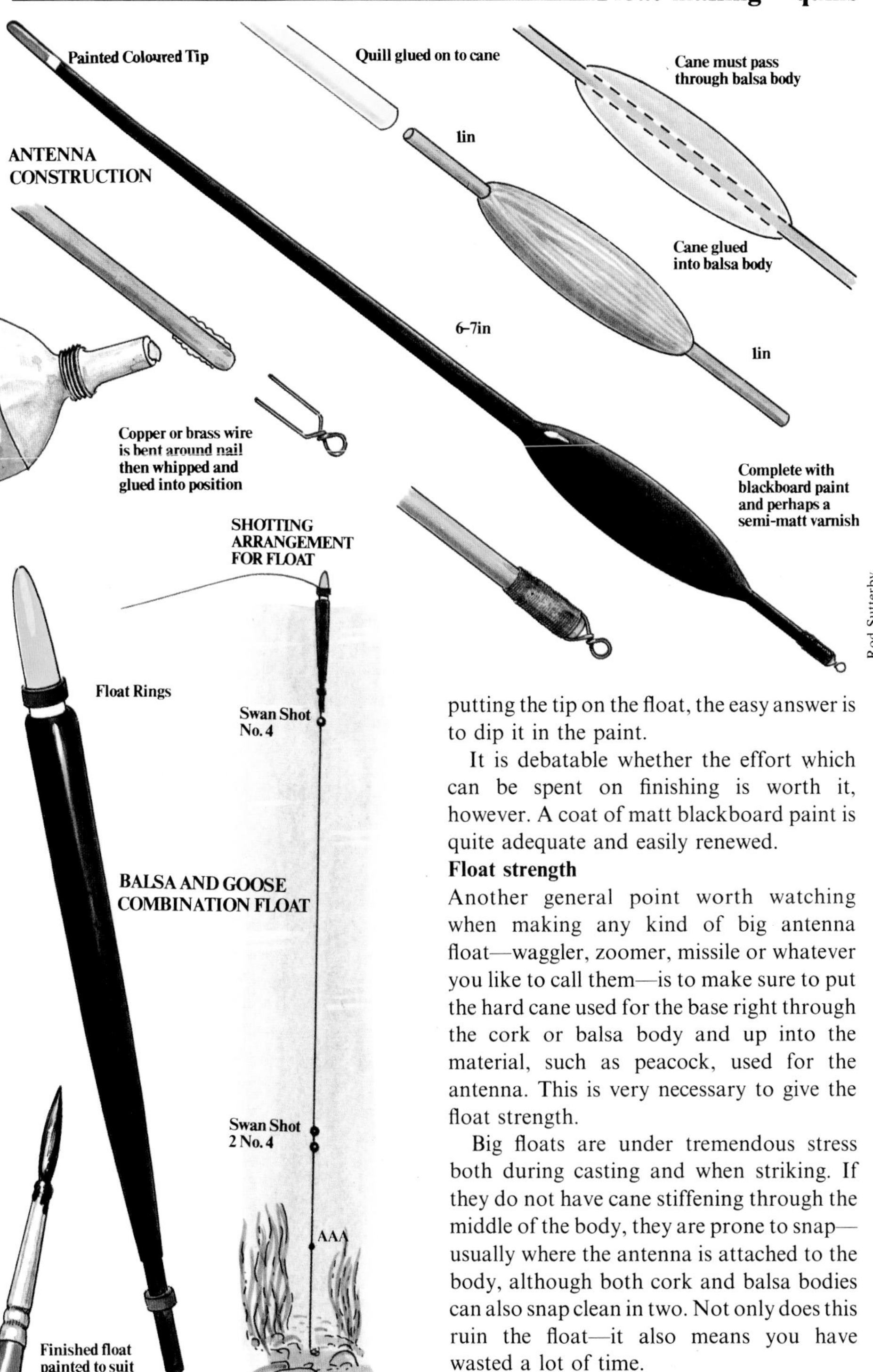


putting the tip on the float, the easy answer is to dip it in the paint.

It is debatable whether the effort which can be spent on finishing is worth it, however. A coat of matt blackboard paint is quite adequate and easily renewed.

**Float strength**

Another general point worth watching when making any kind of big antenna float—waggler, zoomer, missile or whatever you like to call them—is to make sure to put the hard cane used for the base right through the cork or balsa body and up into the material, such as peacock, used for the antenna. This is very necessary to give the float strength.

Big floats are under tremendous stress both during casting and when striking. If they do not have cane stiffening through the middle of the body, they are prone to snap—usually where the antenna is attached to the body, although both cork and balsa bodies can also snap clean in two. Not only does this ruin the float—it also means you have wasted a lot of time.

# Slider floats

*The Ian Heaps slider float, developed by Ian Heaps and his father, who say it is an improvement on old designs.*

Rod Sutterby

Slider floats are enjoyable and effective in use, but curiously neglected. It is difficult to understand why anglers will sit all day watching a motionless swingtip without trying a slider which, by giving a greater variety of presentation and often a little movement, provides a better chance of fish, particularly bream.

**Length of float**

Many sliders have no loading and, although they are effective, the floats developed by my father and myself are better. With these, it is important that the cane goes into the peacock quill, producing a strong joint. The length of the float is not particularly important, although it must be long enough to keep line below the surface drift. The peacock quill should be anything from 6in to a maximum of 10in long.

The amount of lead wire required is just enough to sink the balsa barrel, leaving the full length of the peacock quill standing above the surface.

The swivel is important, for it allows the float to turn in the air without the line tangling. A size 12 swivel is ideal in that it is small enough to stop at the knot tied for that purpose. If you cannot get so small a swivel, however, a larger one with a small bead positioned between the stop-knot and float may help.

As to tackling-up, it must be stressed that this float is intended to slide up and down the line and to stop at a certain depth. The required depth is obtained by using a stop-knot to halt the float. A simple way to tie a stop-knot is to take a few inches of 4–6lb line, form a coil with two tails alongside the reel line and pass either tail through the loop, and around the reel line and the other tail four times before pulling both ends tight. Not too tight, however, because although the knot has to stay in place, it is important that it can be moved without having to break the reel line. If the stop-knot does move when you are casting and reeling in, do not tighten it more, but tie on another stop-knot an inch above it. This will act in the same way as a locking nut.

Another important point to remember is to trim the tails to a length of $\frac{3}{4}$in after tying the knot. There are two reasons for this. If the tails are too short they will be bristly rather than flexible and will not pass through the rod-rings easily enough. Second, when fishing extreme depths, the knot, or knots, will be lying on the reel and short tails will impede line flowing off the spool. The longer ones will lie flat as line is wound over them.

**Shots**

Each kind of shot used with this tackle has a specific function. The job of the stop-shot is to keep the float off the bulk shot and so minimize tangles on the cast—but do not confuse it with the stop-knot. This stop-shot should be as small as possible, say a No. 6, to

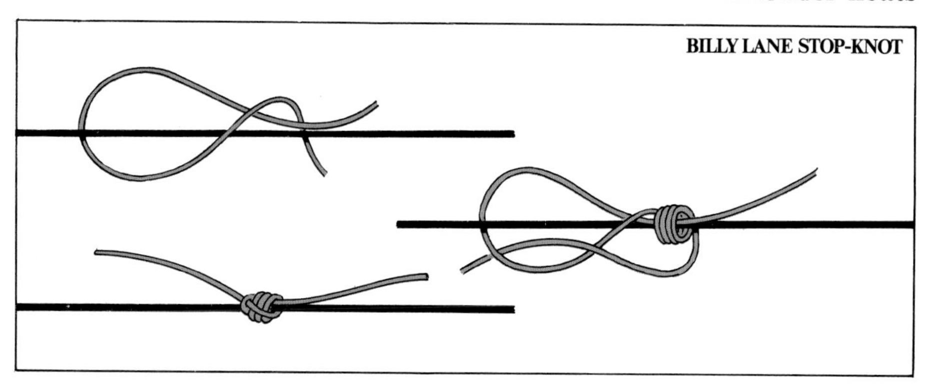


keep bending of the line or 'waggling' to a minimum during casting.

The bulk-shot is used to get the bait down to the fish and also to pull down most of the peacock quill. The weight needed will be found by trial and error.

The tell-tale shot's function is to show bites, and remember, you get a lot of 'lift' bites with this method. This tell-tale must be heavy enough to alter the setting of the float noticeably. In deep water I seldom use smaller than a No. 4 and often a BB shot.

**Lift bites**

Incidentally, why so many 'lift' bites— when the fish actually lifts the tell-tale shot and so causes the float to rise in the water—when using this method? It seems to result from the way a bream feeds. A bream's body is distinctly oval in shape and so has to tilt forward to pick up a bait from the bottom and when it comes back to an even keel it inevitably lifts the shot.

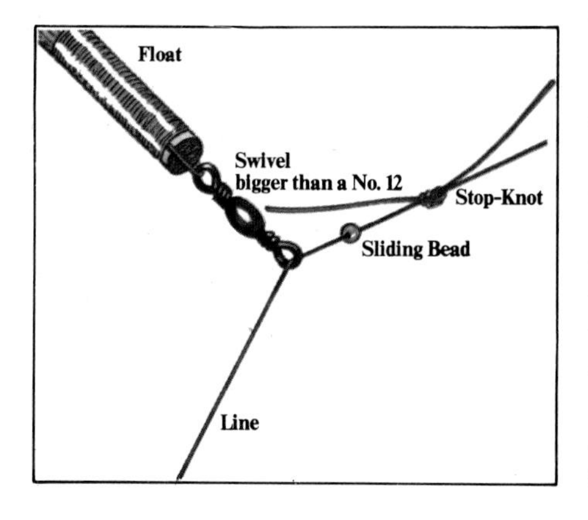


The tell-tale shot also helps get the depth without using a plummet. Keep moving the knot to a deeper setting until the shot does not act on the float; the tell-tale must then be on the bottom. Once this is done, measure the position of the stop-knot by holding the hook at the rod-butt and seeing where the knot lies—fishing 20ft deep with a 13ft rod, for instance, will put the knot around halfway. Make a careful note of this because if tackling up again no time need be lost in resetting the right depth.

Shotting is very important and experiments over the years seem to show that the following distances are correct for use in water over some 14ft deep: from hook to tell-tale shot 17in; from tell-tale shot to bulk shot 43in; from bulk shot to stop-shot 66in. The last two distances can be scaled down proportionately in shallower water.

**Great accuracy and distance**

The loaded slider float really scores when casting, giving greater accuracy and distance. This is because the weight of the float has it pushing against the stop-shot and consequently helping it out while the weight in the nose gives the float a 'flight' as in a dart. An unloaded slider float is far more likely to waggle in the wind and, in the case of a facing wind, actually 'climb back' towards the angler. Both of these situations take the force out of a cast and so limit casting distance.

*For large swivels a sliding bead can be used between it and the stop-knot.*

Many anglers cast a slider underhand, but it might be better to put the float well up in the air with a smooth action, avoiding snatching. Then, when it is starting to drop from the highest point of its flight, draw back the rod and 'feather' the line off the reel with the forefinger. This holds back the rig and straightens it so that it enters the water with the minimum of fuss and also reduces tangles. This last point is important, because the risk of tangling puts many anglers off the slider, which need not be.

When the float hits the water, get the rod tip well under the surface to sink the line, after winding three or four times to take up the slack, then start the 'countdown' as the bait sinks. It is possible to establish a standard time between tightening the line and the tell-tale shot pulling the float to the fishing position. If subsequent counts go more than five seconds past the standard time, strike for there is every chance that a fish has the bait in its mouth, holding up the tell-tale—known as a bite 'on the drop'.

Remember if you tighten up the line to the float that the bait will drop much more slowly than if allowed to run freely off the reel. Make sure you fish to the same pattern each cast, although when fish are taking 'on the drop', slowing down the bait gives the bait more time in the catching zone.

Following these points provides a good basis to practise slider float techniques. These can provide interest—and fish—when other methods fail.

*(Previous page) The Billy Lane stop knot. It holds firmly but can be slid up or down. (Below) Details of the lift-bite method using the specially designed Ian Heaps slider float.*

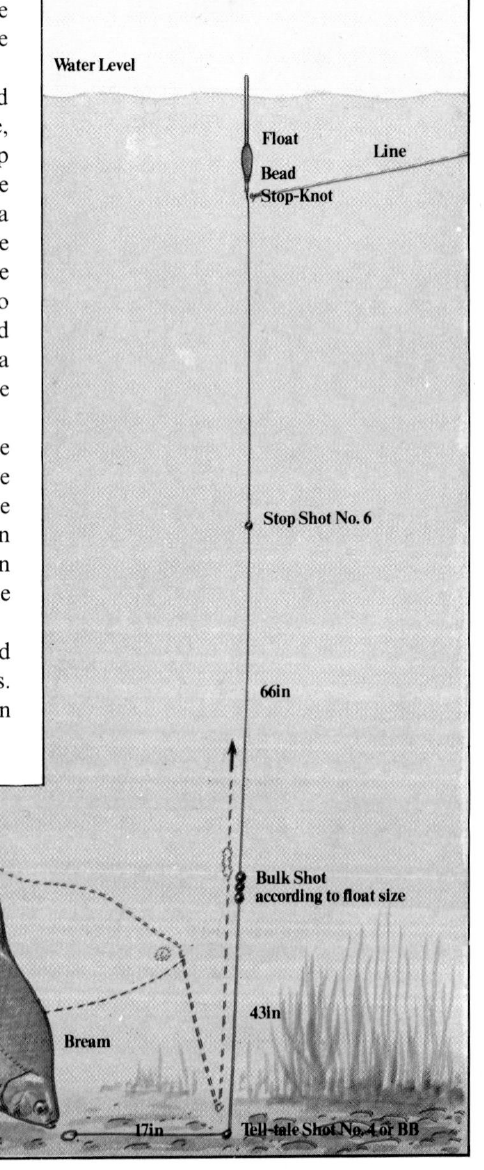

# Keepnets

Most modern coarse-species anglers use keepnets whether for specimen hunting, pleasure angling, or competition fishing. The match-man obviously needs to weigh in his catch at the end of the match to establish who wins the prize. The keepnet enables him to do so without killing the fish. Pleasure anglers once used to return fish as soon as they were unhooked. Nowadays we often carry a camera and record the catch in photographs. The keepnet enables us to do this with no damage to the fish. Specimen hunters often keep a very detailed log of their catches, recording weight, girth and length and other details. They too find the keepnet a valuable accessory.

The important thing about these differing groups of anglers is that they all return their catch alive as soon as possible. All are strongly conservation minded, not only carrying out the law with regard to immature fish, but returning also the big ones which, a couple of decades ago, would probably have finished up in glass cases.

**Introduction of the keepnet**

The match fisherman was responsible for the introduction of the keepnet. Before its arrival, every fish caught during a contest was thrown on the bank to be collected and weighed when fishing ceased. The drain on the fish population, even in the best-stocked waters, eventually led to the use of a net to keep fish alive for the duration of the match. Although those early nets were small and manufactured from heavy twine, they were of vital importance.

Today's nets are available in a vast choice of sizes. Naturally, the bigger the net, the less risk of damage to fish through overcrowding. Although most anglers favour a round net, there is a distinct advantage in using a rectangular one when shallow waters are fished. These models will allow a greater area to remain submerged, providing more water space for their inhabitants.

Many Water Authorities now specify the minimum size of keepnets to be used in their waters. Where the Water Authorities fail to do so, most of the larger and forward-thinking clubs themselves specify minimum keepnet sizes to be used by their members. Some clubs go even further and specify how many fish of each species may be kept in the net. A dozen roach in a net 6ft long with 18in hoops would seem to be in no danger, but a dozen bream, or even carp or pike, would suffer. Bream are especially vulnerable to overcrowding as their narrow body cross-section causes those at the bottom of the net to be forced on their sides and crushed if they are overcrowded. They are also the most sought-after quarry of the competition fisherman.

**Vulnerable species**

Barbel and carp are also vulnerable to keepnets because both species bear large serrated-edged spines on the dorsal and anal fins, and these often tend to tangle in the mesh during movement, suffering considerable damage if the fish struggle to free themselves.

The organized match-angling world is also very concerned with this problem. To prevent overcrowding in well-organized

Ray Forsberg

*A small perch about to be put—not dropped—into a square-shaped keepnet.*

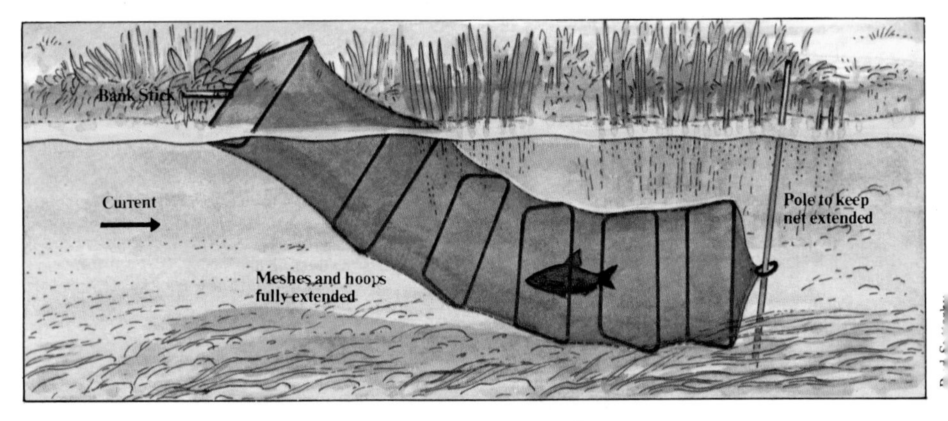


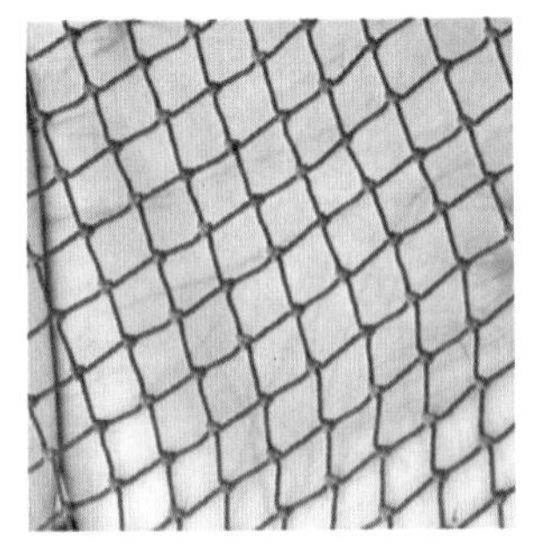

*(Above) Correct positioning of the keepnet in a current. (Left) The micro-mesh polynet, ideal for good keepnet construction. (Far left) This knotted nylon keepnet mesh is known as the 'fish mincer' due to the way it can rip away the scales of fish.*

P H Ward/Natural Science Photos

matches the stewards are required to patrol the bank at regular intervals to empty competitors' nets and weigh and record the contents. When you consider that a match champion may take several hundred pounds of fish in the course of the match, it requires little imagination to appreciate the suffering to fish which could arise in a single match.

Keepnets vary a great deal according to their specific function. The match angler's net is likely to be about 8 or 10ft long, with hoops of at least 15 or 18in. His specimen-hunting counterpart will probably use a far larger net which may be up to 12ft long with hoops up to 3ft in diameter.

**Spacing rings**

Spacing rings, to provide support and strengthen the net, are manufactured either from galvanised wire or plastic. Wire rings are joined by brass ferrules that have an annoying habit of pulling apart. They can be glued with Araldite or soldered, but will always be suspect. Plastic rings rarely break and being soft reduce the chance of damage to fish. But being pliable they tend to become oval-shaped and thus crowd fish together. They are also lighter than wire, which may cause smaller nets to roll in a strong current, but stone in the base of the net will hold it down.

But however big the net, it cannot do its job if it is badly placed in the water. If the net is not properly extended, 10ft of netting is of little value, and hoops of 2ft diameter are useless in 18in of water. They are usually attached by a screw fitting to a bank stick conveniently placed to allow the angler easy access to the open end. They can also be prevented from collapsing with the aid of mesh-spreaders which attach to the rings and hold them apart.

The ring at the neck, into which the bankstick is mounted, is important. Many models have a very small ring, which makes it more difficult to slide a fish into the bag of the net. Choose the net with the biggest ring possible, and plastic-coated, so that if a fish is dropped against it there will be less risk of injury. Some rings have a dent or curve so that a rod can be rested across the net while the angler unhooks a fish—an advantage, if the net is firmly fixed to the bank.

Nylon netting is available in several mesh sizes, from 'minnow' upwards, and if machined in a tubular run will be free of knots. This means that the only stitching should be at the base and neck ring—both weak areas that must be examined even in a new net. A recent introduction and improvement on the nylon mesh is micromesh, a soft nylon material with extremely small holes that is reported to cause little or no damage to fish. A few clubs and authorities are already insisting on its use in an effort to reduce the incidence of disease. Micromesh is expensive, but weighs little and dries quickly.

**Need for maintenance**

Regular maintenance is needed if a keepnet is to remain efficient. Although mesh may be advertised as 'rot-proof' it is still liable to strain, especially if a large weight of fish is lifted awkwardly. Check the base of the net at the join for signs of fraying, and replace it at once if need be.

Fish slime, allowed to accumulate with repeated use, can work its way into the mesh, stiffening the net to such an extent that it will have the effect of glass paper on fish scales. Washing the keepnet in clean cold water and thoroughly drying it after each outing will prevent this and leave the net more wholesome to handle.

Remember that fish naturally face the current, and so the net should lie parallel to the bank, the mouth facing upstream. Provided the net is long enough, there should be no difficulty in arranging this. The mouth of the net should lie close to the angler at a height convenient for handling.

Most damage to keepnets occurs when they are lifted with their contents at the end of the day. Grabbing the neck ring and pulling will eventually split open the bottom. The correct method is to retrieve the net hand over hand by the spacing rings, and then lift it, holding the bottom and the gathered rings in separate hands. Better quality nets have a small ring attached at the base with which to hold and lift.

Once onto the bank, avoid tipping the net on its side and shaking the fish free. This will dash them against the mesh, removing scales and ripping fins. Instead, collapse the net so that hands can be inserted, and lift out fish individually. After weighing or photographing, they should be returned to the water immediately, not re-netted—a practice that can cause further abrasions if the fish are tipped back using the net as a shute.

*Peter Ward uses a long landing-net handle to extend a keepnet to its full length.*

S L Ward Natural Science Photos

# Bite indicators

The most expensive, well balanced, and skilfully fished ledger outfit can only be as successful as the bite indicator used with it will allow. Whether ledgering by day or by night, the angler will require an indicator light enough to allow a fish to run unchecked with the bait, but heavy enough to withstand pressure from wind, current and floating debris, all of which so often register a false bite.

Although the term bite indicator is generally applied to any item that registers interest in the bait from a fish, indicators fall into two distinct categories—those that record the fish's action and movement with the bait, telling the angler when to strike, and those that are simply alarms, giving aural and/or visual signs that attention has been paid to the bait.

**The simple dough bobbin**

The cheapest and most simple indicator is probably the dough bobbin, and moulded dough weight attached either to the line above the rod tip, or between butt ring and reel. Its main disadvantages are that, because of its small size, it is not easily seen, especially in poor light, and that it needs to be replaced after every cast or strike. An improvement in this weight-type indicator is the large bottle cork, split at one end so that it can slide onto the line, and secured at the other by a short piece of cord, the other end of which is tied to a rod rest. The cork indicator, which is usually painted bright red or yellow, responds to a bite in the same way as the dough bobbin, but with the strike it pulls free and drops to the ground where it can be retrieved and used again.

**Silver foil loop**

Yet another simple improvement in the weight-type of indicator is the silver foil loop. Several pieces of baking foil can be carried, folded, in a small box—an empty cigar tin, which will keep them from being crushed, is ideal. The rod is adjusted in its rest, the bale arm of the reel closed, and over the line between this and the first rod ring is looped a folded strip of foil, turned round on itself to form a complete circle. Lying on the ground, it will reflect light, even when other things have merged into shadows, and its slightest movement will attract the angler's attention. On the strike it will fall free without obstructing the line in any way, so allowing the fish to be played.

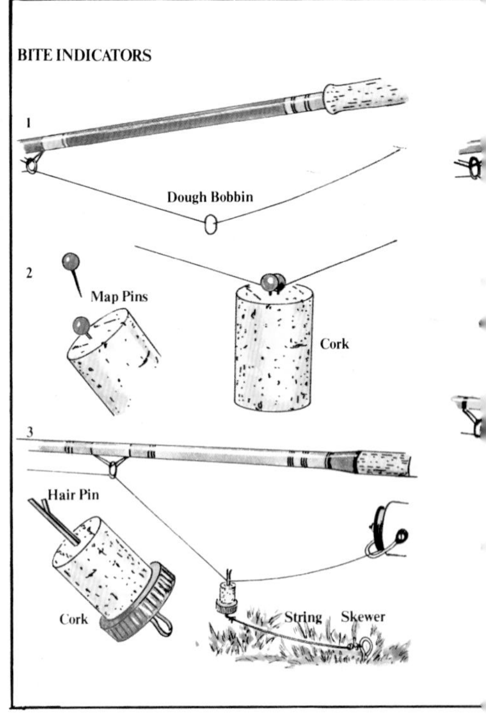


**Problem of wind**

Keeping any form of weight-type indicator still during windy weather is always difficult, especially when it is necessary to use one as light and sensitive as possible. Increasing the weight that is hung onto the line creates a resistance that fish will feel, and that will cause them to drop the bait. Restricting the wind's action on the indicator by building windbreaks generally blocks the angler's

*(Below) Sensitive bite indicators, from 1 to 5, can easily be made.*

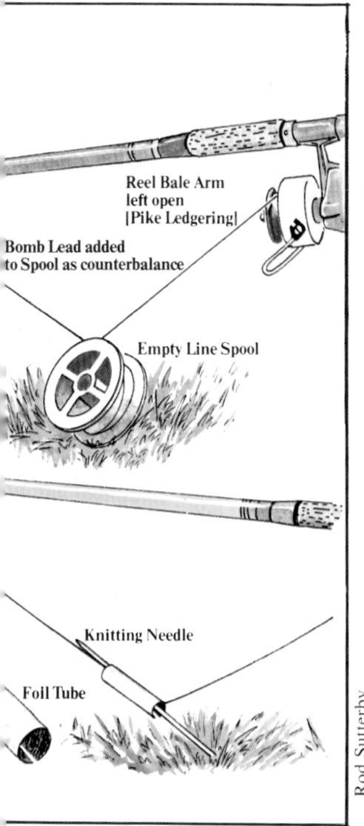

Rod Sutterby

*A tube of silver foil is a sensitive bite indicator. Placed in a small plastic flowerpot, wind will not affect it.*

Ken Whitehead

*The same silver foil, but here with a knitting needle pushed into the ground to prevent wind action giving false signals.*

view, and small takes can be missed altogether. The only solution in these conditions is to use needles or pots to steady the indicator.

**Set the rod-rests firmly**

Before either method is used it is essential that rod rests should be firmly set, and the area immediately around the rest, which will support the butt end of the rod, cleared of all twigs, weed, and other vegetation. After the cast is made and the line has sunk, the rod should be laid into the rests and line wound onto the reel until the lead or bait can just be felt to move on the bottom. The strip of kitchen foil is now circled round the line as previously described, and sufficient line paid off to allow it to drop onto the bank immediately below the reel, and over a metal knitting needle set at an angle in the ground.

As a further assistance in gauging a bite, the needle may be painted with coloured bands, which act as a rough scale. Once set in this way there will be no swinging of the indicator due to wind action—the needle will prevent this—and no obstruction once the strike is made, the silver foil simply pulling off both needle and line in one movement.

Using a pot to prevent wind action is similar in every respect to the needle method, except that the circle of kitchen foil is dropped into a piece of cardboard tubing or small flower pot, where it will lie until the bite of a fish pulls it upwards and into the angler's view.

**Bite indicating at night**

Obviously, bites from an indicator at night are always difficult to see, and so most anglers resort to a torch or other lighting aid directed onto both indicator and line. Useful though this system may be, it begins to strain the eyes after several hours spent in looking at one spot in a subdued light and, worse still, one's night vision for areas other than the illuminated patch, is completely destroyed. Fortunately, there is an aid on the market that surpasses other lights for indicator watching—the Betalite.

**The Betalite**

The Betalite is a small, gas-filled tube which glows brightly, needs no re-charging, and lasts for approximately 20 years. In use it is either strapped onto the rod tip near the top ring by a short length of Sellotape, or clipped onto the line between reel and first ring, a short length of cord securing it to the rod rest, as with the cork bobbin. No matter how dark the night, this little tube's powerful light is easily seen and in no way impairs the angler's night vision.

A final range of indicators—or to be more accurate, alarm raisers—remain, and these are the electric buzzers and flashers. In principle, these mechanical aids work through the line, which is trapped or tensioned against or between metal arms. While it is in place the alarm is silent, but when a fish takes, any pressure or jerk imparted to the line makes an electric circuit, which in turn sounds the alarm.

There are several models on the market, but many angling boffins have constructed their own without too much difficulty. They are as sensitive as the angler allows them to be by observing simple requirements like renewing batteries and protecting the sensitive wire that attaches to the line.

**Two basic buzzers**

Naturally, these alarms must be protected from water, including rain and mist. Models produced in the last few years are carefully sealed in plastic boxes that should not be tampered with unless absolutely necessary.

*(Below) Bite indicators which depend upon visual signals transfer the horizontal movement of the line to a vertical one supplemented by eye-catching objects. The Harlow model does this with a red indicator on a clipped-on wire.*

P. H. Ward/Natural Science Photos

*(Right) The more sophisticated bite indicators act as alarms and give warning buzzes or, for night fishing when noise must be suppressed, a flashing light. The model shown is extremely sensitive.*

P. H. Ward/Natural Science Photos

Two models are on sale—those set into the head of a rod rest and which stand a little way in front of the angler's seat, and those which have the line-attaching mechanism at the same point, but have an alarm and/or flashing light set in a box connected to a length of flexed cable and which can be placed right beside the angler.

**Advice for sleepy anglers**

This latter type is excellent where an umbrella-tent or shelter of any sort is rigged, and in which the angler will probably sleep or doze. However, they are not large, and it has been known for equipment to be dropped over them, and even for the angler to roll onto them in his sleep, thus muffling the alarm signals. The answer to the problem is to try to arrange that the alarm box stands off the ground, preferably at eye level and away from potential accidents..

**How to magnify the sound**

Whether the alarm or flashing light is best is a matter of personal preference; there have been plenty of fishermen who have slept through both. If you are a deep sleeper, standing the alarm in an empty tin box to magnify the sound can often help. Whichever model you purchase, read carefully the maker's instructions on setting and try a 'dry' run with it during daylight hours to get the feel of its sensitivity.

Finally, remember that electric indicators are designed to do exactly what their name implies—to indicate by an alarm that a fish has moved the bait. Judging when to strike is the angler's responsibility. Those who achieve greatest success with this aid are anglers sufficiently in tune to respond to the alarm by checking the amount of line running out either by feel, or with the aid of a torch. A blind strike when the alarm rings cannot guarantee a hooked fish.

N. J. Fickling

(*Left*) *A triple battery of rods set with visual bite indicators. This is a neat and efficient-looking set-up, with the angler seated well back from the water's edge. But what happens if all indicators twitch at once?*

# Forceps and disgorgers

Of the many tackle items that the angler will invest in, disgorgers, gags, forceps and pliers will be the cheapest, most essential, and generally the most easily mislaid. These simple pieces of equipment enable him to remove a deeply embedded hook and are vital to fish life and fisherman alike. They are important time savers too. There is a bewildering array of them—good, bad and indifferent—on sale at any tackle shop.

Despite their usefulness, the angler should be aware that, in many situations, these tools only become necessary because of bad fishing techniques and that deep-hooking can often be avoided altogether.

Of course there are times when a fish bolts the bait with such speed that throat or cheek hooking is unavoidable, but many such cases could be avoided if proper attention were paid to the rod, with the angler close at hand and not several yards away from it. A small hook is another cause of deep hooking.

A rank barb—one that protrudes too far from the body of the hook—can cause further disgorging problems, and each hook that is tied to the line should be inspected and a few strokes of a file or sharpening stone used to remove excess metal. Badly tempered or soft hooks that straighten under pressure can also present difficulties: a few seconds should be spent in examining hooks. Those that distort when flexed against the thumb nail, should be rejected.

It is in the realm of pike fishing where most unnecessary disgorging is seen. Reasons for it include bad timing of the strike ('give him a few seconds more to make sure he has really taken it'), and the use of fancy dead-bait rigs that are reminiscent of gorge tackle.

If all these precautions have been observed and the angler is still presented with a deeply hooked fish, quick action with the correct unhooking aid will always prevent a death.

**Disgorgers**

Many anglers wrongly believe that one type of disgorger will release a hook from any fish. At least two types will be required, depending on where the hook has lodged and on the type of hook being used. Where the hook is deep inside the mouth, but still visible, then the straightforward flattened 'V'-shape disgorger, with a long handle, may be used to ease the barb back through the skin. Where the hook is deep and cannot be

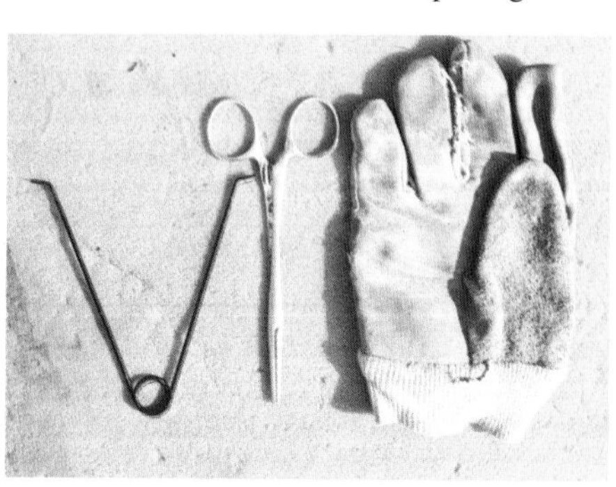

P. H. Ward/Natural Science Photos

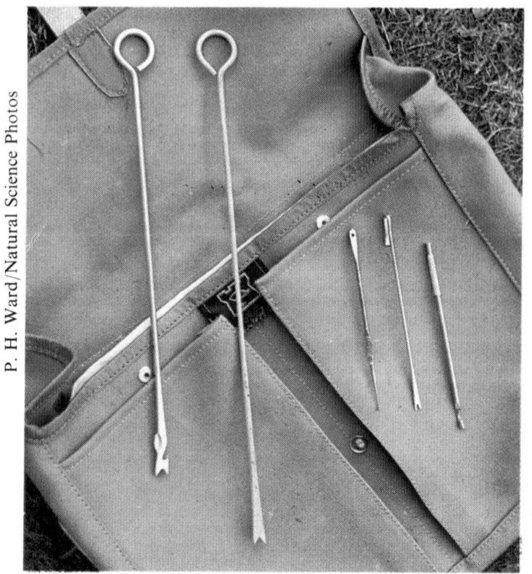

Ken Whitehead

*(Above) Heavy-duty gardening gloves are a good substitute for the spring gag, and artery forceps, for pike and zander fishing. (Right) V-end and tubular disgorgers for all other fish species.*

seen, a disgorger with some sort of loop or ring will be necessary. This can be slid down the line until the bend of the hook is found.

Several of the ring and guide types are available, but most fall down in practical use either because they do not slip easily onto the line, or more generally because they jam at the eye or spade of the hook. Only one type will slide onto the line and ride easily onto the bend of the hook, and that is the simplest design of them all—the open wire loop.

Simply sliding the disgorger down the line and blindly stabbing with it will, in many instances, push the barb further into the flesh. The easiest method—and the safest for the fish—is to support the creature with one hand gently but firmly behind the gills. If it is too large, lay it along the bank with the head raised against a tackle box or rod handle. Hold taut the line leading into the mouth, put the disgorger onto the line, slide it down and ease it over the eye or spade of the hook and onto the bend. Press directly downwards until the hook moves freely and withdraw from the mouth—still supported in the disgorger—taking special care not to catch it against the tongue.

The disgorger is ridiculously easy to lose, but there are two things you can do to reduce the number that you mislay. One is to tie the handle by a piece of thin, strong line to your jacket lapel or through a buttonhole. The other is to paint the whole object either bright red or yellow, preferably with luminous paint. This also makes the business end easier to see inside a fish's mouth.

A lost disgorger can be replaced, in an emergency, by a small, forked twig or a twig into which a groove has been cut or filed.

**Forceps**

Within the last few years, medical artery forceps have become popular as a means of releasing a deeply-embedded hook, and several firms have produced them specifically for the angler. Undoubtedly they are useful, but like most pieces of angling equipment, they have their limitations.

Some fish have a relatively small mouth opening even though the actual mouth cavity is quite large. The width of a pair of forceps, particularly when they are open, can block the view of the mouth, and if they are opened widely, can cause actual damage. It is all too easy to grasp a portion of flesh, together with the hook, and tear it in the process of unhooking. For fish with bony or leathery mouths, therefore, artery forceps are an efficient means of freeing most hooks. Even so, the very large treble hooks used, for example in pike fishing need a lot of leverage, and forceps are not always adequate. When choosing a pair at the tackle shop, look for strong, long handles and a fine nose that can get to grips with very small hooks.

Pliers are infinitely better for removing treble hooks than either forceps or disgorgers—even the king-sized, foot-long models sold as 'pike disgorgers'. Obviously, those with a long and narrow nose are best, and stainless metal preferable to cheap tools that rust. There is at least one pair on the

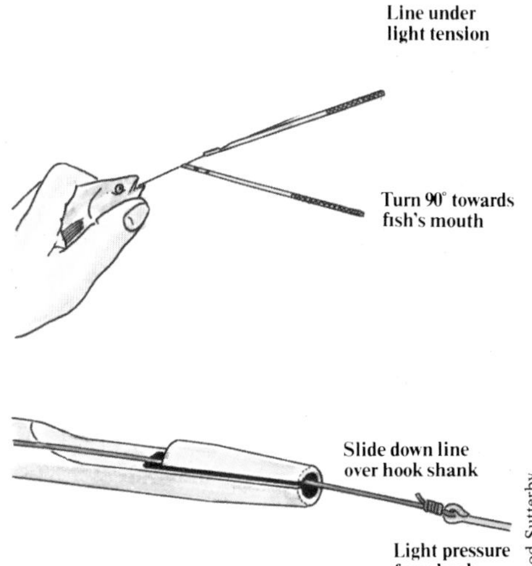


Rod Sutterby

*(Left) The tubular disgorger is run down the line to the eyed or spade-end shank. Held by the disgorger the hook is pushed down to dislodge the barb, then drawn out.*
*(Overleaf left) It is wrong to put your hand behind the gill cover.*
*(Overleaf right) A spring clamp can exert too much force and damage the pike's jaw.*

market that are especially designed for this heavy work on large and 'toothy' fish.

Like disgorgers, forceps are best tied to the jacket with a length of line and not clipped onto a lapel or pocket flap.

**Gags**

These are usually thought of as pike disgorging aids, and there is no doubt that they become essential where large pike have been deeply hooked. But their use is not appropriate with small fish. In fact, considerable damage can be caused to both mouth and tongue where gags are forced and stretched into immature mouths.

The gag is a simple, safety-pin-style piece of sprung steel that, when opened, will hold the jaws of a pike apart. This enables the angler to use two hands to remove the hook without fear of the mouth closing and damaging a finger or two. Small ones are useless—and big ones brutal. Six inches is about right, and the first thing a purchaser should do is to crimp up one of the loops on the keeper that holds the gag closed. Failure to attend to this detail will lead to the gag springing open at the wrong moment and being lost.

Next, the prongs at the jaws—those parts that are actually going to be pushed inside the pike's mouth, should be filed down until they are completely round, then either covered with pieces of plastic sleeving or bound round with electrician's tape until well padded. After this, the gag can be used without fear of damage to the fish.

In correct use on a fish, the two protected prongs on the gag are wedged against the hard ridge of teeth just inside the upper and lower jaw—not into the outer lip, or halfway down the throat. By keeping them into the centre maximum space will be created through which a disgorger can be operated.

It is worth remembering that where hooks are well down towards the throat area in a pike, a careful approach can always be made through the gill openings, avoiding the actual gills themselves.

Where hooks are well down in the entrance to the stomach, great care is needed, and rather than pull and push against the soft skin, it is better to use a pair of pliers to crush the barb, after which it can be withdrawn with ease.

Finally, if the situation becomes impossible and every effort fails to free the hook, cut it off as close to the eye as possible and return the fish to the water. The flesh of the fish may well heal over wound and hook alike and the body acids gradually destroy the metal. If it is not bleeding badly when you return it to the water, a fish may survive perfectly well.

Ken Whitehead

Ken Whitehead

# Spinners

A spinner can be defined as an artificial lure that usually comprises of a blade or body which rotates quickly about a straight line axis consisting often of a wire bar. Spoons, in contrast, have a wobbly retrieve and do not usually spin. Plugs are artificial fish-like objects, made of various materials, which wobble on retrieve. These distinctions are not clear cut, and it is possible to buy, or make, spinners that are headed by a sizeable body and are therefore halfway between spinners and plugs (such as the famous Voblex), and spinners with so much hair or feather that they approach flies in construction, but with the added flash of a small rotating blade. There is great scope for inventiveness among anglers and many new combinations are possible, if not many new basic designs.

**Five basic spinners**

There are five basic kinds of spinners—artificial minnows, wagtails, mackerel spinners, fly spoons, and barspoons. It is unfortunate that the last two incorporate the word 'spoon' in their names, for they are in fact spinners with a straight axis around which the blade spins.

Of all the kinds of spinners, artificial minnows most closely represent fish,

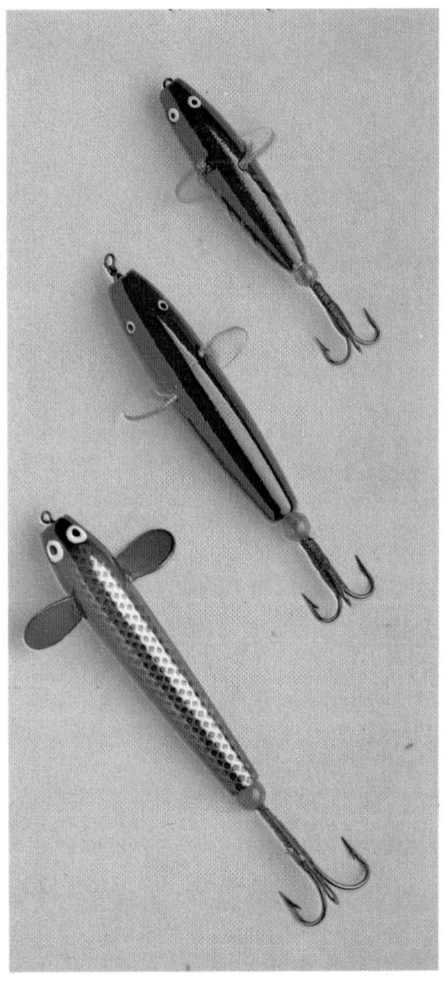

*(Right) Devon minnows, the most fish-like spinners. The vanes cause rotation.*
*(Below) The Voblex, another favourite.*

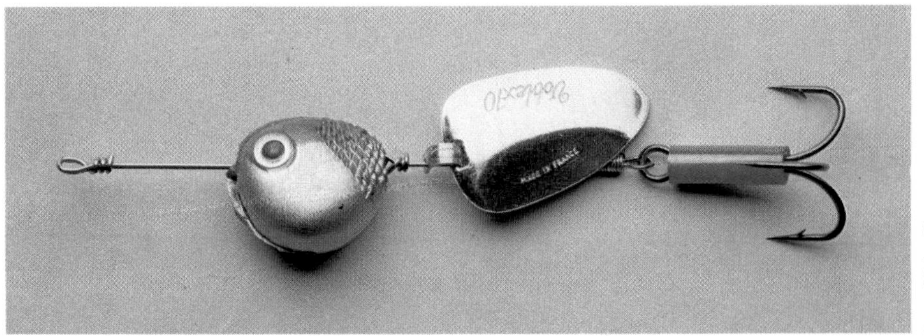

Steve Bicknell

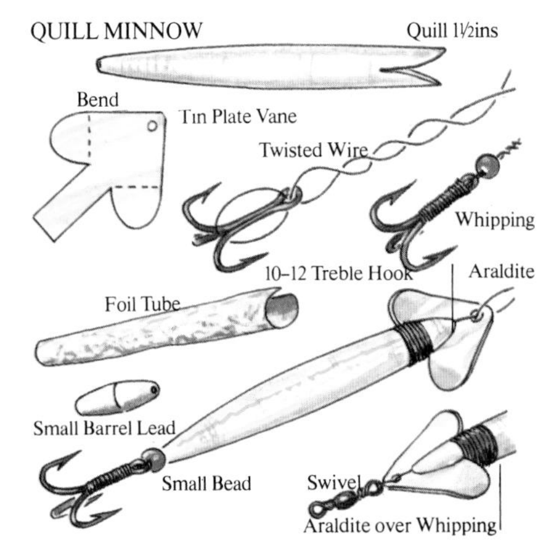


*A home-made quill minnow, identical in action to the Devon minnow. The barrel lead is slid down the wire inside.*

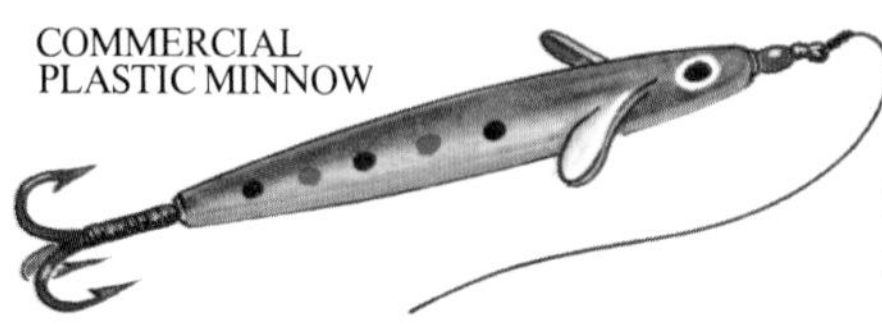


both still and on the move. The body, made of either wood, plastic or metal, is round in cross section, minnow-like in profile, and has a hole along its length through which a metal bar or wire trace passes. At the tail is a treble hook and at the head a swivel which can be attached to the reel line or, if fishing for pike, to a wire trace link swivel. Generally, the swivel at the head has a smaller overall diameter than the hole through the middle of the lure so that on the take the fish tends to blow the lure up the line, giving itself nothing to lever against as it tries to throw the hook. This is an excellent feature of the design which is occasionally incorporated in such other lures as plugs.

The head of the minnow has a pair of vanes which cause it to rotate. Some makes have adjustable vanes so that the spin can be reversed, and lure twist reduced.

**Minnow variation**

A variation on the minnow theme is the quill minnow, a superb lure for fishing for trout in hill streams. The whole body of the quill minnow rotates, often including the bar wire through its middle, so that the swivel has to work well to avoid line twist, and an anti-kink vane is usually necessary. These lures usually have up to three sets of treble hooks and since many hill trout take the spinner crossways, this is an advantage despite the tendency of the lure to become hooked up in rocks and other snags.

**Wagtail movement**

Wagtails look more creature-like when still than when moving. They usually have a head complete with eyes, spinning vanes, a swivel and tube-like body hidden inside two long rubber flaps which are pointed at the tail end, close to the treble hook. The name comes from this loose, flapping rubber. All this detail disappears, however, when the whole body rotates quickly and, other than in body softness, the wagtail probably differs little from the various minnows. Wagtails can be made to quite large sizes and with a slow spin. This can occasionally be an advantage over the commercial minnows. Like minnows, wagtails are mostly used when fishing for salmon, sea trout and trout, but can be very effective for pike.

*Wagtails look unnatural when still, but in action they work in a life-like manner. One side piece is shown removed to illustrate the wagtail's structure.*

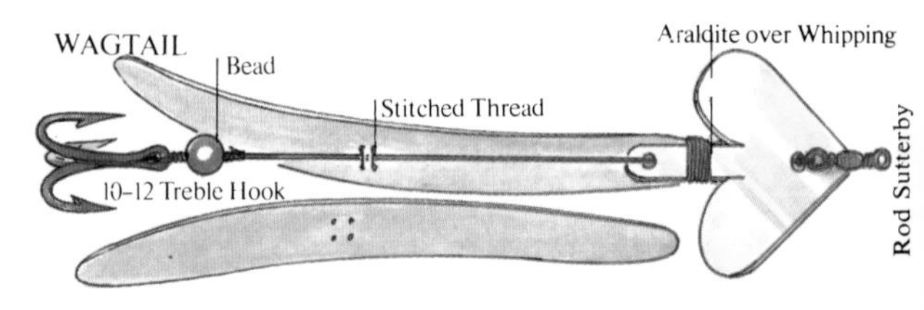

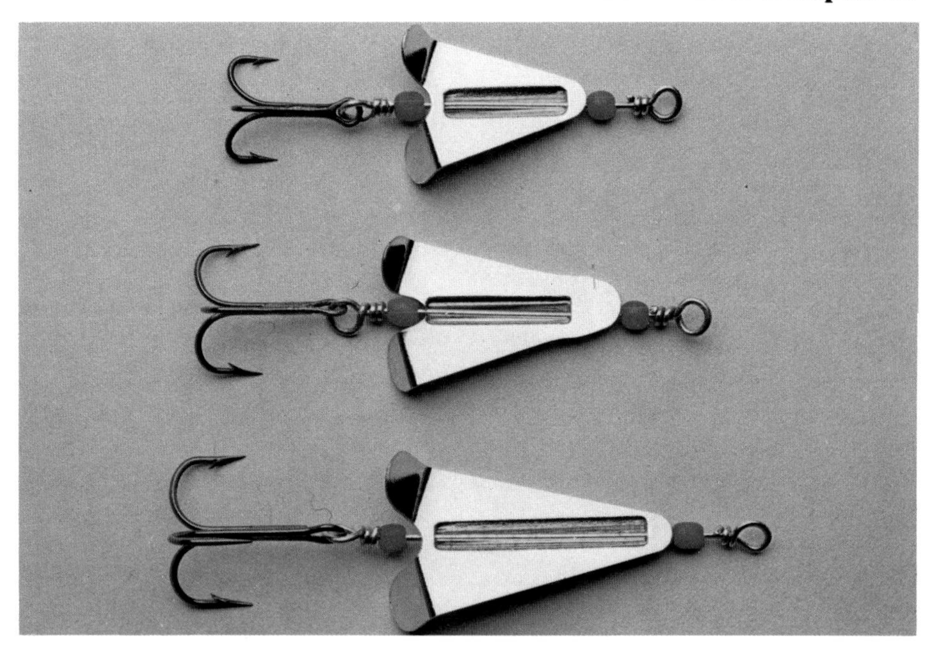

Mackerel spinners are superb lures for any predatory fish. They do not work well if more than $2\frac{1}{2}$in long, but most commercial ones are 2in or less. They have a tube around the axial wire, and this tube is brazed to a triangular-shaped plate that has the spinning vanes at the rear, near the treble hook. Mackerel spinners can be retrieved in very shallow water and with extreme slowness at any depth. For catching large numbers of perch and pike they are perhaps the best lures ever designed, and should be fished on lines of 6-8lb b.s. to obtain the best casting results out of their aerodynamic shape. Mackerel spinners have advantages over other spinners, as they are very cheap and nearly indestructible but they are the only spinner that is not easy to make unless you dispense with the tube and make do with a couple of bent eyes at the front and back of the blade.

Fly spoons, as their name implies, have traditionally been used for game fish, but are very effective for chub and perch on small streams. They are small, twinkling lures, most of which spin rather than wobble, and are essentially spinners for

(*Above*) *Both simple and superb, mackerel spinners work at low retrieve rates.*

(*Below*) *Fly spoons, for light spinning.*

short casts on light tackle of 2-6lb b.s. monofilament lines. This can even be fished on fly tackle with fly lines. This is probably how they originated but today it is unusual to see them fished in this way. Many fly spoons are constructed with a spinner blade attached at only one end to a split ring connecting two swivels. A treble hook is attached to the other end of one swivel and the reel line to the opposite end of the other swivel.

Barspoons are more correctly classified as spinners since they have a straight axis of wire around which the blade, attached at one end, rotates with a strong vibration. Weight is added to the bar, just behind the spinning blade, and this weight can be made to look like a body and can be painted different colours. Bar spoons are among the most versatile of lures and all except the very heavy ones are retrievable even in very shallow-water conditions.

Heavy barspoons, however, can be cast a long way, and many can be fished very deep and slow. Making your own is easy provided you attach the blade to the bar with a separate link, rather than passing the bar through a hole in the blade. Popular commercially made barspoons are Ondex, Veltic and Mepps.

A change in the blade shape has given rise to some classic lures: the Vibro has the end away from the bar quite sharply pointed, and the result is a spinner which vibrates very strongly. The kidney spoon has a kidney-shaped blade which gives a pulsating spinning action.

Perhaps in a category of its own is the Colorado which has a spoon-shaped blade attached at both ends. It spins about a bar axis by means of spinning vanes at the head end. It is one of the oldest lures

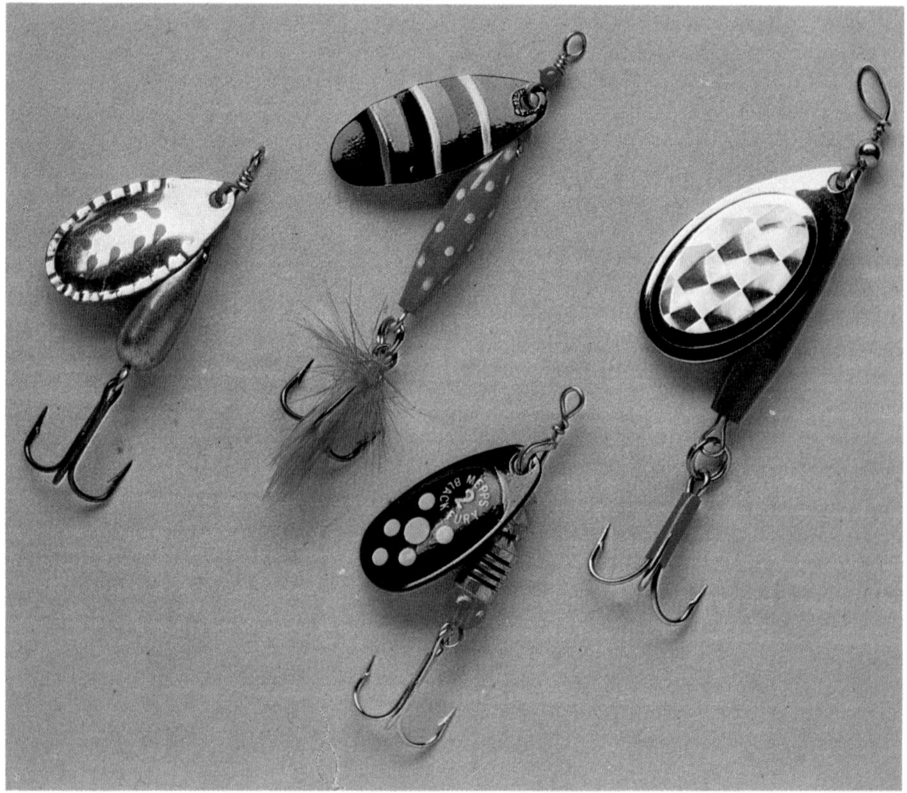


Steve Bicknell

available, and in its smaller sizes can be extremely effective for perch.

Do-it-yourself enthusiasts can have a field day with spinners. Spinner blades are lighter than most spoon blades and they can be easily cut with tin snips. Even plastic blades can be used successfully. All you need are lengths of wire, round-headed long-nosed pliers to bend the wire into terminal loops, and the ability to cut various weights of metal sheet into blades that can be beaten to the required curve.

**Antikink vanes**

There is one more thing the spinning angler needs—antikink vanes to prevent line twist. Half moon leads which can be clamped to the reel line or trace are one of the best. They range in size from minute to very large and for really heavy spinning they can always be used in multiples. Many more antikink devices are available, and it is wise to try them all, but make sure they are firmly fixed to the line or trace, otherwise they are totally ineffective.

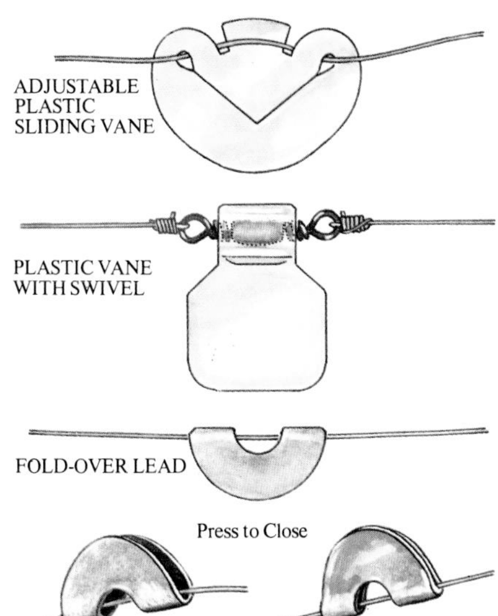


Rod Sutterby

*(Above) Devices to prevent line twist. (Below Colorado (top) and kidney spoons. (Left) Colourful bar spoons for deep fishing.*

Bill Howes

# Plugs

The best description of a plug is a cross between a spinner and a deadbait. In shape it resembles a dead fish with hooks ready-set. In use it is retrieved in much the same way as a spinner. But a plug possesses advantages that neither spinner nor deadbait has – it can be made to work with innumerable variations on a straight retrieve at any of many chosen depths.

Plugs fall into four general categories that coincide with the depth at which they should work. There are surface lures, floating divers, sinkers, and deep divers. Their shape, especially at the nose, often gives a clue to their working use. But it is left to the angler to actually get the best action from them when he is fishing.

**Kinds of plug**

Floating plugs are light, usually made from wood, and have a 'V'-shaped wedge inserted in the nose. There are models made to represent mice, and one has broad arms, or sweeps, that vibrate backwards and forwards during the retrieve; they are intended to represent a surface-swimming fish in distress – rather in the fashion of one with swimbladder trouble.

*A chub, with a selection of plugs with varying actions. The placing of the vanes dictates whether the plug dives or rises.*

Ken Whitehead

They should be cast close to the bank, under overhanging trees and bushes and retrieved alternately fast and slow, causing them to dive a few inches under the surface, then pop up to the top. The bow wave caused by this sudden dive is the lure's main attraction.

**Most versatile plugs**

Floating divers are the most versatile of all plugs. They have lightweight bodies with a medium-sized diving nose (or lip) set into the head. After being cast, they will lie on the surface, only diving when the angler commences the retrieve. The faster the motion, the deeper they will dive – short, hard turns on the reel and then a few seconds with the handle stationary, produce a series of swoops and rises that few fish can resist. They have an added advantage in snaggy waters. By stopping the retrieve when an underwater obstruction is reached, the plug is allowed to float up, and can be coaxed gently past the danger area before continuing with the normal dive and rise action.

**Sinking plugs**

Sinking plugs are for very deep gravel pits and reservoirs where the lure has to sink some way before it can be fished usefully. In order to find and keep the 'taking' depth, the count-down method should be used. After the lure has hit the water, the angler counts from, say, one to six, then starts his retrieve. On the next cast, he may count to seven, then eight on the following casts – and so on until a fish is taken. This will probably be the taking depth, and future casts should be allowed the same length of time before retrieve begins.

Few plugs in this category have a diving vane, all are heavy, and some models have a metal ball sealed into a cavity in the body.

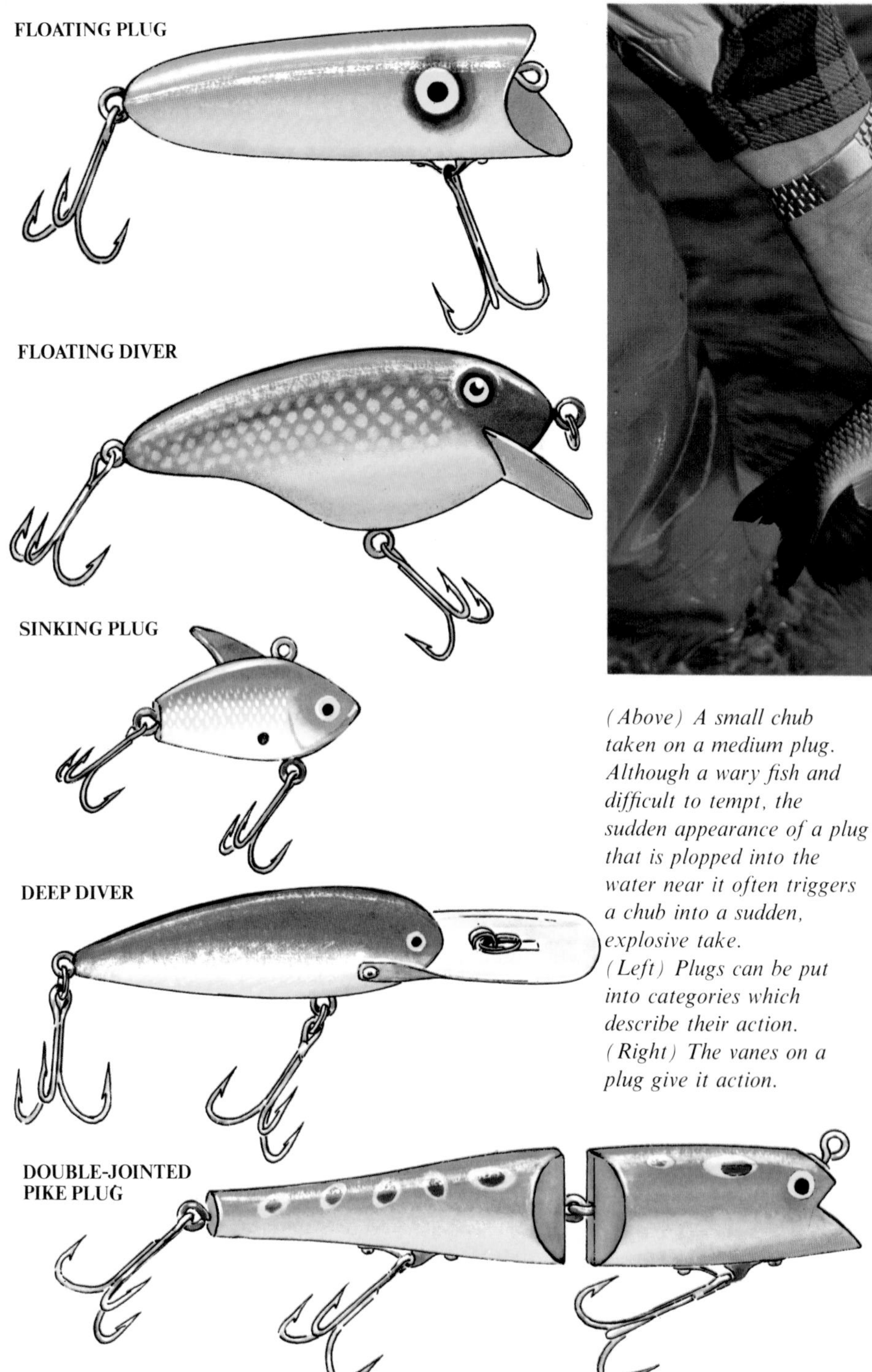


*(Above) A small chub taken on a medium plug. Although a wary fish and difficult to tempt, the sudden appearance of a plug that is plopped into the water near it often triggers a chub into a sudden, explosive take.*
*(Left) Plugs can be put into categories which describe their action.*
*(Right) The vanes on a plug give it action.*

Ken Whitehead

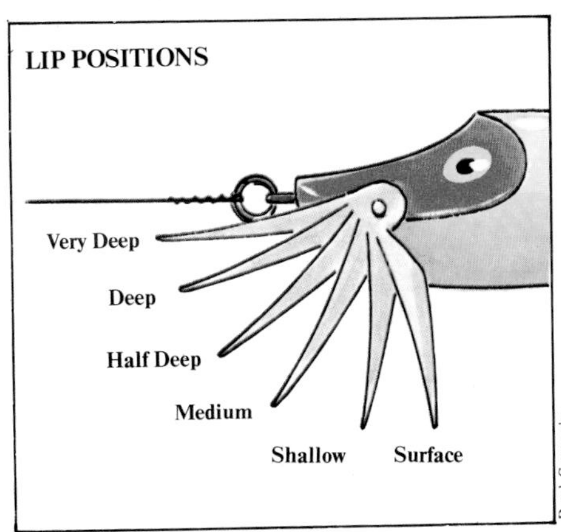

Rod Sutterby

When the retrieve begins, the action of the plug under the water causes this ball to rattle, making vibrations that attract predators.

**Deep divers**

The last selection of plugs, the deep divers, are easily recognized by the extra large metal vane set into the head. This broad lip sets up drag against the water when the retrieve starts and causes the plug to dive quickly, at a sharp angle. As with sinkers, the count-down method is the best when exploring with this type of lure.

The colour range of plugs displayed in a tackle shop can be quite staggering. But action is more important than colour in a plug, and generally those with green, yellow and a little red coincide with the natural colours of fish and appear the most acceptable.

Most important of all is the construction of the plug. Hooks should be neither so large that they dwarf the body, nor so small that they will fail to set into the jaws of a fish on striking. The best hooks are made from fine wire, with well-defined barbs. Most of them are mounted into the body by screw eyes or metal bands secured with screws. These should be most carefully checked, and, if they appear loose, should be removed and re-set with a little Araldite glue to hold them firm. The eye-loop at the head, to which the trace will be mounted, should also be carefully looked at to ensure that it is firmly closed, otherwise the trace will slip free from it during a cast.

**Size not important**

One naturally thinks of pike fishing in connection with plugs, and most of the sinking and deep-diving models will take good fish. Size does not seem important where pike are concerned – 4 and 5in double-bodied plugs that simulate the flowing movements of a swimming fish, down to tiny 1½in minnow imitations, will all produce results. Perch take a running plug, too, especially in reservoirs and gravel pits. Their large, 'telescopic' mouths are perfectly capable of tackling the large lure intended for a pike. Chub are appreciative of surface plugs that can be persuaded to make a large disturbance on top of the water – especially the more gaudy, tassle-embellished models. Shallow divers of the minnow size are worth a trial during the winter months.

But there are few fish that have not, at some time or other, fallen for a plug – particularly in the early season when many of the old adult stock have turned cannibal.

# Maggots

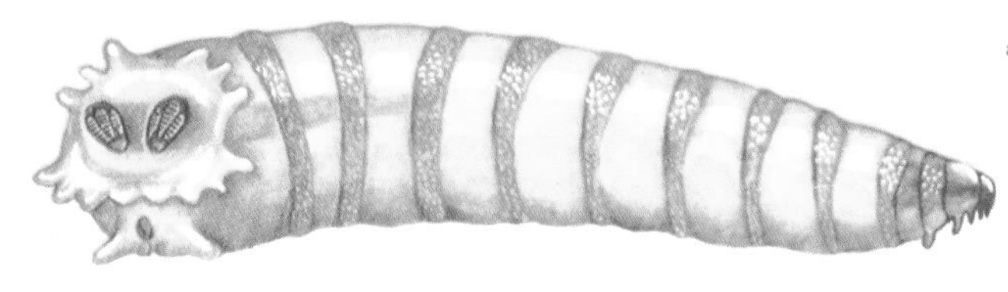

*Maggots are bred as bait from flies, most often the bluebottle (above).*

The maggot is the most popular coarse fishing bait used in Britain. Almost all our freshwater species may be taken on it, major competitions have been won on it, and it has also accounted for some record fish.

Maggots are small, easy to buy, transport and use. Not so long ago they were cheap, but prices have risen steeply. Maggots now cost about 60p a pint. They are sold this way because pint beer glasses were once used to scoop them up for sale.

The maggot is the larva, or grub, of the fly. The maggots of the bluebottle, greenbottle, and common housefly are the ones used by the angler.

There are four stages in the life-cycle of a fly: egg–grub–pupa–fly. The female of the common housefly lays between 120 and 150 eggs at a time and deposits several batches in a lifetime.

**Maggot breeding**

Breeding maggots is big business. Millions are sold every week by tackle dealers all over the country. Professional breeders use bluebottles for mass production of the ordinary maggot. The common housefly's maggots are known as 'squatts', and being smaller than the bluebottle larvae they are used as 'feeders' thrown in to attract fish. Maggots from the greenbottle are called 'pinkies'. These are also small and used as 'feeders', but may be used on the hooks when circumstances require very fine tackle.

Special fly-houses holding the breeding stocks are maintained at constant temperatures 21.1°C-23.9°C (70-75°F). This enables maggot production to meet the year round demand.

Maggot breeding starts when meat or fish is placed in the fly-house so that the breeder flies can lay their eggs. When this is done the meat is said to be 'blown'. The meat is then removed from the fly-house and placed on trays in long sheds. When the maggots hatch they begin to feed and grow. On reaching bait size they are transferred to another tray filled with bran or sawdust. As they wriggle

Bill Howes

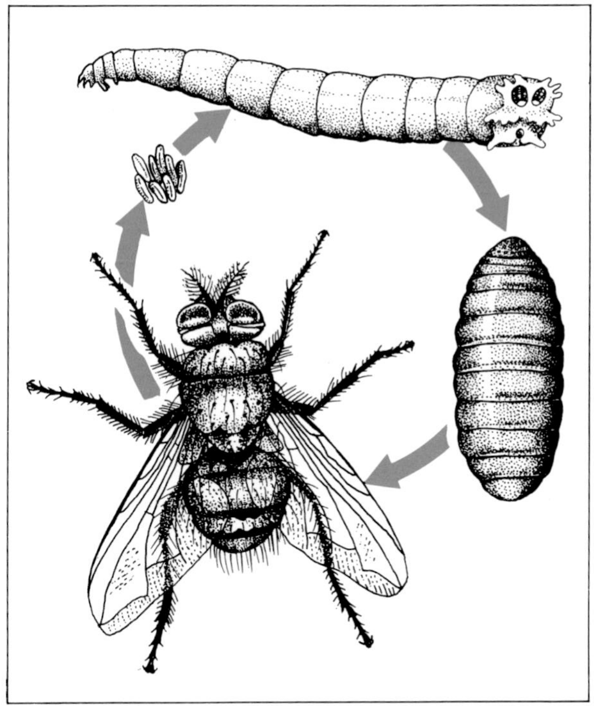

*The greenbottle (top) produces the maggots known as 'pinkies'; the housefly (lower) those called 'squatts'. (Right) The life-cycle of a fly: egg-grub-pupa-fly.*

Lyn Cawley

through this they are cleaned and then ready for despatch, usually in large biscuit tins, to tackle shops. There they are kept in fridges to prevent them reaching the pupa (or chrysalis) stage too soon.

Maggots are usually sold in the sawdust or bran. To improve their taste remove them from the sawdust or bran and transfer them to a clean bait box containing custard or blancmange powder, flour, or a similar substance. As they crawl through this they become well-coated and tiny specks flake off to add an extra attraction for the fish.

**Breeding your own maggots**

Many anglers are now breeding their own maggots, and producing very high quality hook-bait. This must be done in garden sheds or somewhere away from the house. (Even professional breeders are often asked by local authorities to move on because of the smell associated with their business.) Quality maggots may be obtained from chicken carcasses. Put these in a container—a large biscuit tin is ideal—and make sure the lid fits perfectly. Make a 2-3in diameter hole in the top and leave the tin outdoors. After a couple of days the chicken flesh will be blown, with clusters of eggs visible.

Wrap the blown chicken carcass in old newspaper and replace it in the tin. The eggs will hatch a few days later and the grubs will begin to feed on the nutritious meat. To help the maggots grow fat, add soft brown sugar or even the cream off the top of the milk.

Keep the chicken wrapped in the paper, watching at intervals to see how the maggots are growing. When they stop feeding, place the maggots in bran for 24 hours. Next, tip onto a sieve and allow the bran and maggots to separate. Now add clean bran, plus more sugar, which will ensure that the maggots remain soft until needed.

The 'gozzer' is a very soft, white maggot, the larval form of a type of bluebottle, reared mainly on pigeon carcass, pig's or sheep's heart. After five or six days of feeding, these should be given a final bran 'bath' and left until required.

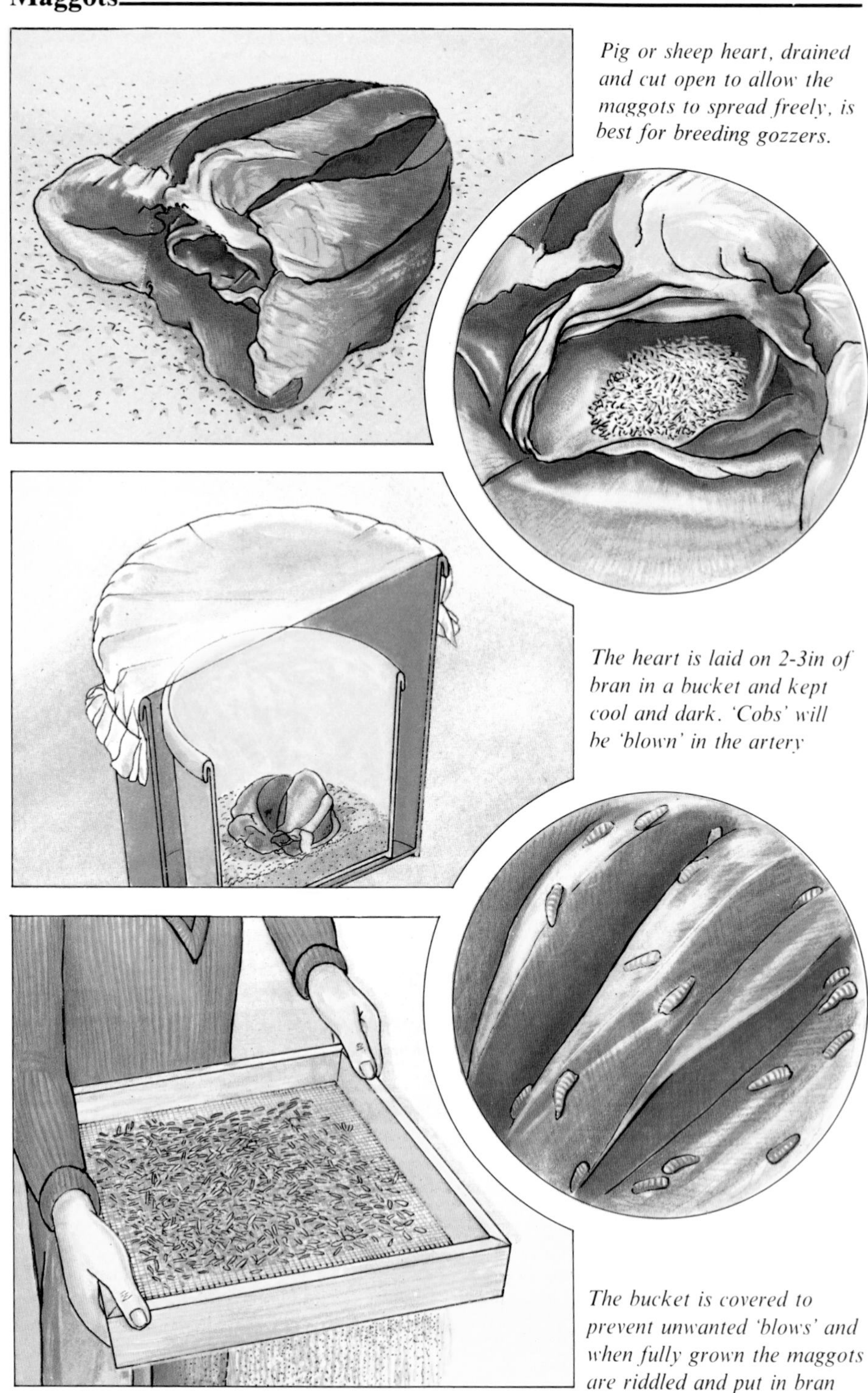

*Pig or sheep heart, drained and cut open to allow the maggots to spread freely, is best for breeding gozzers.*

*The heart is laid on 2-3in of bran in a bucket and kept cool and dark. 'Cobs' will be 'blown' in the artery*

*The bucket is covered to prevent unwanted 'blows' and when fully grown the maggots are riddled and put in bran*

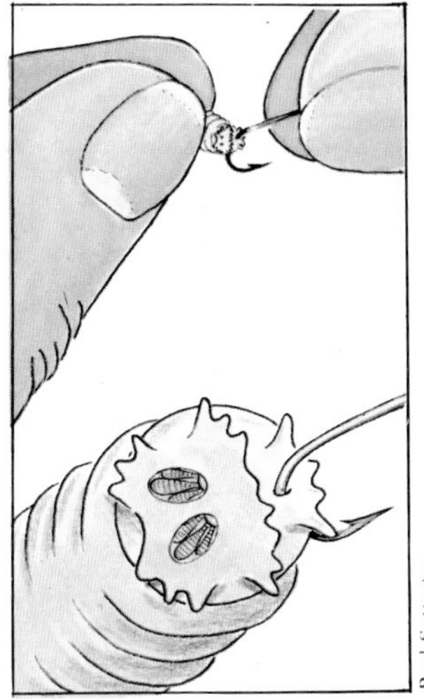

Rod Sutterby

Kim Seyer

*Hook the maggot through the vent at the blunt end. This will allow it to wriggle attractively to tempt the fish. Be careful not to pierce your thumb*

A very succulent maggot, the 'gozzer's' powers of attraction are highly valued, especially by match fishermen.

**Coloured maggots**

To increase the attractiveness of maggots to fish, they may be dyed a variety of colours, and indeed can be bought coloured orange, red or yellow. Tackle dealers supply Chrysiodine R for colouring maggots orange, Auramine O for yellow, and Rhodamine B for red. These dyes may be used in one of two ways. First, the maggots can be coloured by raising them on foodstuffs treated with a small amount of the dye. The second method is best for maggots that have already been cleaned, as they are when bought. For this, sprinkle dye on them and stir well, then leave for three or four hours according to the depth of colour desired. Next, add bran or sawdust on which they will deposit excess dye. Lastly, sieve them to remove the bran, and they are ready for use.

The 'annatto' is a special colour-fed maggot whose yellow colour comes from the dye used to colour butter. Gozzers and other extra-soft maggots produce the best results with this dye. Annatto is bought in roll form and must be cut into slices and mixed into a thin paste with water before use. The best time to introduce annatto is when the maggots are about half-grown. Spread the paste on the meat and replace in the bran. When the maggots stop feeding they are ready for use.

To prevent your maggots from turning into chrysalids, or casters, before you want them to, when the weather is warm, place them securely in a plastic bag and store them in your domestic fridge where they will become cold and still. No harm will come to food there if they are secure. Remember, too, that maggots need air, so ensure your bait containers are ventilated with pin-holes.

Lastly, if buying maggots from a shop, be sure they are fresh and do not include remnants of last week's stock. They should be shiny and wriggle vigorously.

# Casters

The chrysalis, or pupa, of the fly is known to anglers as a caster. At this point in its life-cycle (from egg to grub, or maggot, to pupa, to fly) it is an excellent bait. First made popular by match anglers in roach waters, some experts consider casters to be the most important new bait adopted in recent years. Although the maggot remains the most popular general bait, the time may be near when the caster will have replaced it. As well as roach, chub and dace are partial to it and it has accounted for bream, gudgeon and tench. When first introduced to a stretch of water the fish may be uninterested but, once sampled, every caster is likely to be taken. The fish probably gets its food more easily from the insect at this time in its life-cycle than when it was a mere maggot.

**Home production**

Casters can be purchased from a tackle-shop or bait dealer and kept in a refrigerator for about a week. Home production can work out to be more expensive than buying them ready-bred, but the angler needs chrysalids (or casters) as sinkers: too fast a metamorphosis and the caster becomes a floater, of no practical use except as a means to check on the presence of fish in unknown water. The keen angler who needs a constant supply, therefore, will want to produce his own, in order to control the speed of change. After a little trial and error the angler can have casters in perfect condition and colour in the quantities he needs as and when he wants them for a day's fishing.

**Test for freshness**

Whether you buy casters from the dealer or raise maggots, and casters as well, yourself you will need about five pints of maggots to produce three pints of good quality casters—enough for a match or a day's fishing.

For large casters, choose large maggots. To test for freshness if you are buying the maggots, look for the food pouch—the small black speck under the skin. This pouch

*(Above) Five pints of maggots give a day's supply of casters. (Below) In five or six days most of the maggots turn to casters.*

*(Below) The casters are separated at regular intervals from the maggots. (Right) Casters and maggots laid out at the swim.*

Bill Howes

carries all the food the insect needs to complete the stages of its development to a fly, and should still be visible.

It takes a fresh maggot, one that has just been taken from its feed medium, five to six days to turn into a chrysalis with the temperature at between 65° and 70°F (18° to 21°C). To slow development, put the maggots, in a plastic bag, into the refrigerator for three days—more in very hot weather, less in cold.

Tip the maggots on to a sieve to be riddled and cleaned, then into tins of dry sawdust, so that maggots and sawdust cover the bottoms of the tins to a depth of not more than a couple of inches. The tins of maggots should now be kept in a cool place: a garage or cool outhouse is ideal.

After about 24 hours the first of the casters will be seen. Once this stage is reached put the contents of the tins on to a riddle over a larger container and the maggots will wriggle through, leaving the already-turned casters on the mesh, with any dead maggots which should be thrown away.

Return the live maggots to their tins. Repeat this inspection and selection process every 7 or 8 hours. Each batch of casters can be rinsed in water to remove bits of sawdust, drained on the riddle and then placed, in sealed plastic bags, in the refrigerator, at not less than 34°F (1°C).

By rinsing the casters, any floaters can be removed at this stage. Damp casters, however, can sour in the refrigerator and some anglers prefer to omit rinsing at this stage, as a final check should may be made before setting off, or at the water-side.

If you do not want to use the refrigerator for collecting the bags of casters, you can put

Don Bridgewood

them direct from the riddling into a bucket, just covering them with water and adding to their number as they develop. Floaters can thus be eliminated as they appear and the bucket kept in the same cool outhouse as the tins of maggots.

**Uniform colour**

Whichever method you use, you will find that the casters vary in colour. Casters of a uniform dark red colour—the favourite—can be achieved quite simply. On the evening before use, put all the casters into a wet towel, fold it over them and leave in a bucket overnight. Next morning all the casters will be the same colour.

The size of hook will be governed by the size of the caster. The biggest you can use will probably be a 14, but generally a 16 or 18 will be necessary. The hook must be buried in the caster. Hold the caster between thumb and forefinger and, with the hook in the other hand, pierce the head of the caster with the point. Turn the hook very gently into the caster and, with some of the shank still showing, lightly tap the top of the shank until the hook sinks into the caster.

**Casters as groundbait**

In deepish, fast flowing water, casters are best introduced as groundbait. Where there are plenty of fish and once they are taking them, you can put as many as two dozen casters in every cast. A 'cocktail' mixture of worm tipped with a caster is particularly deadly with bream.

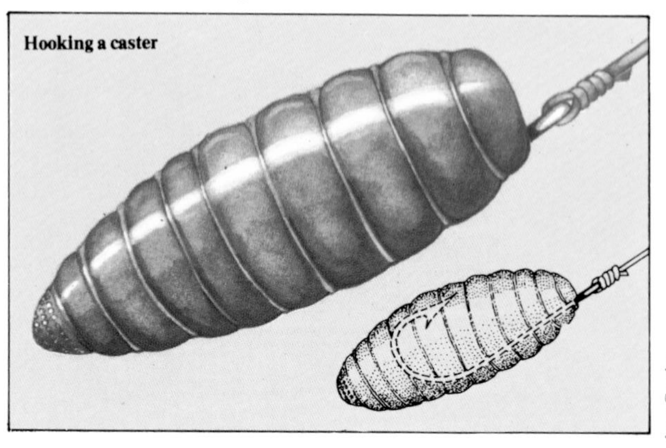


Lyn Cawley.

*(Right) To hook a caster, hold it gently between thumb and forefinger, pierce the head with the point and sink the bend and most of the shank in the bait. Tap the shank lightly so that all of the hook is now concealed.*
*(Below) A catapult is used by match anglers to hurl casters with accuracy into a distant swim.*

Don Bridgewood

# Caterpillars and mealworms

P. H. Ward/Natural Science Photos

The idea that any caterpillar accidentally found along the river bank should be mounted onto a hook and dapped through the bushes, is one of angling's popular misconceptions. There are better techniques, and although it is true that many fish, including dace, chub and roach, will feed on the surface during very warm weather, not every caterpillar is attractive to fish, or useful as a bait.

**Natural protection**

Many species of grubs and caterpillars are naturally protected either by their startling colour or shape, or by a repulsive taste or smell made when danger is sensed, usually effected by means of a discharge through the skin. So the angler using a bait which has either of these protections is likely to find that, although a fish may show an interest, his offering could well be rejected almost immediately, and long before there has been a chance to strike.

Caterpillars are best gathered before the angler goes fishing and not left to a chance finding on the day. Despite the number of modern sprays and insecticides in use, the larvae of the Large White (better known as the Cabbage White) butterfly are still plentiful: few gardeners or allotment holders will resent anglers searching the leaves of the cabbages, mustard, turnips or radish plants for full-grown grubs.

**Storing and carrying**

These grubs should be stored in a large plastic box with ample ventilation and with a few leaves of the host plant. If there is a handle by which the box can be tied onto a waist-belt, so much the better—it will allow the angler complete mobility as he fishes and save constant trips to where the box has been left. Keep the box in a cool, dark place before going to fish, and try to protect it from the sun as far as possible when actually fishing.

Dapping is one way in which the caterpillar can be fished. Usually a long general-purpose trotting rod is best, and this is rigged without a float but with just one large swan or BB shot pinched above the hook. The caterpillar is mounted by its tail end—an easy task providing that the hook is of very fine wire and has recently been sharpened. Loose line below the rod tip is wound round the rod, which can then be poked through gaps in overhanging bushes and the bait released to dap on the surface of the water.

In theory this method is sound and will generally produce a few fish. But in practice, the disturbance through vibrations made by the angler, either on the bank or by the rod tapping against branches prohibit the better fish from being attracted. Even if a fish is hooked, the angler is often unable to play or land it because of obstructions surrounding his rod.

A far better approach can be made when the angler is in the water, either wading where this is possible, or from a boat. A short, light rod—a fly rod is ideal—and a free-running centrepin or light fixed-spool reel with a light line in the region of 3lb b.s. will enable accurate casting to be achieved with the minimum exertion. Accuracy is all-important, but you should nevertheless aim to use as little lead on the line as possible, and cast the caterpillar under bushes and between reeds or weedbeds from the mid-stream position.

fact, where brickwork lines or crosses water. Many insects live or hibernate in masonry, and naturally fall onto the surface from time to time in these areas.

**Mealworms**

Mealworms make an excellent bait. The long, straw-coloured grubs, segmented and rather similar to a centipede in appearance, are the larvae of a large beetle found in granaries and flour mills. They can occasionally be purchased at pet stores, where they are sold as food for insectivorous birds and mammals. Although they are expensive, they can be stored for a very long period in a ventilated tin of fine bran or oatmeal. If an even temperature is maintained, they will often go through the chrysalis stage, adult insect, and breed, allowing a succession of baits from the one purchase.

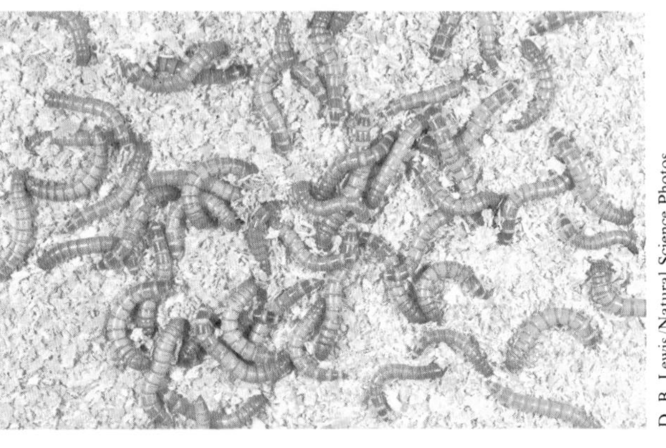

D. B. Lewis/Natural Science Photos

*(Left) Probably the most commonly seen caterpillar, the Large White. Fish take but may also reject like lightning, so be prepared to miss some bites.*
*(Right) Mealworms are not worms, but the larvae of beetles found in granaries and flour mills. They make good baits right through their larval, chrysalis and adult stages.*

Time is well spent in watching the surface for movements from a fish before casting to it. The angler can wade slowly upstream and position himself below the fish he has located. Two tail-hooked caterpillars will create sufficient disturbance as they land to ensure that immediate interest is shown, and no attempt should be made to strike until the fish has turned away with the bait—an action that can be judged by movement of the line across the water's surface.

**Dapping**

Dapping in one form or another can also be successfully undertaken in the region of locks, bridges, canal wharfs—anywhere, in

The two rigs described for using caterpillar baits are equally successful when fishing mealworms, although they should be mounted through a middle segment rather than one near the tail end, which is rather delicate and likely to break away during the cast.

Even if there is no acceptance of a mealworm bait on or just below the surface, it should be allowed to sink and lie on the bottom for a short time before being retrieved gently. The larva is not strong enough to withstand constant casting, and its light colouring makes it a distinctive mouthful appreciated by any bottom-feeding fish.

# Worms

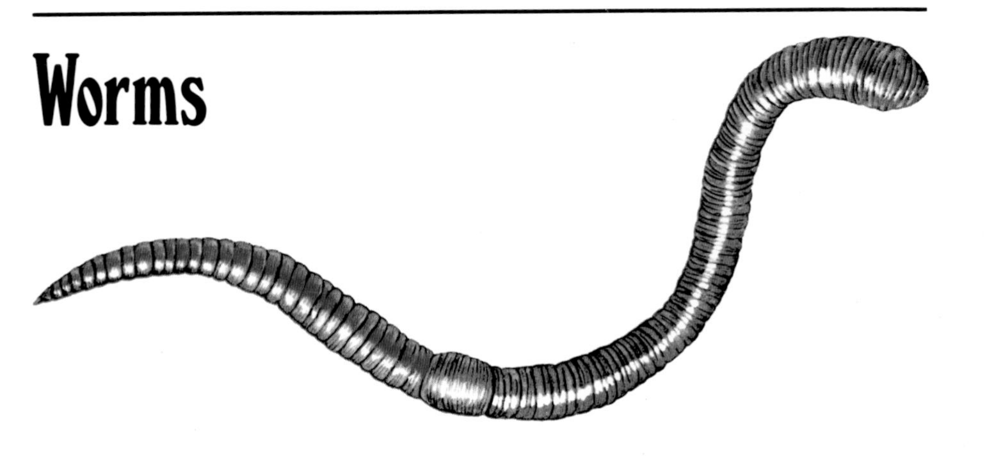

Earthworms have been used as a bait for fish for a thousand years and more, and today they are just as effective. All species of freshwater fish can be caught on worms, and indeed several record fish have fallen to this bait. And to the horror of game fishermen, even the salmon or trout may be taken in this way, sometimes deliberately, sometimes by chance.

There are some 25 kinds of earthworm found in Britain, but only three species are of real interest to the coarse fisherman—the lobworm, the redworm and the brandling. The lobworm, sometimes called the dew-worm, is the largest, the most used as bait and probably the easiest to find. It is fished whole for the bigger fish, but just the head or tail, commonly offered to roach, will often take larger species.

**Best places and times**

Lobworms may be gathered from a lawn, but if the grass is long it may be difficult. Cricket pitches and close-cut sports fields will also yield lobworms in plenty if access, at the right time, is available to the angler. The best periods are after dark and following a heavy dew or shower or, when conditions are dry, after a lawn has been watered. Early morning can also prove fruitful for worm collecting. It is important to move stealthily, for worms are very sensitive to vibrations and will soon dig themselves in if disturbed. At night it is necessary to use a dim torch or a

*The three kinds of earthworm used commonly by the coarse fisherman.*

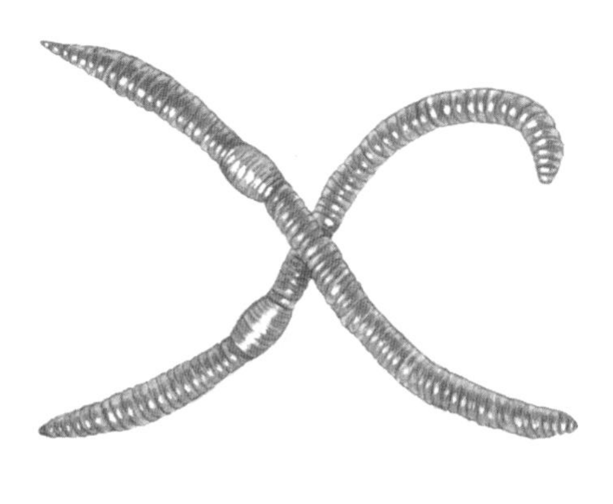

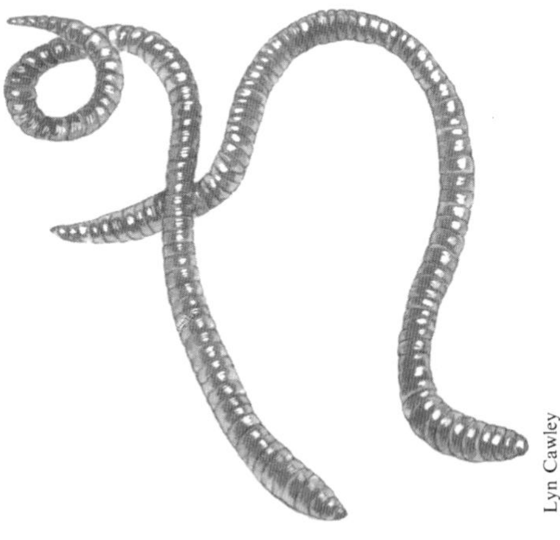

Lyn Cawley

Peter Burt

beachcaster's lamp that straps on to the head and leaves both hands free.

A worm must be seized quickly and firmly when it has come partly out of its hole on to the wet grass. Carry a tin of fine sand in which to dip your fingers to give them a grip on the slippery creature. The lobworm has tiny clusters of erectile bristles at intervals along its length, and these enable it to grip the sides of its burrow. So having got hold of the worm, maintain a steady pressure until it relaxes and comes out with its fish-attracting tail intact.

**The redworm**

The redworm is a smaller species, not usually over 4in long, and is a very useful roach, dace and rudd bait, although any species of worm may appeal to all freshwater fish. This worm is found in compost heaps, under large stones or rotting logs, in fact any sizeable object in the garden could conceal enough worms for a good day's fishing.

The brandling is of similar size to the redworm but is distinguishable by a series of

*Earthworms can be obtained from most garden lawns, especially after rain.*

*The worm is hooked at least twice or, if preferred, two hooks can be used.*

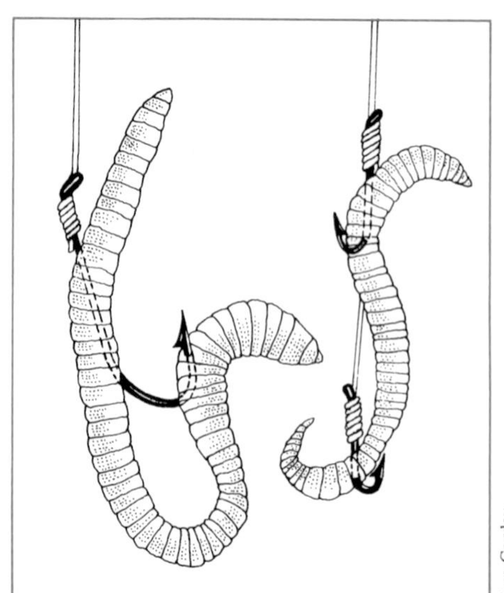
Lyn Cawley

*The best time to gather worms is after rain. In dry weather water the lawn to bring the worms to the top.*

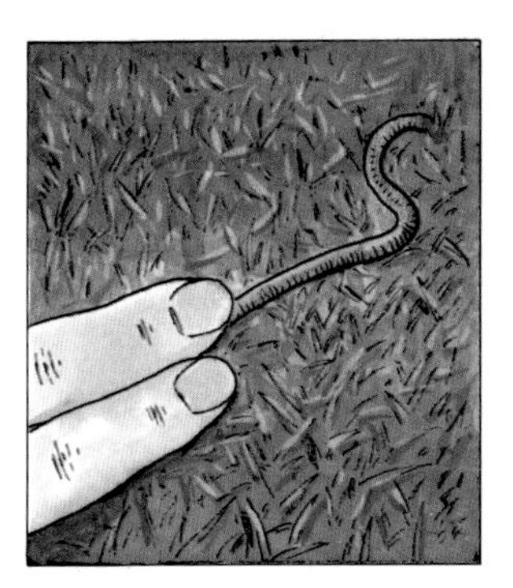

*The worm's body can grip the sides of its hole. Stop it from going back down by using light finger pressure.*

*Grip the worm firmly, using fine sand to improve your hold. Gentle pressure will coax the worm from its hole.*

Rod Sutterby

yellowish rings around its red, often shiny, body. It can be collected from manure piles or compost heaps. The presence of a compost heap will, of course, mean a regular supply of worms. If the wormery is tended by adding vegetable matter, tea leaves and vegetable waste the worms will grow much bigger and probably breed there, thus supplying a constant store of bait. Where grassy conditions are suitable, worms can be dug at the river bank. Be careful to fill all the holes in and not leave places which other anglers can stumble over.

**Keep them alive**

Although very effective on the hook, most worms become soft and lifeless very quickly in water and often drop off the hook during casting out. Their quality can be improved to overcome this by allowing the worms to work through a good soil for a few days prior to use. Sink a box in the earth, providing small holes in the bottom for drainage. Place the worms on a bed of soil (a dark, loamy kind is best) and cover with sacking. In wriggling through the soil they will scour themselves to emerge brighter and so more attractive to the fish. They will also be tougher, and will stay on the hook longer and wriggle more enticingly. 'Faddist' used to recommend that worms be kept in fine red sand or brickdust, suggesting that this gave them an added colouring as well as making the texture of their skins tougher.

Alternatively, a bucket containing sphagnum moss (obtainable cheaply from a florist) provides a medium for cleaning and toughening your worm bait. They will burrow through the moss, which should be damp but not wet. To keep worms fresh immediately before and during use, put them in clean moss and place in a linen bag. Tins and jars should be avoided, for they do not allow the worms to breathe properly. Remember also to weed out dead and dying worms, for one dead worm in a bait tin triggers off an extremely fast mass mortality among the rest.

**Hooking the worm**

It is important to hook a worm correctly, for this ensures that it stays on the hook and that it will wriggle naturally to attract the fish. A whole worm can be hooked anywhere along its length, but make sure that pieces cannot be bitten off by the fish without it also taking the hook. If necessary, pierce a long worm several times and feed it along the hook. Tails or pieces of worms should present no problem and stay on the hook. In general do not try to cover the hook, for a worm is a very tempting bait and, if lively, will probably wriggle enough to expose part of the hook anyway.

Look after worms, they are an all-purpose all-weather angling bait

# Bread

Ball

Flake

Crust

Fresh uncut loaf

Lyn Cawley

*(Above) The different forms of bread bait: flake, crust, ball taken from an uncut loaf. (Below) Flake pressed onto the hook. Be careful not to pinch too hard.*

Bread is not only an old-fashioned bait but also a very successful one. In recent years, and on many waters, it has been neglected, perhaps because its uses are not fully understood. Four different baits can be made from a white loaf—flake, crust, balanced crust and paste. The first two of these come from a new loaf, the third from an old loaf, the fourth from either.

**Flake**

Flake is the name given to the crumb of new bread. The crumb of two-day-old loaf is difficult, if not impossible, to place on the hook. When removing the crumb from the loaf a light touch is essential. Take hold of the required amount of crumb and lightly pull it from the loaf: it should be like a sponge with one edge sealed between thumb and forefinger. With the other hand take the hook, push the shank into the 'sponge' and gently pinch the crumb over it. Both the bend—or part of it—and the point of the hook will be exposed. The two sides of the crumb must be joined together with the minimum of pressure. If the sponge falls apart, the bread is too old: one light edge-pinch should be sufficient to keep it together. If the flake is pinched too tightly the bait will be hard and unattractive.

The size of flake, and therefore the size of hook, depends upon the fish you expect to catch, the water you are fishing and the time of year. Chub, barbel, carp and tench during

P. H. Ward/Natural Science Photos.

the early part of the season, big roach in waters not too heavily fished, can all be taken on a No. 6 hook. For bream, chub in winter, roach in some waters, tench, grayling and crucian carp, use a No. 10. For dace in heavily fished waters, or in winter, use a No. 12; in exceptional circumstances, when, for example, the fish are shy or in very cold water, a No. 14.

**How to cast flake**

Many anglers dislike flake because it is difficult to cast. The cast must always be a soft one, smooth and unhurried. Generally a sideways cast is best or, when fishing close in, an underhand one. When proficient, overhead casts can be made without bait and hook parting company in mid-air. An advantage of flake is that, whether trotted or ledgered, small particles constantly break off, thus attracting fish from downstream. into ones swim, especially in fast water.

Crust is self-explanatory. It must come from a newish loaf, not more than two or three days old, The loaf should be kept in the shade because, once hardened, the crust is useless. Depending upon the species being sought, sliced and unsliced loaves can be used. For such small fish as roach, dace and grayling, a cut loaf is best: where larger pieces are required for such species as chub and carp, an uncut loaf is necessary, especially when using floating crust. Floating crust is not only popular among carp and chub fishermen, but is also highly successful. The crust must be soft, so the baking of the loaf and its freshness are very important. Hard, brittle crust is useless. Some fastidious anglers order specially-baked loaves but this should not be necessary if you choose a loaf baked to a light brown colour.

*(Below) One of the standard bread baits used by carp fishermen is the floating crust. It can be fished close to lily pads, with the line running across them. This method shows no tell-tale line in the water. It also indicates the smallest twitch bite.*

P. H. Ward/Natural Science Photos

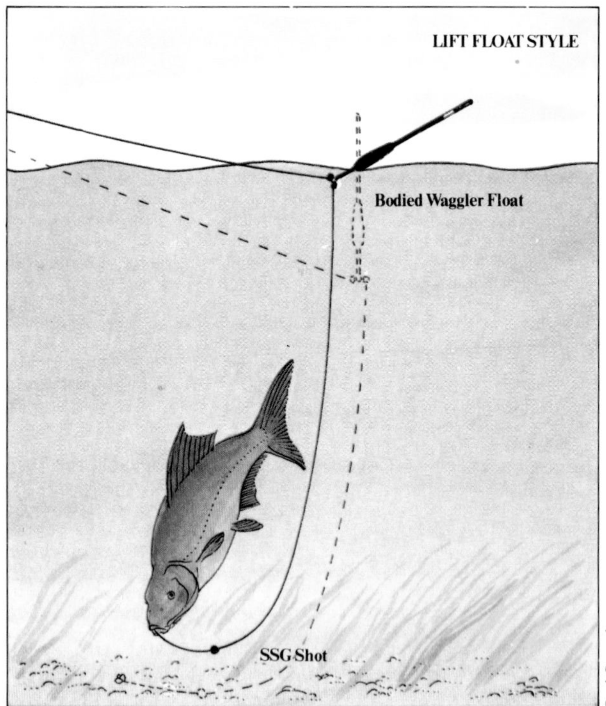


Rod Sutterby

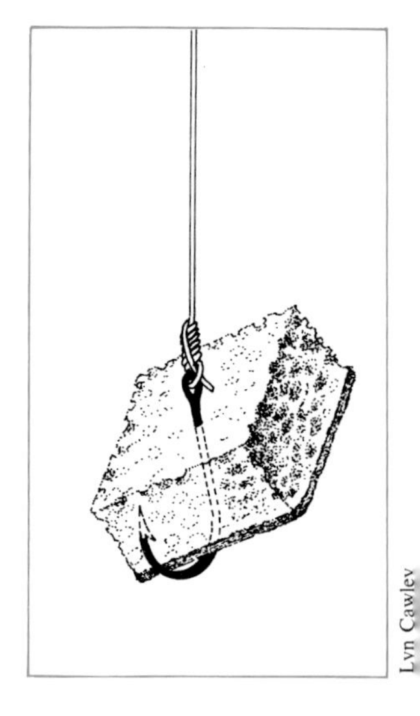

Lyn Cawley

*(Above) Crust for hooking must not be stale.*
*(Left) The lift method relies on the float popping to the surface as the fish takes, thus lifting the shot.*

Crumbly or too-hard crust from stale loaves is also useless, breaking up as the hook is pushed through it. A fairly large piece of crust, say 1½in square, is often used with a cast of 20 yards or more. For distance-casting the corners and edges of the loaf are, for a given size, heavier than the flat areas and therefore cast better. As no floats or weights are used, however, some weight might be given to the bait, so just before casting the crust is dipped into the water for a moment. This is called 'dunking'.

**Hooking the crust**

Opinions differ as to which side up the crust should lie. To make the bait hang crust side down take the crust and the hook, push the hook into the crumb side, out of the crust, then back through the crumb until both bend and part of the shank of the hook protrude. The opposite actions will make the bait hang with the crust up. About half the shank with the point and barb should always protrude from the crust. A hook slightly larger than the crust must be used. If the hook is completely buried, the wet crust is liable to fall or cast off.

Crust will catch fish at all seasons but it is especially useful in winter, fished stationary, close to the bottom. The distance it is presented off the bottom is determined by how far the weight is stopped from it: 6in from the crust and the crust will be fishing about 6in off the bottom.

In June and July crust is especially good for tench, fished either under a float, 'lift' style, or simple ledgered. It can be fished in rivers, trotted and ledgered, floating on a weightless line. In stillwaters, ledgered and floating crust has probably accounted for more carp than any other bait.

Although a soft bait, crust will withstand quite a hard, forceful cast. An overhead cast is best, especially when fishing big pieces of crust on the surface for chub and carp. With this style of fishing, remember, the cast must be made immediately the crust has been dunked, otherwise it will become waterlogged and tend to fall off the hook during the cast.

# Meats

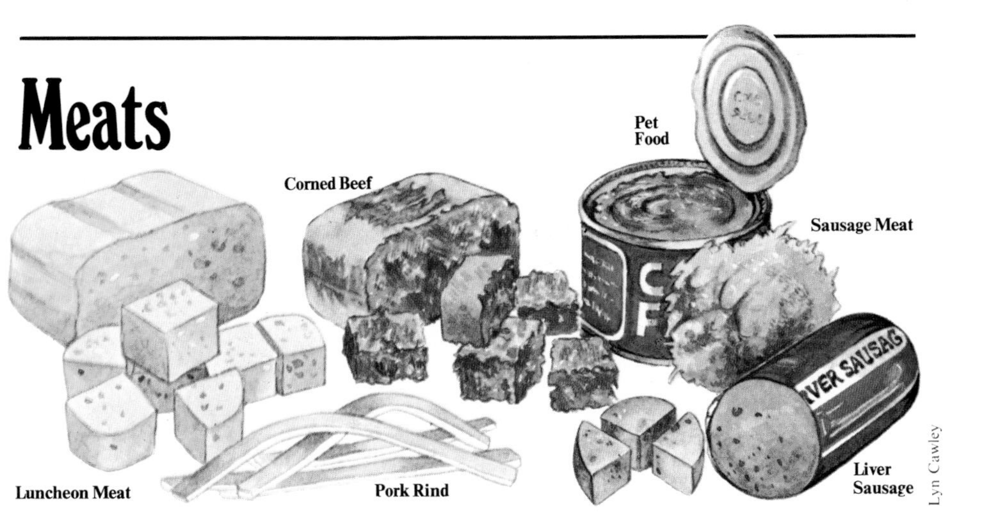


*(Above) A selection of meat baits used in freshwater. Barbel and chub are the prey usually associated with these.*

At the turn of the century the angling press was astonished by the report of a man who had caught a fish on a sausage out of his luncheon pack. It was, the experts said, an exceptional happening. No one should consider catching a fish on a meat bait. There was only one form of bait used at that time with any association to meat, and that was greaves, a waste product of tallow obtained from candle manufacturers and used both as hook and groundbait at Thames weirpools to catch barbel.

Today, meat baits—pure meat and not merely by-products—are commonplace, and barbel, roach, bream, chub, tench and carp are regularly caught on them throughout the year. Much of the present day angler's success is the result of modern meat preparation of meat products which are packed with a consistency that not only allows easy mounting on the hook, but also a slow break-down in the water allowing flavour and smell to remain around the lure.

**Luncheon meat**

The best known and most used of the meat baits is undoubtedly luncheon meat. The tinned types are easily carried and provide a hefty chunk of meat from which substantial sized cubes can be cut. Blind buying of the first tin on the shelf is not advised. There are many cheap varieties of luncheon meat which have a very high fat content, and this means a soft cube of hookbait that will either break away from the hook during the cast, or fall apart within a few minutes of lying in the water, especially if the swim lies in fast water.

A few extra pence will purchase a good meat mix that should be kept refrigerated until required, and thereafter kept as cool as possible while the angler is fishing. Once the tin is opened, keep the contents out of the sun and packed away in an airtight box. Drop any unopened tins held in reserve into the shallows at your feet—probably the best refrigerator on a warm day.

**Mounting the bait**

Mounting cubes of bait onto the hook requires care. Choose a hook too big rather than too small—sizes 8-4 are usual—and push the point of the hook slowly into the centre of the cube before threading it round onto the bend, making sure that the barb shows. To help the bait from jerking free on the cast use a small portion of green leaf or fine clear polythene bag folded double. This should be pushed over both point and barb to act as a platform behind the cube, and into which it will press during the thrust of the cast. It will not effect the hooking properties, and will save endless re-baiting.

There are variations on the luncheon meat theme—Prem and Spam are excellent baits, as is liver sausage. But strangely enough, the majority of Continental processed meats that are highly seasoned, usually with garlic, seem to be inferior to the straight tinned varieties. Corned beef is excellent, but used straight from the tin tends to shred very quickly. A better method is to cut the cubes beforehand and then fry them for a few minutes to seal the fibres.

**Sausage meat**

Sausage meat, purchased in bulk and not made into sausages is another excellent meat bait. Again, it is too soft in its natural form to stand hard casting or long immersion in water, and it is better stiffened with breadcrumbs or, better still, sausage rusk, until it assumes the properties of putty. Another deadly bait is sausage meat mixed together with rusk and soft cheese with a little plain flour to harden the balls once they have been shaped into bait-sized pieces.

Tinned pet food, especially the cat types with a high proportion of fish in their ingredients, hit the headlines a few years ago as a deadly carp bait. Preparation of the bait for the hook is messy, and requires a little trouble, but results are usually worth the effort. Ideally the tin should be opened at the bank, hook-sized lumps moulded, and these dipped into boiling water to form a hard glaze over the surface which helps hold them in place during a cast. Obviously some soap and a towel are essential items using this method, otherwise the whole of one's tackle smells very strongly by the end of the day.

One variety of meat that is used in

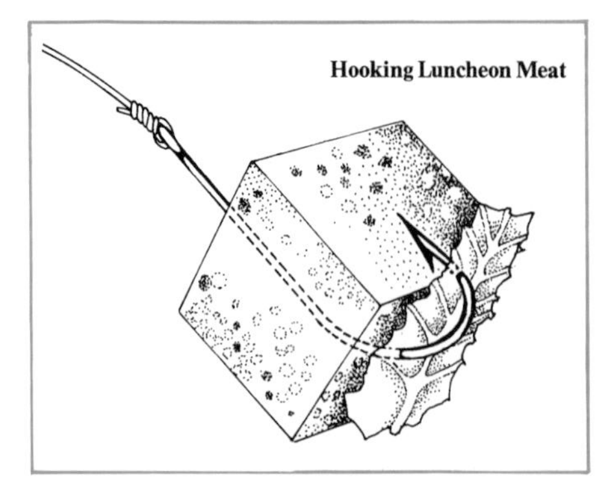


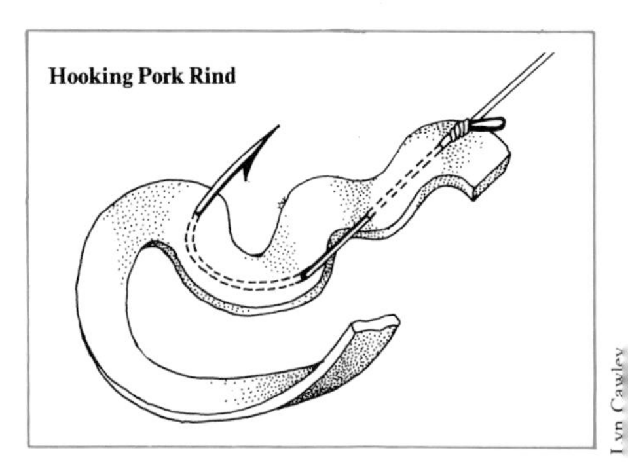


*(Above) Pork rind firmly mounted on a single hook. (Below) A cube of Spam set on a leaf to cushion the cast.*

freshwater fishing, although not in the way discussed so far, is pork rind, or strip. The use of this bait has been in vogue for some years now in America, where it can be purchased uncooked, vacuum-packed and ready for the hook. Usually the strips are hooked into the treble of a spinning lure, and it is claimed that baits treated with this addition of two or three work-like strands towed astern really tempt the big fish.

The other way of using bacon strips is to hook-mount it as one would a worm, on a single large hook, and slowly reel this without a float and with the minimum of lead through areas where predators are found. As yet the method is practically untried in this country, but well worth some experiment, especially during the winter months.

**Where to fish**

Where one should fish with meat is an important decision. Naturally, it has a better chance of success in waters where it has been accepted for a number of years, and some species take it more willingly than others. Probably the natural place for its use is when fishing for barbel and chub in a weirpool, where luncheon meat is best.

A solitary piece flung just anywhere into the pool and left is hardly likely to be effective. To reap the maximum from meat, back up its use with groundbait. Fast water that washes away free offerings or hook bait from the hook, is a dead loss.

Bill Howes

*Tinned meats are an excellent bait for barbel, chub and large coarse fish. For groundbaiting, add a cereal.*

Choose an edge of the pool, preferably as close to the sill as possible and at one side of the main flow of water. Depth is decidedly useful, and if there is an undercut to the structure so much the better—an eddy will probably be created holding the bait in one place. Make several trial casts and search for the slack water that always lies at the head of a pool before deciding to bait the area.

**Other places**

Other places where meat will often do well are above the weir—where the river and navigation channel divide provides deep water under the rod—and where erosion has taken a bank away, leaving a deep cut and slow stream. Lock cuttings are worth a try, but there is always a risk of too much attention from eels, especially during the autumn months.

Other natural places that suggest themselves as places to try meat baiting are where human food is readily available. This means boatyards and houseboats moored along the banks of a canal.

To use meat on its own as a groundbait would obviously cost a fortune. The solution is to use a little, and to eke it out with cereal bait to give bulk, then to add, where it is possible to obtain it, some blood to spread scent over the area. An alternative, especially with sausage meat, is to roll a large supply of very small balls that can, if necessary, be catapulted into a distant swim.

Fish that accept meat baits generally do so with a bang, and the angler should always be prepared for the bite. Rods left in rests are in danger of being pulled onto the bank, and floats left unwatched can lose the angler fish after fish. By far the best way of using meat in all of its forms is with the ledger, and the rod should be hand held, with one rest only giving support along the upper third of the rod itself. Once the tip bounces, then the strike should be immediate.

# Wasp grubs

G. E. Hyde

For float fishing in clear, fairly fast-flowing river water, there are few deadlier hookbaits than wasp grub. From late August onwards sport is often hectic and bites so positive they are hard to miss.

So effective has the bait proved to be that its use is banned in many contests. It is even barred completely on some controlled waters, so always check before using it.

Fishing the bait is simple, finding it a bit more difficult. A lot of anglers are just too lazy to take time to go out and collect this quite remarkable bait, and you will need at least three nests for a good day's fishing. Even so, wasp nests are more prevalent than most people think.

**Where there's muck there's wasps**

Wasps are not the most clinically particular creatures. Where there is muck, there you will find wasps. Strange as it may seem, there are more wasp colonies per acre in towns than in country. The author has collected, in one evening, as many as ten nests from city parks, commons and gardens.

Evening is usually the best time for wasp spotting. To find a nest, pick a likely area of waste land, banks or hedges, then watch. If you see a wasp idly meandering, stopping here and there, ignore it. If you see one flying straight and with purpose, mark mentally the direction of its flight path; the nest is rarely more than 100 yards away.

Another wasp will soon come along the flight line. Follow it fast, and as far as you can. It may beat you, but the next will probably lead you to the nest entrance. This is usually underground but rarely deep down. Found in soft earth, often under a hedge or bush, nests are round or oval in shape and made up of layers closely resembling papier mâché.

The next problem is in removing the nest while avoiding painful stings. Reassuringly, a wasp sting is not as dangerous as that of the honey bee which carries a venom akin to that of a cobra. The danger in a wasp sting comes usually from the bacteria injected at the same time–so take care!

Although cyanide-based insecticide compounds are on the market (Cymag is the most efficient), their general use cannot be recommended. Unless stored and used correctly, they can be dangerous (you will have to sign a poison register to obtain them) and safer proprietary insecticides are preferable, although not so effective as Cymag.

**Beware—Cyanide Fumes**

Whether you use a cyanide-based mixture or another type, it should be applied using a large tablespoon tied firmly to a 3ft stick. Put one spoonful as far into the nest entrance as possible and make quite sure that you are upwind of the nest so that noxious fumes blow *away* from you. Another spoonful is sprinkled around the entrance. All this is best done in the early evening when the wasps have returned home. Next, block the entrance with a clod of earth and wait for at least two hours, preferably overnight.

The nest should be removed as carefully as possible, since every bit of it can be used by the angler. Dig round the nest, scraping away all loose earth and lift it whole.

In comparison to the maggot, wasp grubs are big, creamy and soft. The biggest and plumpest were destined to be queen wasps; they also make the best hookbaits. Remove and lay aside all you want for this purpose

*(Above) Plenty of big-fish bait in this wood-wasp nest, Stamford Spinney, Devon. (Below) Ray Forsberg extracting grubs from a piece of wasp-nest 'cake'. The cake helps make a useful attractor groundbait.*

Ray Forsberg

Taff Price

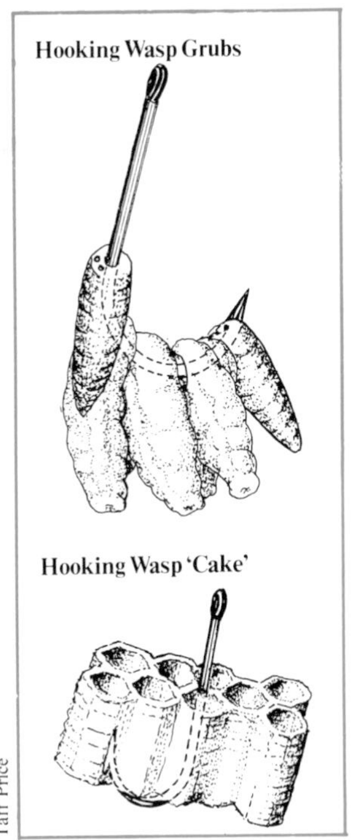

Ralph Stobart

from their tube-like homes in the nest centre.

The smaller grubs and any damaged ones are then scalded, along with the nest of 'cake', for use as the attractor groundbait. This can be used mixed with breadcrumbs or on its own. It is also worth trying as hookbait once in a while.

**Champion wins on wasp grub**

Wasp grubs are best used with float tackle of the kind suited to fishing bread flake. Bob Morris became Severn Champion using wasp grub bait to take a record 55lb of chub from the breamy lower end of that river. His tip was to put a piece of bread flake on the hook every half dozen casts or so. This often tempts the bigger chub which tend to lie at the rear of the shoal.

Now and then it is necessary to fish wasp grubs hard on the river bed. Most fish take 'on the drop'. There is no mistaking the bite, particularly with chub. With a size 10 or 12 barbless hook, all that is needed is to tighten line quickly–and your fish is on.

Apart from the Severn Championship win, wasp grub has accounted for a record-breaking Trent Championship victory. It will tempt most species. Single grubs on the hook will lure roach, and at least one carp of over 20lb has fallen to a ledgered grub.

As soon as a tinge of colour creeps in to cloud the water, sport comes to a halt. The reason for this is not yet fully understood. Possibly the suspended sediment causing the coloration dulls either the fishes' senses or that peculiar flavour that makes wasp grub so irresistible to them.

There are other successful grub baits, too. Dock, or docken, grubs, which grow large and live long, are excellent baits for roach, chub, dace and grayling. Barbel have been caught from the Severn with these, as they have with caddis, the larvae of the sedge fly, and with meal worms.

Most caterpillars make great grayling baits, and if you are not squeamish, wood-lice, earwigs and most bankside beetles will catch fish. It pays to try, and the unusual often gets results.

# Silkweed

Ken Whitehead

(*Above*) *The ideal silkweed fishing gear.*
(*Left*) *Always keep silkweed moist. Once dry it is useless as a bait.*
(*Right*) *Shrimp and* (*far right*) *diatoms live in the silkweed and are eaten by fish and fish fry.*

From June to October weir structures, bridge supports, lock gates, posts and piles which support the river banks are covered below the water line with thick green bands of silkweed. Hidden within the weed is a mass of minute animal life that provides an abundance of food for fish and can provide the angler with one of the best natural baits available. From August onwards, roach, dace and chub graze or feed on the weed, browsing like cattle when the water is quiet, or lying in the weirpools to take small particles of weed as it is dislodged and worked downstream by the current.

**Origins of silkweed fishing**

Silkweed fishing has a style and method that originated in the Thames weirpools. Acceptance of silkweed as a bait, at least on the part of the fish, is not, however, confined to the Thames, and any weirpool throughout the country is worth trying in the warmer months.

Collecting silkweed to use as a hook-bait requires care. Pulling tufts by hand from the weir surrounds will crush all animal life that it contains. It is better to rub a patch free with the handle of a landing net or bankstick, then scoop it into a large plastic bait box that is half-filled with water. Do not place a lid on the box—on a warm day it will cook and spoil the weed.

**How to use silkweed**

Baiting is accomplished by pulling the hook through the ball of weed within the bait box, then folding the weed round the hook several times to form a sizeable clump before pushing the hook through again. It has been suggested that the hook can be baited by pulling it through growing weed on the lasher of the weir. Certainly it is a quick method, but also one guaranteed to take the edge off the hook within seconds.

The ideal tackle for silkweeding is a long 11-12ft rod with a free running centrepin reel loaded with line of 3lb b.s. Selecting a suitable float needs thought. Anything with a fine stem cannot be seen in the swirl of water and froth of a weir pool and a float needing very few shot is unlikely to get the bait down below the surface. Suitable floats are big-topped celluloid ones, or round corks coloured bright red that are usually associated with minnow fishing. Clumsy though these floats seem, they are not required to register a bite in the accepted sense of the term but merely to allow the angler to see where his bait is.

**Find your fish**

The depth at which fish are feeding on weed is usually 2-3ft below the surface, but bright sunlight or water temperatures that are lower than normal will send the fish down to the 5 or 6ft mark. When fish appear not to be feeding or suddenly go off the silkweed, experiment by trial and error over a range of depths until the fish are located again.

A spin-off from silkweed is often overlooked. It is a natural hiding and feeding place for small fish fry, a fact known to every predatory fish in the river. It is well worth spinning any area alongside weed-covered marks, either with a small leaf-type spinner or a shallow diving plug—a trick that any Thames trout fishing enthusiast will confirm.

**Standing on the weir**

Where the angler should stand when fishing depends largely on the construction of the weir. Traditionally the Thames angler stands on the apron or sill (the concrete stretch which the water hits after

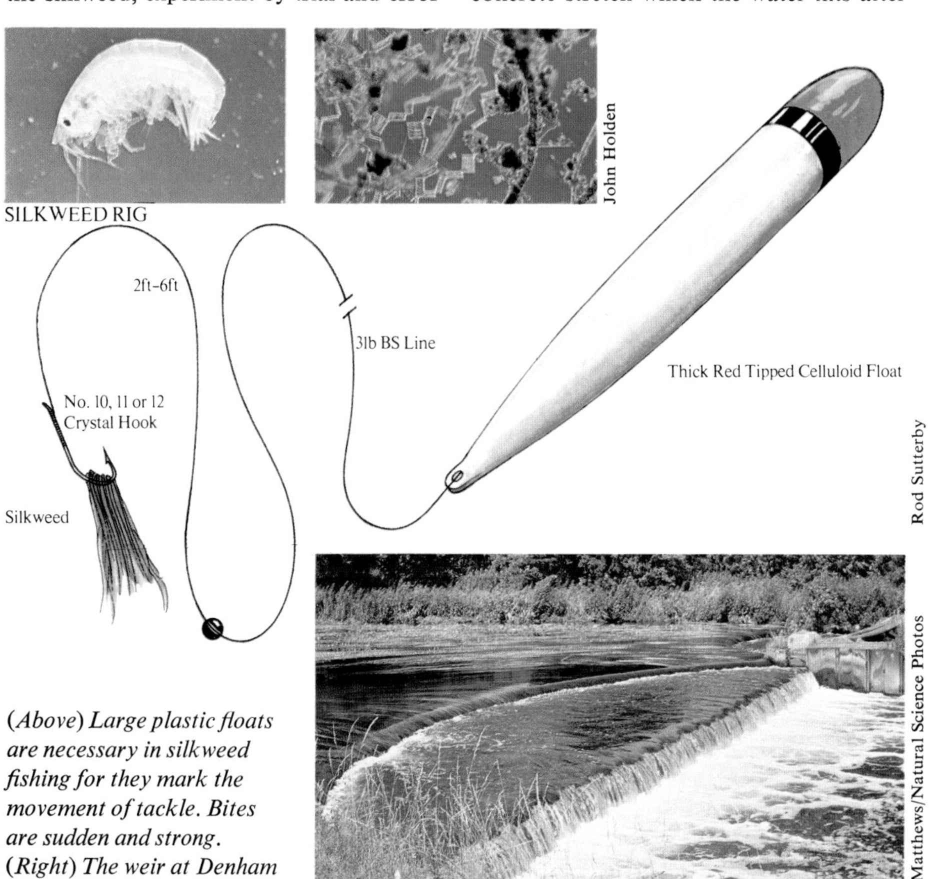


John Holden

Rod Sutterby

G. A. Matthews/Natural Science Photos

*(Above) Large plastic floats are necessary in silkweed fishing for they mark the movement of tackle. Bites are sudden and strong. (Right) The weir at Denham on the River Colne, a fine silkweed fishing spot.*

spilling over the gates) and drops his float at his feet, allowing it to run downstream. This method is simple, but it does have some disadvantages.

**Importance of waders**

First, water flows over the apron, making wellingtons or waders a necessity. The apron will be covered in weed, making it as slippery as an ice-rink. One false step and the angler goes into the pool below, with little chance of recovery once his wellingtons are full of water. They act as anchors. So thigh-length waders are preferable, for they tend to hold pockets of air. It does not support the body of the angler, but does show where he is.

Another disadvantage for the angler standing on the sill is that he is visible to the fish below and silhouetted against the sky. A better position, and a safer one, is at the side of the weir, where the current is still within easy casting distance, and also where there is usually a dry patch to stand on.

**Keep a tight line**

Following the cast, all line between the rod tip and float should be kept as tight as possible, with the rod kept at an angle of 45 degrees. Feed line out slowly, keeping the float in check, and be prepared for bites which will be felt, not seen, against the rod tip. The thumb can be clamped against the reel in a split second and the hook driven home.

Landing fish in a weirpool can present difficulties, more so when the angler is sited well above the water level. Use a net with a very long handle, and fix a stone or ledger weight into the mesh at the bottom. This prevents it being turned inside out when dipped into the running water below.

*An angler silkweed fishing on the River Lea at Kingsweir, near Broxbourne, Herts. His position is just right for casting into the swirls and eddies under the sill. The large red tip of the plastic float can be seen bobbing in the foam. He is standing firmly on dry rock without fear of a sudden slip into the water.*

Ken Whitehead

# Float fishing

Bill Howes

(*Above*) *Peter Burton using an extending landing net to bring in a fish caught on the very popular waggler float.*
(*Right*) *Shot pattern for the waggler.*

Float fishing is probably the most popular form of coarse fishing. There are a great number of different types of float and methods of float fishing, but all too many anglers, having found that one tactic and one float work reasonably well, stick to this without considering other methods. Rather than just settling for the most convenient method, the angler should try to achieve the best possible presentation of the bait in each situation. He should go for the most effective method. This might not be the easiest, but it is the angler with the techniques and ability to do this who will more often than not catch the most fish.

**The waggler**

The large antenna float—the waggler—seems to be the float most abused by lazy anglers. Certainly, in the past two or three years, it has been responsible for winning a lot of matches. Yet is this because it is the most effective float, or because it is being used when it shouldn't be?

This is not so contradictory as it sounds. People are winning matches with the waggler, but with other floats, such as a stick, they would have won with even more fish. And while a waggler is comparatively easy to fish, it will not enable the angler to get the best out of every swim.

The reason for this is simple. The waggler does not allow the same degree of control over the presentation of the bait as a double-rubbered float. When it is being properly used it is fished attached by its bottom end only and has a lot of tip showing above the water. This is because it is fished with a shot dragging the bottom and the float must not be sensitive enough to be dragged under.

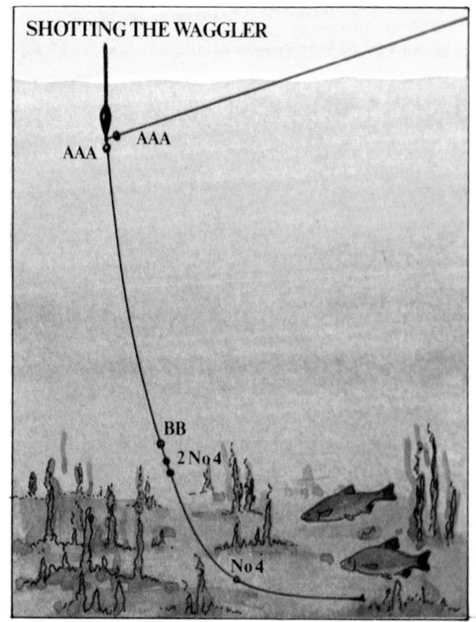


Rod Sutterby

*Shotting the balsa is important and must be carefully balanced. The tell-tale's weight depends on strength of current.*

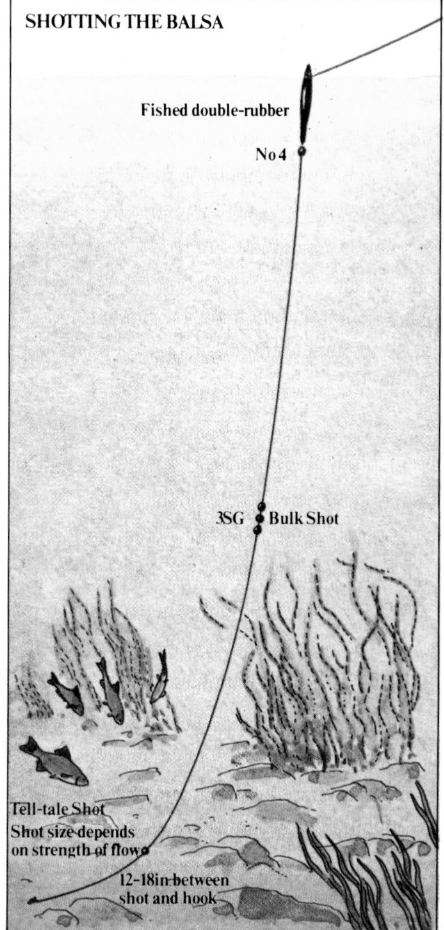


Even so, despite its size, try to hold it back against the water flow, so that the bait is presented in a slow, attractive manner, and what happens? It just drags under because of the effect of the line between rod tip and float—unless you have achieved a degree of expertise and control of the float possessed by very few anglers. By contrast, a stick or balsa, fished double-rubber, can be held in the stream so that the bait just trickles along.

All this is not to say that the waggler cannot be a very useful float in certain circumstances. In difficult conditions, rough water and a fierce downstream wind, for example, or when the fish are biting freely three or four rod-lengths out—when it has the edge in speed—it can be ideal. In other circumstances, on rivers such as the Ribble, which has an uneven flow, other floats are more successful. Here, use an Avon, or balsa fished double-rubber.

**The Avon balsa**

The size of the balsa is important. It must be big enough to carry sufficient weight to allow you to pull back on the rod without it dragging into the bank too quickly—a float which can carry about two or three swan shot serves the purpose. Shotting is simple: all you need is a small shot, say a No.4 (directly under the float to stop it sliding down the line under the pressure of striking), the bulk shot roughly halfway between the float and the hook, and the tell-tale which goes 1ft to 18in from the hook. The purpose of the tell-tale shot here is to regulate the presentation of the bait. The size of the tell-tale will depend on the strength of the flow.

The method with this rig is to cast out to the area you wish to fish—with this rig the under-arm cast is a must if tangles are to be avoided—and then to mend the line—that is to lift the line and swing it upstream if it threatens to put drag on the float and bait—until the float settles. Then lift the rod-tip high in the air so that the line goes directly to the float tip without touching the water.

If you choose a float with plenty of bulk and weight-carrying capacity, it will strip line from the reel at the pace you dictate and carry on the current far more smoothly than a waggler. Furthermore, if you check the line on the rim of the spool with your fingertip, you can slow the float right down or even momentarily stop it—something you can't do with a waggler.

There's no doubt that this pays off. If you have studied the swim properly, you should know what part of it is most likely to produce a fish; you can then slow up the float when it is approaching the area, relaxing again when it has passed on downstream.

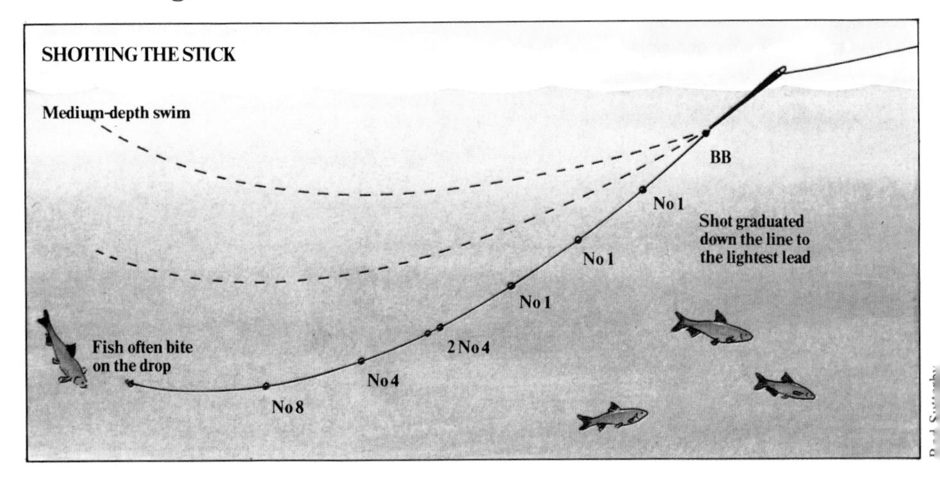


*The shotting pattern for big stick floats is a steady graduation from the top down. A BB stops the float running down the line on the strike. No. 8 is the lightest.*

**Big stick floats**

Big stick floats are another useful tool ignored by many anglers nowadays. With wind blowing upstream and out from the bank, the big stick is probably easier to handle than a waggler. This is because the effect of the wind on the line when the float is being fished double-rubber slows down the bait without any effort from the angler. Again, underarm casting is essential.

Another 'old-fashioned' method of fishing which receives too little attention nowadays is stret-pegging. It has largely been abandoned in favour of swingtip rods and there is little doubt that when the bait is wanted hard on the bottom in the middle of a river it is by far the best solution. Nevertheless, if the fish are closer in, then stret-pegging is deadly, particularly if the river is carrying a lot of water. In fact, in flood conditions, it is as likely a method as any to pick up a fish.

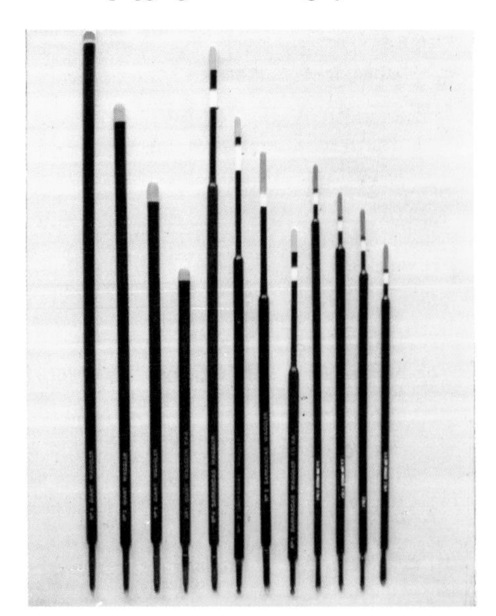

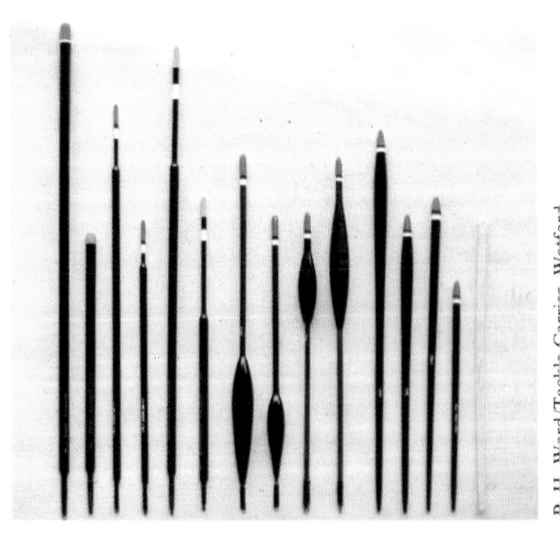

*(Above) Wagglers, Avons and reversed Avons with some stick floats. On the right is a 6in peacock quill, which should be fished double-rubber for stret-pegging.*

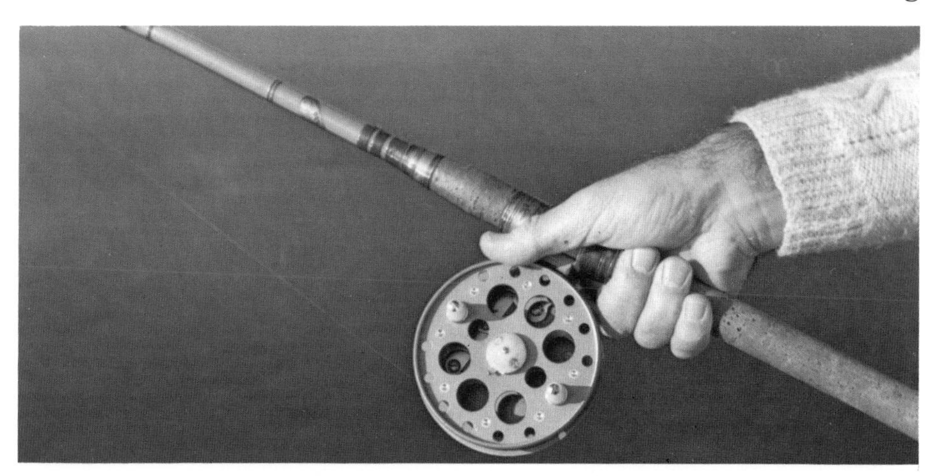

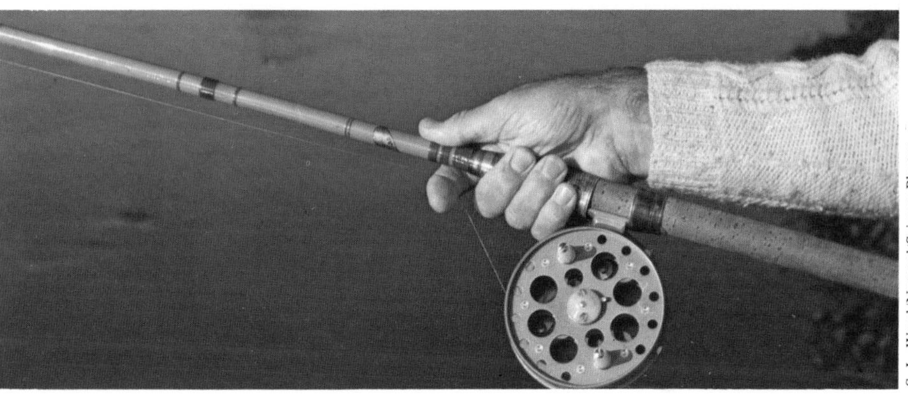

S. L. Ward/Natural Science Photos

*(Top) One method of slowing the tackle is to use the thumb on the reel drum. (Above) Another way of controlling the line is by running it over the forefinger.*

**Stret-pegging**

When stret-pegging, the float—a peacock is ideal—is fished double-rubber, over-depth and over-shotted. Basically, this means that the line between float and hook should be about twice as long as the water is deep and should carry roughly double the amount of shot the float can support. For example, if you have a 6in length of peacock quill capable of carrying half a dozen BB shot, load it up with 12 BB, concentrated around 6in from the hook and if the water is 4ft deep, set the float at 8ft. The bait then bobs around in the current just off the bottom, while the line stretches at an angle of 45° from the float to the weight at the bottom.

The technique is basically simple. Just cast out and allow the tip to pull round. But although this sounds simple, it is not that easy. The line must be held tight between float and rod tip and the float literally held up—otherwise, being heavily over-shotted, it just dives to the bottom. However, if used properly, you'll be surprised at just how positive the bites are.

If the fish are not biting, try varying the presentation of the bait by slightly lifting the rod and 'inching' the business end of the rig across the bottom. This diversion will often take a 'bonus' fish.

A stillwater alternative to ledgering is the lift method of float fishing for which, conveniently, you can use the same piece of

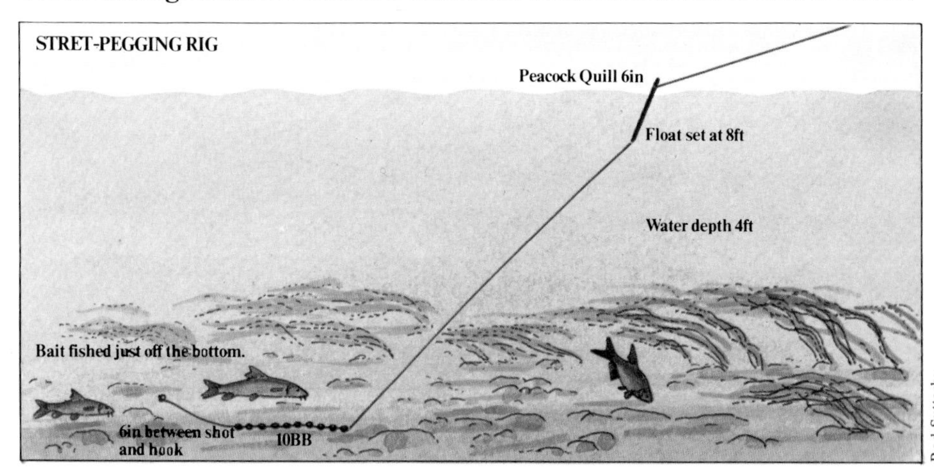


peacock as for stret-pegging. But instead of a bunch of small shot, use one big one, say a swan, although once again the rig is fished over-shotted, and over-depth as with stret-pegging. The difference is that the float is fished peg-leg—that is attached by its bottom end only. Furthermore, unlike stret-pegging, the hook should be very near to the shot, say, only two or three inches away.

With the lift method, cast out to your swim, and allow the shot to hit bottom. The float will, of course, lie flat. Then gently tighten the line until the float cocks and is dotted down—that is, it has only the smallest amount possible showing. When a fish picks the bait off the bottom—this method is particularly effective for tench—the result is the most dramatic bite in fishing. To swallow the bait, the fish must also pick up the shot and the float pops up like a Jack-in-the-box!

*Stret-pegging, sometimes the only way to fish fast-flowing rivers successfully. A typical river is the fast, weedy Avon.*

Curiously enough, the big shot does not seem to put off the fish—although obviously the method can be scaled down using, say, a reversed crowquill or an even more sensitive pheasant-tail quill.

S. L. Ward/Natural Science Photos

*(Above) Be careful not to miss out any rod rings when tackling up. This can lead to difficult casting when the line becomes wet.*
*(Left) When putting the rod sections together, starting with the top, make sure that the rod rings are ranged in a straight line. If not, the line is slowed during the cast.*

# Ledgering

Once, ledgering was considered a crude and clumsy way of fishing, only resorted to when float fishing had failed to catch fish. Now, ledgering has a separate and valued status as a means of fishing, and the varied styles and techniques have led to the capture of many large fish.

Basically the method presents the bait on the bottom of a lake, reservoir, stream or river where coarse species such as bream, barbel, carp and tench normally feed.

The short, stiff and insensitive rod once used for ledgering was poor for detecting bites. Now, needlessly heavy tackle has been replaced gradually by more suitable and effective equipment. Today purpose-built ledgering rods are available which incorporate a fine tip to greatly improve bite detection. Heavy leads, often of the 'coffin' variety, have given way to lighter weights which are designed to lessen resistance of the tackle felt by biting fish. A nylon monofilament line of 5-6lb b.s. is suitable for most freshwater ledgering.

Ledgering has some distinct advantages over float fishing techniques. First, waters deeper than the rod-length can be bottom-fished. Second, there is the advantage that the weight of a ledger rig allows long casts so that a greater area, or swims inaccessible to float tackle, can be fished.

**Anchored bait**

Also important is the fact that the bait is anchored (unless intentionally allowed to drift slowly) in the spot the angler wishes to fish. This is not possible with float tackle in a current. The bait stays on the bottom, where it will be most effective and appears more natural than one suspended in mid-water beneath a float. Ledger tackle, furthermore,

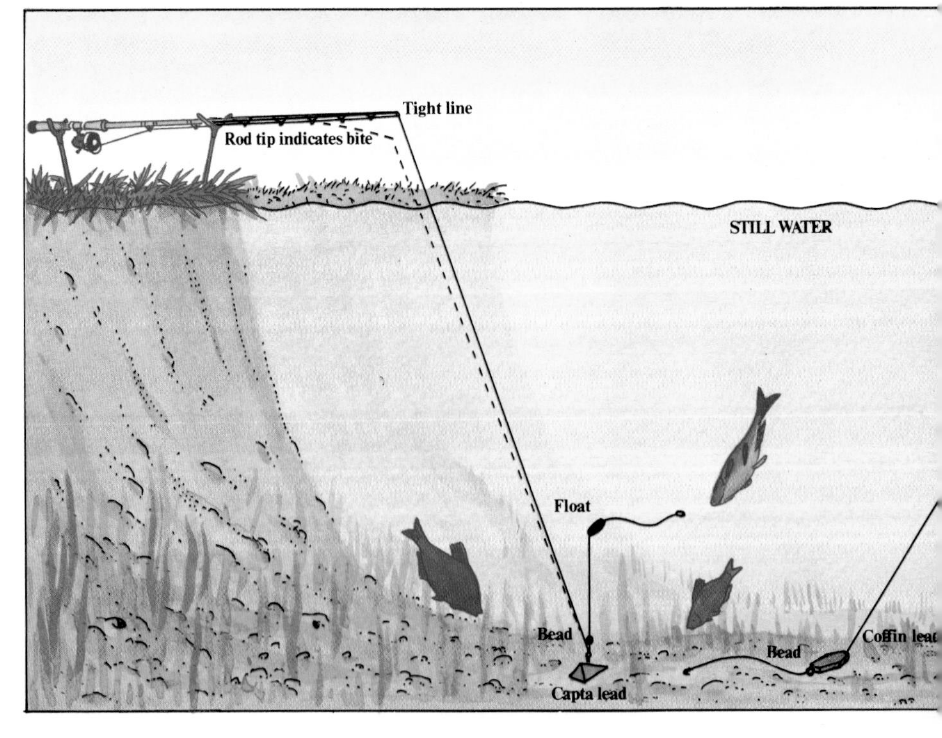

Bill Howes

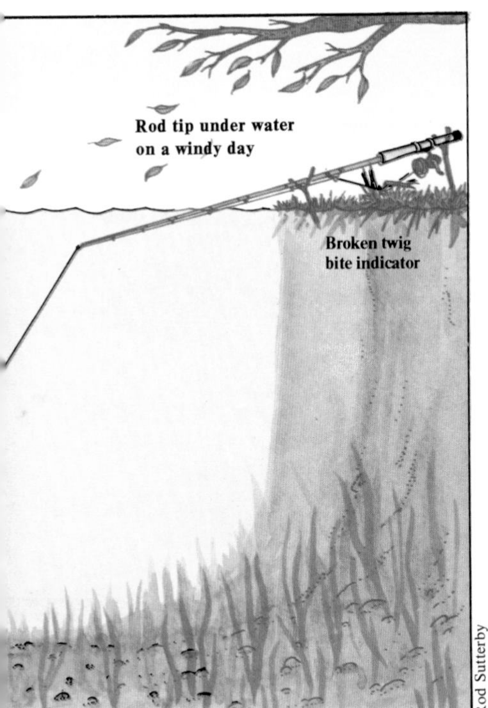


Rod Sutterby

*(Above) Two methods of ledgering, one with a swing-tip, the other keeping the rod-tip under the surface. (Left) Stillwater ledgering. Two methods of anchored bait.*

is not so obtrusive as the float silhouetted on the surface, which can easily frighten off fish. Lastly, ledgering allows night fishing, which is impractical with a float.

**Leads**

Rigs for ledgering vary, usually according to water conditions. A fast river will require a heavy lead if the bait is to be anchored and the same weight will be useful where a long cast, on river or lake, is required. A lighter lead will provide sufficient weight to take the bait to the bottom and keep it there in stillwater or in a slow current. For many years the most commonly used leads were the 'coffin' and the 'bullet'—a lead sphere with a hole through which the line passes. The weight lies on the bottom and the line can be pulled through it by a fish taking the bait. In this way, the fish does not feel the resistance from the tackle—in contrast to float fishing—but only from the rod tip. A compromise is a lead of the 'Arlesey Bomb' kind devised by Richard Walker. The line passes through a swivel at the top of this pear-shaped lead and less resistance is transmitted to the fish. The 'Capta' lead performs similarly but is preferable for use when the bait is to be anchored rather than rolled by the current or slope of the bed.

**Link-ledgering**

The technique known as link-ledgering has become increasingly popular in recent years. For this, a short, lead-shotted trace is attached at right-angles to the reel line by a free-running swivel. This rig combines the advantage of reduced resistance with that of allowing the bait to 'roll' with the current or by flexing the rod tip. In link-ledgering, as with all ledgering styles, a stop must be attached to the line—usually 2-3ft above the hook—to prevent the ledger from running down on to it, thus producing a bait that is unnaturally heavy and, of course, appears strange to the fish. A split shot is commonly used, but care must be taken to pinch it immovably on to the reel line. This can weaken the line, and some anglers prefer, especially with a link-ledger rig, to insert a split ring or a swivel to keep the weight the required distance from the baited hook.

To ledger in stillwater, cast out the tackle and give it time to sink. The line is then tightened, without dragging the ledger off the bottom, and the rod laid horizontally on twin rod rests. Bites will be indicated by the movement of the rod tip or line or by the action of one of a number of kinds of bite indicator.

In river fishing, where the pull of the current can make it difficult to detect a bite, it is advisable to hold the rod and so be prepared to strike quickly. The rod can be supported on one knee and the line held between thumb and forefinger so that a bite can be felt. The tip of the rod must be sensitive, so that it trembles to indicate a bite. With practice, a take by a fish will be distinguished from the natural movement of the tackle with the current. The tackle can be cast into one spot and anchored there, but it usually pays to cover a larger area,

ROLLING LEDGER

*(Right) Simplest of all ledger rigs: two swan-shot on a short nylon leader.*
*(Below) Moving-water ledgering and two methods which are successful. The rolling ledger (bottom left) shows the effect of current.*

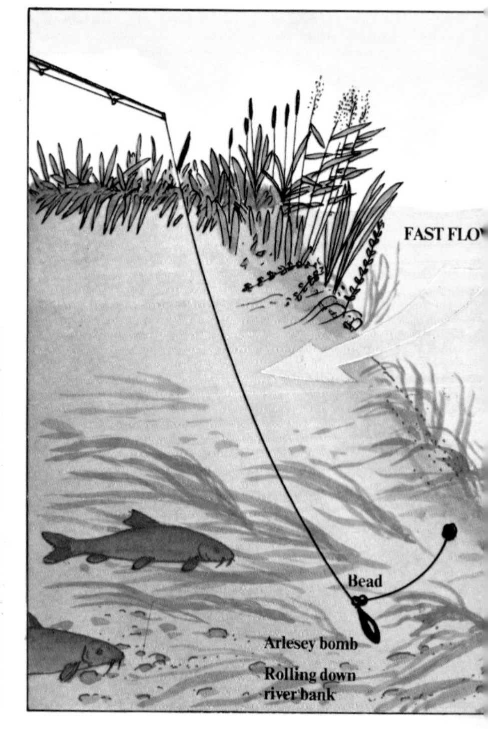

particularly if the water if unfamiliar, by allowing a light rig such as a link-ledger to drift across the bed. Cast down and across stream and cover a stretch of river with repeated arcs, progressively moving downstream.

Upstream ledgering is less often practised, but seems to have good results with barbel. Striking is more difficult as the fish, having taken the bait, will run downstream, towards the angler. This means that a slackening in the line will indicate a take. In order to connect, the strike must be calculated to take up the slack as well as driving the hook home.

The question of bite detection is of prime importance in ledgering. There are various methods of detecting a fish. First, the rod tip acts as an indicator. Alternatively, greater sensitivity can be gained by the use of the swing-tip or the quiver-tip, both of which are available in various patterns.

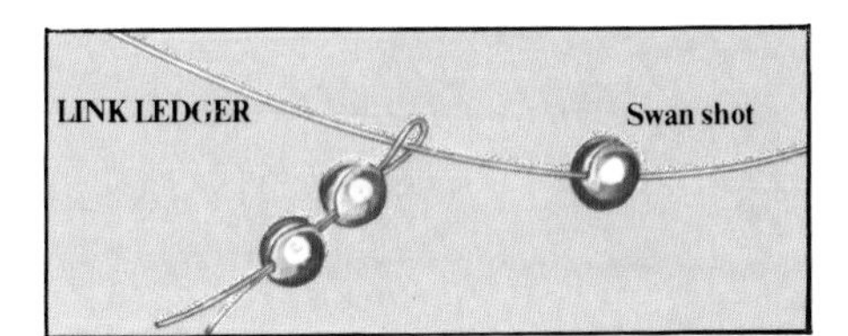


**Bite indicators**

For ledgering in stillwater these tips may be used, but other indicators are equally useful. The simplest consists of a ball of bread paste hung on a 'v' of the line between reel and butt ring. This will twitch noticeably with a bite. A metal bite indicator can be purchased (or improvised). This consists of a straight length of metal strip attached to 2in of rubber, or sometimes a spring, and clipped to the rod butt. The line runs through some models; others are attached to the line after casting. After tightening the line the indicator is allowed to hang down, as with the swing-tip. A bite will cause this very sensitive mechanism to move. Electric bite indicators can be bought. These are used for night fishing but their use is regarded by some as unsporting.

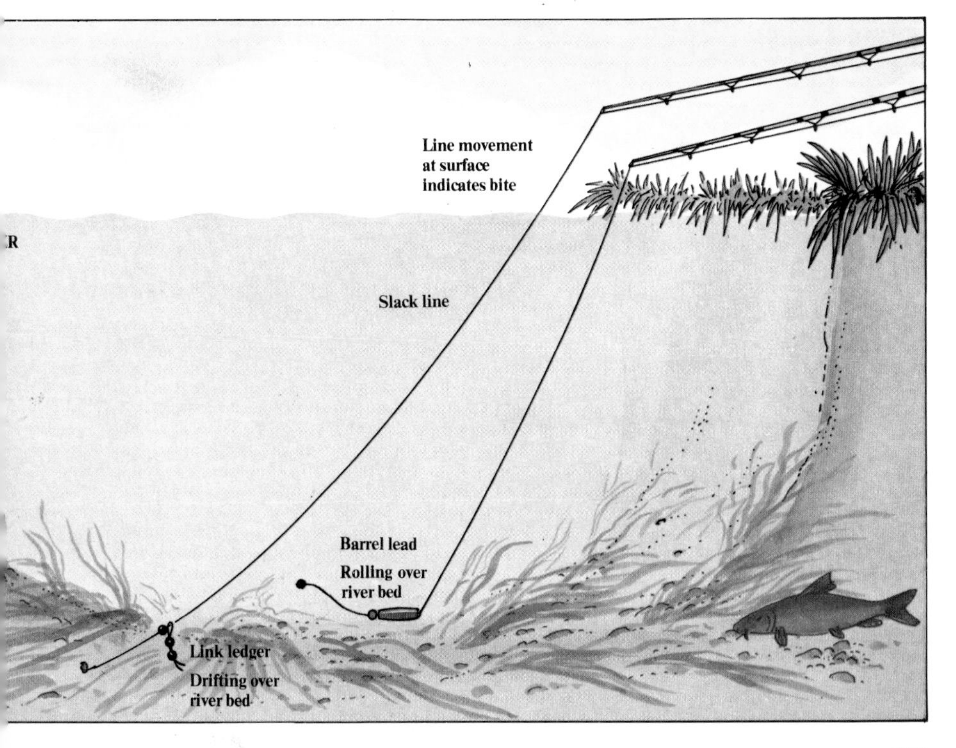

# Pole fishing

Although we regard the present day roach pole as one of angling's latest and most important discoveries it is, in fact, one of the oldest weapons in an extensive array of fishing rods. Dame Juliana Berners described a prototype of it in the *Boke of St Albans* published in 1496, and Izaak Walton described and enthused over it in his *Compleat Angler* of 1653. London's anglers have used it along the Thames for countless years to the extent that in the early part of this century the 'Pole' became a cult and the hallmark of an expert roach catcher.

In theory, the super-long tapered pole, with the line fastened to the end, uses a short link below the rod tip to convey the strike, which must drive the hook home very rapidly in this kind of fishing. In practice, there is an added bonus in the slim taper of the rod, for this produces sufficient spring to allow the careful angler to land fish well above the size of a roach that it was originally designed to catch.

**Hallmark of strength**

Excellent poles have been produced by the firm of Sowerbutts since 1815. They are still made to order in the traditional way; selected white cane was carefully cleaned and cut. Small distortions were straightened by heating the cane gently over a soft flame, and mending against the bench side. When the whole rod, which was usually 18-22ft in length, was aligned, heavy brass ferrules and butt caps were added. The final hallmark of strength was conferred in the form of hundreds of yards of best silk, which was whipped around the nodes in the cane and then repeated, at regular intervals, until each band of support was, on average, a mere ½in apart. Finally, several coats of copal varnish were applied, and the pole was ready. An extra top section was generally supplied with each rod. This was made from spliced whalebone and the tip section was stiffer than that made from cane.

After World War II other companies began to import low quality poles superficially resembling the Sowerbutts original in the form of cheap Japanese and Brazilian ready-shaped and whipped canes, usually 14-16ft in length. These were poor substitutes for the originals, but welcome enough at a time of acute shortage.

**Transition from cane to fibre**

The transition from cane to glass-fibre poles probably took place through the growing demands of match fishermen. For several years the sport had been growing in popularity, and by the 1960s many matchmen were looking to the Continental angler, whose techniques with the pole, an instrument that was a national institution, were far in advance of those of this country. With its fixed line and deadly strike, 'fish whipping' could take prize after prize.

**'Roach' pole a misconception**

The name 'roach pole' suggests that a pole can be used only for catching small fish. This is a misconception. Used properly, a pole can also handle big fish, such as chub, tench, bream and barbel.

Poles vary in length from 14ft to 24ft, and those made of ultra-lightweight hollow carbon-fibre have been made up to 30ft long. The more common hollow glass pole, however, designed to suit the average pocket, is about 18ft in length, and the assembled pole can be shortened according to the angler's needs, simply by not using the butt end.

*(Left) A 15th-century angler with fishing pole. (Below) The original bamboo pole by Sowerbutts. (Right) A fibreglass pole.*

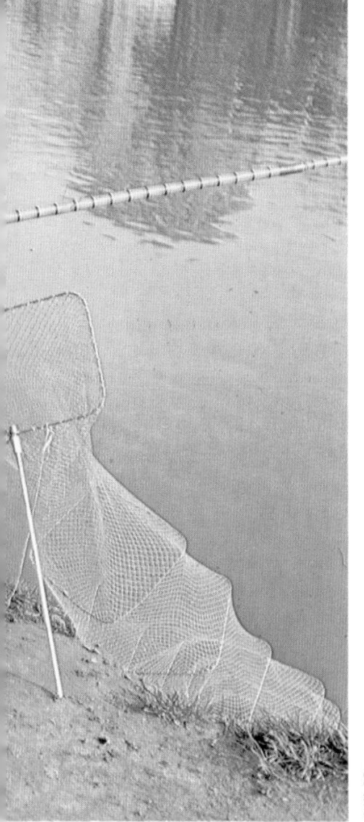

Bill Howes

Bill Howes

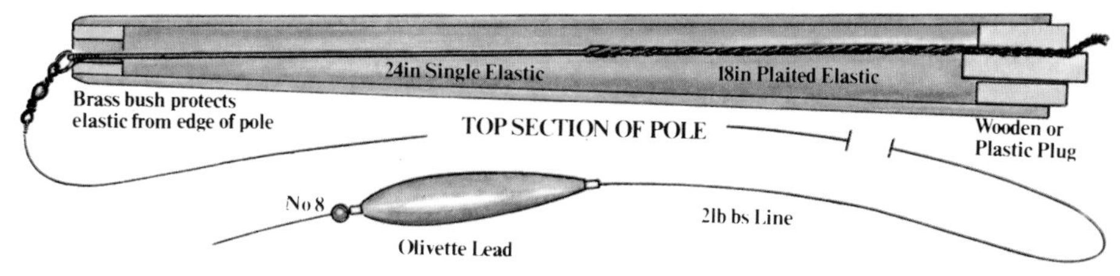


When you buy a pole, you are advised to obtain also tackle specially designed for pole fishing. You *can* make do with ordinary elastic, floats, shots and so on, and still catch plenty of fish, but, on the other hand, the tackle specially designed for pole fishing is neater, more streamlined, and makes pole fishing easier.

The most important item of tackle is that length of elastic. Most poles are designed to be fairly rigid at the tip, and as a reel is not used with a pole, the elastic acts as a shock absorber when hooking and playing a fish. Our grandfathers used a length of knicker elastic fixed to the end of their bamboo poles. Nowadays, special angling elastic is attached to the crook (or swan neck) tip, which is in turn fitted into its slot, and secured with a plastic sleeve which slides over the slot when the elastic loop is in position. The line is tied to the free end of the elastic, and carries the float, shot and hook, so it is useful to have several traces with end tackle on winders, ready for use. A ready-for-use assembly like this could consist of line, plus a float, weighted with either a celery shot pinched onto the line, or a hollow olivette lead with the line running through its centre. (A split shot is pinched onto the line to stop the olivette lead sliding down to the hook.)

**Made-up end tackles**

End tackles are carried ready made-up on plastic winders to save time and troublesome fiddle on the bankside, something that could be a considerable problem when one appreciates that line may drop to as low as a ½lb b.s., hook sizes be as small as size 22, and lead shot for float cocking be so tiny that the angler needs an eye-glass in order to see the split through which the line is run. In order to avoid confusion with various hook and line sizes, tackle winders can be purchased in various colours so that a code may be devised by the individual, allowing him to select or replace end tackle of equal balance immediately.

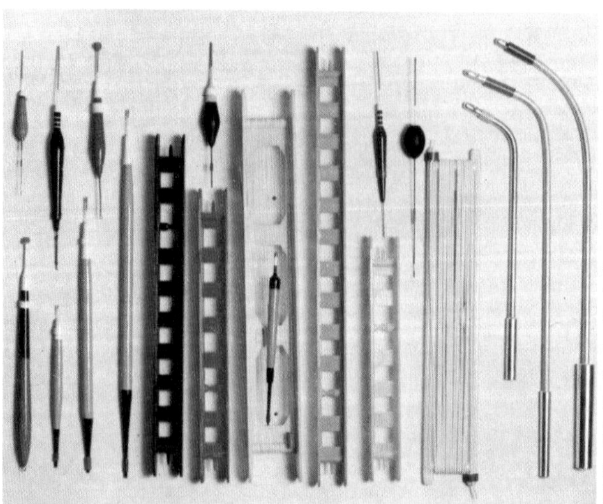

P H Ward/Tackle Carrier, Watford

*(Above) The action end of a modern pole. From primitive beginnings is has developed into an effective, sensitive angling unit.*
*(Left) Pole-fishing tackle: floats, multi-coloured winders, some elastic, universal swan-necks.*
*(Above right) A selection of floats for the pole-fishing specialist.*
*(Right) A float-rig for pole fishing.*
*(Far right) The cross-over-hands method of unshipping pole sections.*

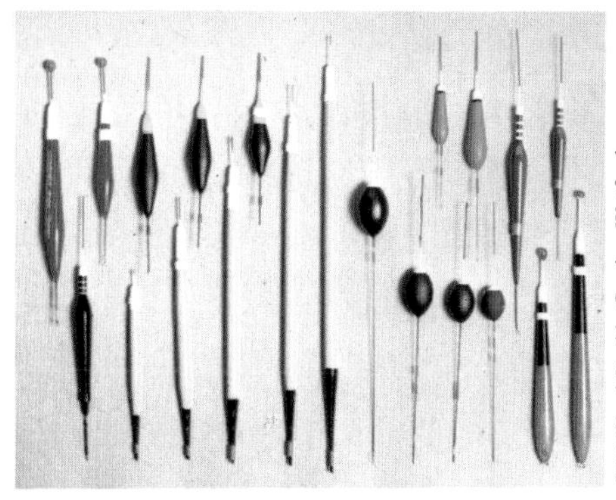

P H Ward/Tackle Carrier, Watford

In the same way that the pole has accepted a definite European slant, so have the floats that are used with it. Originally, a small porcupine or crow quill would be used for fine weather and calm water, with perhaps a tapered cork on quill for winter use. These were shotted down as low onto the water-line as possible, so that the tiniest bite would pull them under. Today's floats respect the same principle of delicacy, but by means of a drastically reduced stem or body circumference so that there is little or no drag when the bite takes place. The float, in fact, is designed literally to crash-dive.

There are different types of poles. Telescopic models, with sections which slide into their lower neighbours, like a telescope, are generally used for small dace, roach, gudgeon and so on, when the fish can be swung in from the water to the hand. The length of line used for this is about three quarters, or less, of the length of the extended pole. If, when using this rig, an angler is fortunate enough to hook a big fish which cannot be swung to hand, he must use the essential 'pole angler's' long-handled landing net. These nets are usually made of hollow glass-fibre, and can be extended to 12ft or more – especially useful when a big fish is hooked with a long, lightweight, telescopic pole.

Other poles are designed to be unshipped section by section, when a large fish is hooked. It may be necessary to bring the fish near to the bank before the net can be used, so after striking, the angler has to play the fish gradually towards the bank, nearer and nearer to his feet. One way he can do this is by walking backwards gradually, shifting his grip on the pole so that his hand moves from the butt towards the tip. However, this is not always possible – nor is it good practice.

**'Cross-over hands' method**

The proper and most convenient tactic is to stay seated, and use the 'cross-over hands' method of unshipping the bottom pole sections as the fish is brought nearer the bank. Here, the right-handed angler continues to grip the pole with his best hand,

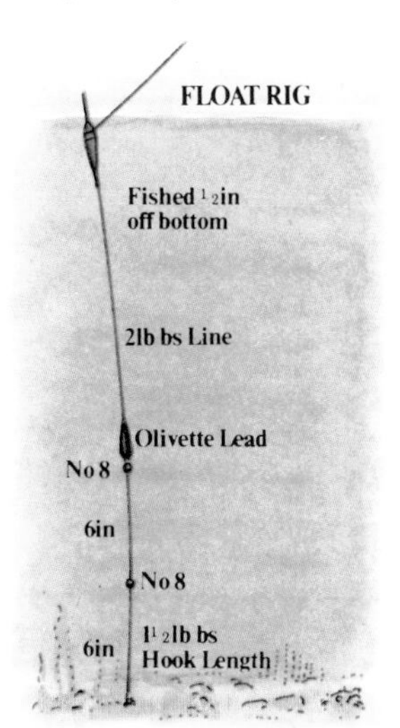


Rod Sutterby

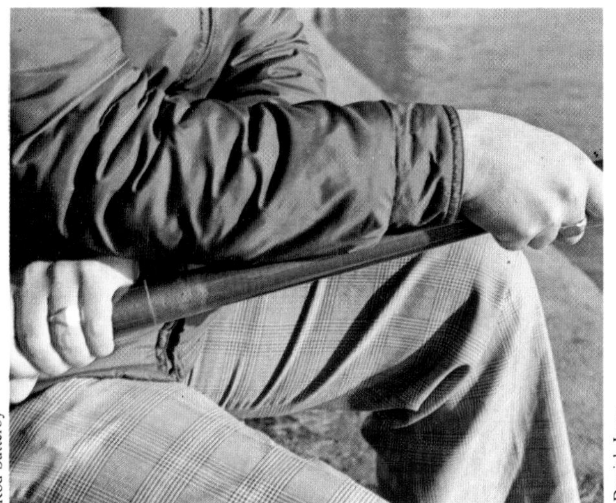

Derrick Jones

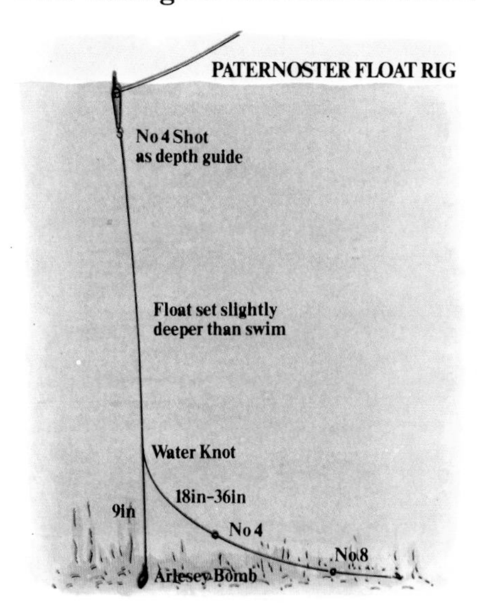


*(Above) A pole-fishing ledger rig.*
*(Right) Fitting the elastic loop into the slot of the crook-tip. When in position, the plastic sleeve is pulled over it.*

while unshipping the bottom sections with his weaker hand. This keeps the fish under constant control, and the weaker hand is eventually used for wielding the landing net.

**Essential factors**

Several important facts must be remembered when fishing with the pole. It is essential that the bait be kept where fish are feeding and normally that means keeping it on, or at most a few inches from, the bottom. A plummet – the new spring-clip types are ideal – must be used at regular intervals, particularly when river fishing where water levels often rise or fall imperceptibly. Should fish move up to the surface, any alteration to the float will result in a longer length of line between it and the rod tip, leaving slack line that defeats the pole's most advantageous feature. The angler must, therefore, at all times be prepared to alter the length of his line in order to avoid slack line at any time.

The rod tip, or point, is the vital part of the pole and it should follow the float and remain directly above it, otherwise the strike will be delayed fractionally by slack line, which may well mean the difference between a hooked or missed fish. It also follows that once a fish is hooked, the rod point should follow, and be kept immediately above it.

**Keep the fish under the tip**

Once a fish is allowed to move away from the tip, then direct strain is placed on the line, all spring absorption from the the rod being lost. A break is almost inevitable under these circumstances, and on more than one occasion an ardent pole angler has been seen running up and down the bank, following a fish to prevent this happening.

Rod Sutterby

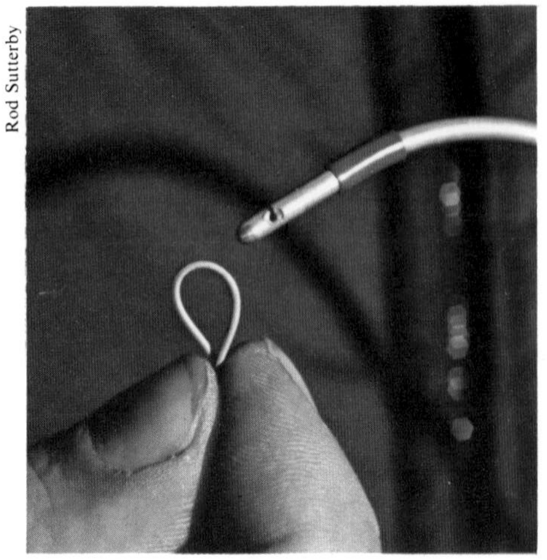

Derrick Jones

Although pole fishing may be new to you, it should not prove difficult. It is simply another way of fishing with a rod and float or ledger tackle. When you first go pole fishing, try for the smaller fish – gudgeon or bleak. You will soon get used to the fact that there is no reel on the rod, and quickly learn to use the stretch of the elastic instead of the slipping clutch of a reel.

You will also learn, as have many top match anglers, that the delicate precision of the pole will often catch fish when other methods fail – a fact confirmed by the thousands of British anglers who have turned to pole fishing during the past few years, not simply to catch small fish, with which the pole is mistakenly associated, but the big ones too.

# Groundbaiting

Bill Howes

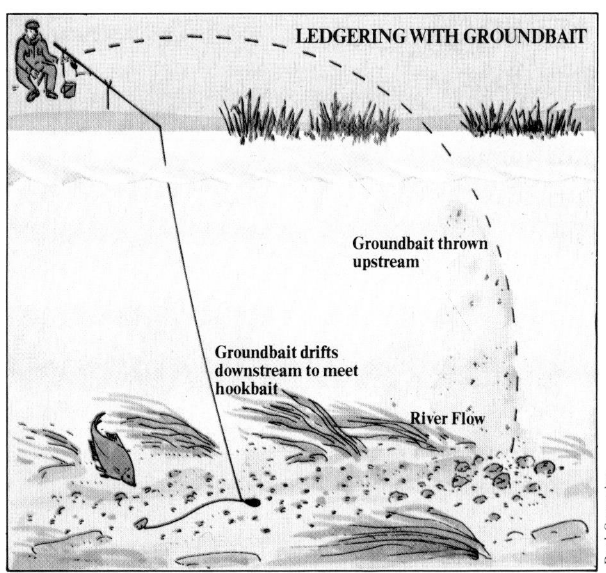


Rod Sutterby

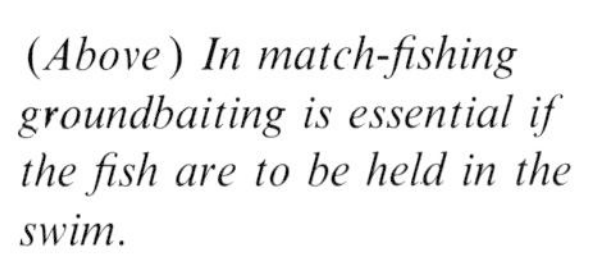

*(Above) In match-fishing groundbaiting is essential if the fish are to be held in the swim.*
*(Right) Groundbait is cast upstream, to break up and settle near the hookbait.*

Groundbaiting is carried out to attract fish into a swim and set them feeding. There are various methods of groundbaiting, depending mainly upon the type of water, the rate of flow, and the species of fish sought.

**Groundbaiting in fresh water**

Groundbaiting with a heavy mixture which drops to the bottom fast is needed at times, but once there it should break up quickly. In fast-flowing water, when barbel or bream are the quarry, a ball of groundbait which sinks quickly is thrown in slightly upstream so that when it hits the bottom and breaks up, the particles drift along the bottom and through the swim. Bream usually swim in large shoals, feeding on the bottom, and large amounts of groundbait are often needed to concentrate the shoal in the swim. A large bucketful of groundbait is generally the minimum required for a day's fishing.

Baiting up a swim several days in advance can pay dividends, particularly when bream, tench or carp are sought. This can draw a big shoal of bream into the swim and hold them there until fishing starts, even though their usual tendency is to be on the move.

A ball of groundbait can be used to land a quantity of loose maggots on the bed of a deep swim. In strong-flowing water, such as a weir stream, bank clay can be worked into the mixture for this purpose. It is then moulded in the shape of a cup, the cavity filled with maggots, worms or another bait, and the top closed over. A strong flow, coupled with the action of the wriggling bait, will soon break up the balls, sending the hookbait samples trickling along the bottom to bring fish close.

**Groundbaiting from a boat**

When fishing from a boat, groundbait can be dropped over the side or lowered to the bottom in a meshed bag weighted with stones. An occasional tug on a cord attached to the bag will release and circulate particles of the groundbait into the swim.

When ledgering, it is essential to get the groundbait in the right place, and then to fish the baited hook in the middle of it or as close as possible—on the downstream side.

Groundbaiting is frequently done with the

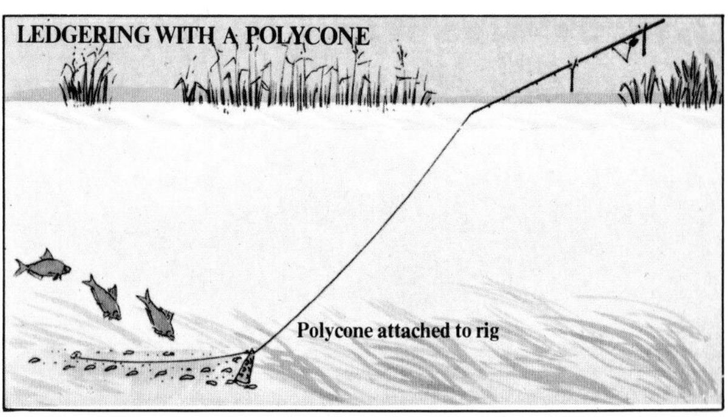


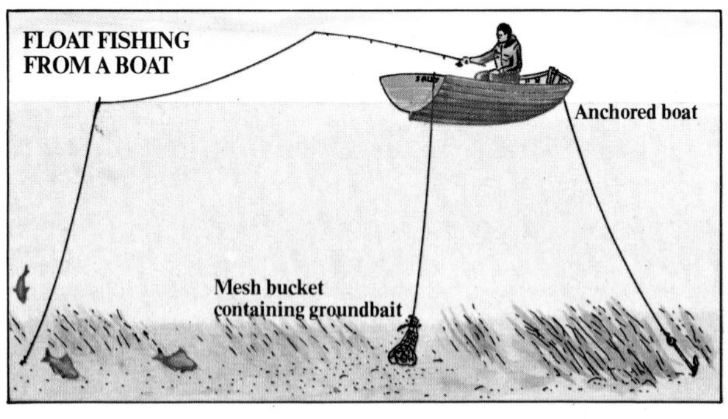


*(Top left) The Polycone swimfeeder allows maggots to be placed near the hook.*
*(Above) The Polycone swimfeeder used as a weight in ledgering.*
*(Left) Feeding a swim from a boat by the use of a mesh bag or bucket. It can be placed directly upstream.*

use of mechanical devices, such as bait-droppers, swim-feeders and catapults. One sure way of landing loose maggots, or other hookbait samples, on the bottom, is to put them there by means of a bait-dropper, of which there are various kinds on the market. The loaded bait-dropper is lowered to the bottom of the swim, when a trip wire opens the lid and releases the contents. The match angler usually starts by putting down several droppers full of hookbait samples. Once the fish move into the swim, the bait-dropper should be used with caution, for it may scare the fish.

**Scattering by hand**

Bait-droppers are obviously not so useful when fishing on the drop, or if taking fish from under the surface when small fish are relied on to make up the match weight. Scattering bait loosely by hand or by catapult is more effective in that case.

Good catches of fish are often made by using choice maggots as hookbait and groundbaiting with inferior maggots, or feeders as they are known. Feeders are generally used in conjunction with a cloudbait. As one becomes expert in casting with one hand and tossing the feed or attractor in with the other, both hookbait and groundbait will enter the water together. The choice maggots on the hook will sink slowly and enticingly amidst the dissolving cloudbait and the feeders.

**Use of the swimfeeder**

When ledgering in midstream an effective way of getting maggots down to the bed of the river is to use a gadget known as a swim-feeder. These come in various designs and sizes, but the basic model is a celluloid tube that is attached to the ledger tackle. The open-ended type is packed with maggots, with breadcrumbs as plugs at both ends.

With groundbait plugs the feeder can also be used to concentrate hempseed or casters in the vicinity of the baited hook. The closed or blockend type is filled with maggots only.

After the tackle is cast out it reaches the bottom and the flow of water swings the baited hook to a position downstream of the swim-feeder. From this the maggots will

Ken Whitehead

Derrick Jones

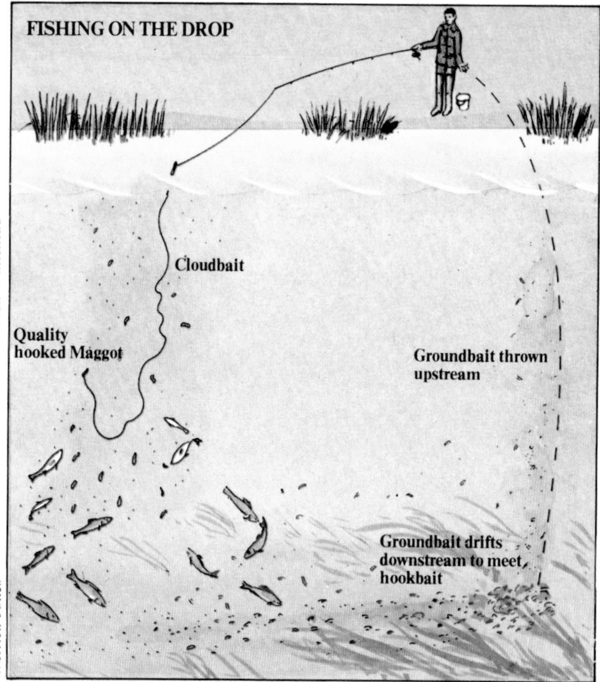


Rod Sutterby

*(Top left)* *Balls of groundbait can be liberally laced with maggots.*
*(Left)* *A stone in groundbait aids casting accuracy and distance.*
*(Above)* *The use of cloud and groundbait.*

wriggle out through the holes and in the right place—around the baited hook.

A swim-feeder deposits groundbait exactly where it is needed—but it does not always put enough there. This is why, when ledgering, groundbaiting the swim manually is sometimes employed at the same time as offering the hookbait samples in the swim-feeder.

Care must be exercised when groundbaiting a swim where specimen fish are the quarry. On a river, the introduction of a large quantity of groundbait will invariably attract shoals of small fish, and these can prove a nuisance.

**Cloudbaiting**

A form of groundbaiting which is effective in many types of waters, particularly for surface and mid-water species, is cloudbaiting. This means clouding the water by introducing minute particles which the fish will search through for more substantial food.

After taking note of the rate of flow of the water, the angler regularly throws small balls of cloudbait into the swim. This is done upstream, so that the cloud drifts down and through the area being fished. The float tackle is cast out immediately after, following the groundbait closely through the swim.

**Drip-feeding**

For roach, dace and chub fishing on a small, secluded river, regular swim-baiting can be made by the use of a 'drip feed'—a tin with a few holes punched in the bottom, which is filled with maggots and hung from a bridge or overhanging branch. The steady trickle of maggots over a long period will entice fish from some distance into the swim.

As match fishermen know, regular groundbaiting of the swim is very important no matter what hookbait is used. Without it, the angler is fishing on a hit-and-miss basis.

# Gravel pit fishing

Most species of coarse fish, including bream, roach, rudd, perch, pike, carp, tench and eel inhabit gravel pits. Chub, barbel, dace and grayling, more commonly river fish, will also be found. But all these species will not be found together and so, before going fishing, it is advisable to find out which fish are present so that suitable tackle can be chosen.

**Study the waters**

Gravel pits vary considerably in size, shape, depth and character, and to get the best from fishing them concentrate on just one or two of a group at a time. Study the waters, especially the effects of changing conditions on the feeding habits of the fish and the locations of the most populated swims.

A gravel pit rarely has a uniform depth. Instead, the bottom slopes drastically, creating shallows of a few feet and sudden deep holes of 20-30ft, perhaps more. This apparent unpredictability can daunt the angler on his first visit, but observation, a little planning and the right technique can produce good results first time.

The prime gravel pit species, bream, roach, carp and tench (but not rudd), are mid-water or bottom feeders. During the summer and early autumn they tend to feed by night in the shallows and by day in deeper water. Therefore, where possible, fish an area containing shallows and medium depths, with deep water close by. If weedbeds are present, so much the better.

A successful method, which will be explained in greater detail in later issues, is to ledger with a simple open-ended swimfeeder rig. Use this with a sturdy but sensitive 12ft rod, a fixed-spool reel, and a line strength to match water conditions and the size of the prey. A 3lb b.s. line is suitable for sizeable

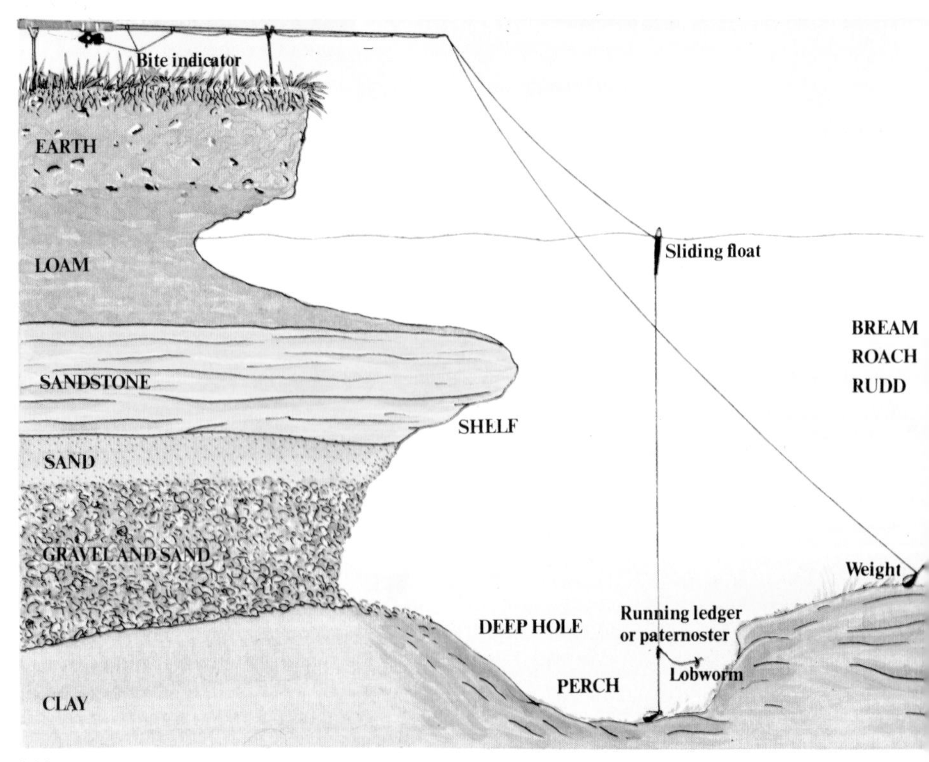

roach and rudd, 5 or 6lb b.s. for average tench and bream, and 8-10lb for shoal carp. Set up the end tackle so that there is an 18in trail between hook and swimfeeder. The latter is held running-ledger style by a plastic-plug stop. Attach an eyed hook securely to the main line. Use front and rear rod-rests and adjust the outfit so that the rod points slightly downwards to the water. A small blob of groundbait hanging on the line between reel and butt ring will serve as a bite indicator. The bale-arm should be closed for roach, rudd, tench and bream, and open for the strong-pulling carp.

**The proven bait**

Proven baits for this method are maggots (hook size 16-18), bread flake or flake and maggot mix (12-8), and whole or just the tail of lobworm (8-6). Make sure the groundbait in the swimfeeder is soft enough to disintegrate quickly so that after casting out and waiting for a couple of minutes, the swimfeeder can be dragged back some 18in to release samples, among which the baited hook will settle. The advantages of this technique are that there is no need to check the exact depth fished and that the hook will be close to the groundbait, no matter how far out you cast.

**When to groundbait**

Throughout most of the day fish the slope leading to the deeper water, groundbaiting occasionally with balls of fine sausage rusk laced with hook-bait samples, and filling the swimfeeder with hook-bait sandwiched between plugs of softish groundbait. From evening until the middle of the night, and again from dawn until midmorning, try moving to medium-depth water. Groundbait heavily to attract and hold the fish as they head for the shallows during these very

*Gravel pits can offer varied and interesting fishing in shallows, medium-depths waters and frequent deep holes. These conditions also account for the variety of species encountered in gravel pits—perch, pike, roach, rudd, carp, tench and bream.*

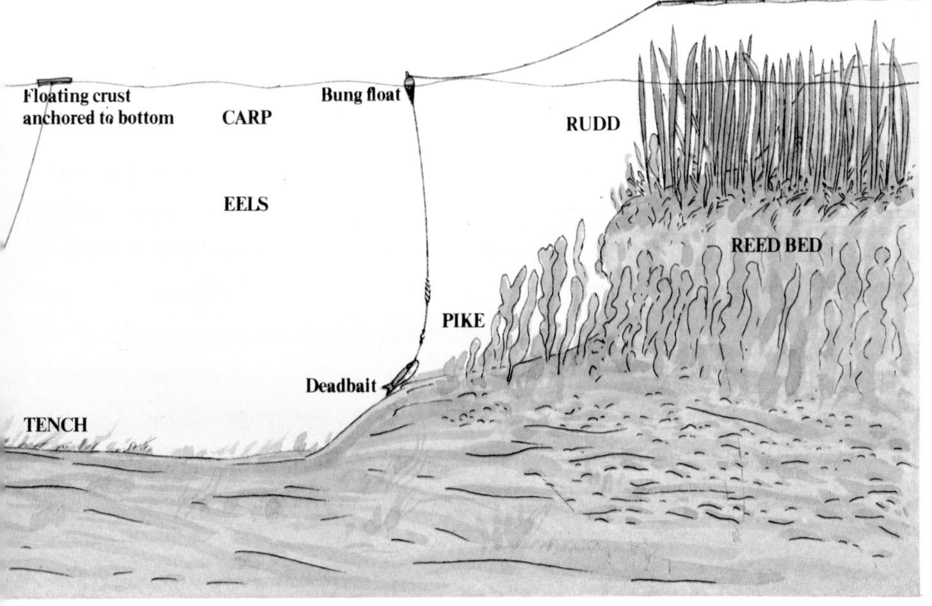


Rod Sutterby

*(Right) A typical gravel pit area can include reedy shallows, ledges, gravelly spots, very deep holes and medium-depth fishing. Adjust your angling style to match these different conditions: floating crust over mid-water, sliding float in deep holes, float fishing or ledgering off reedy areas. Be ready always to switch methods.*

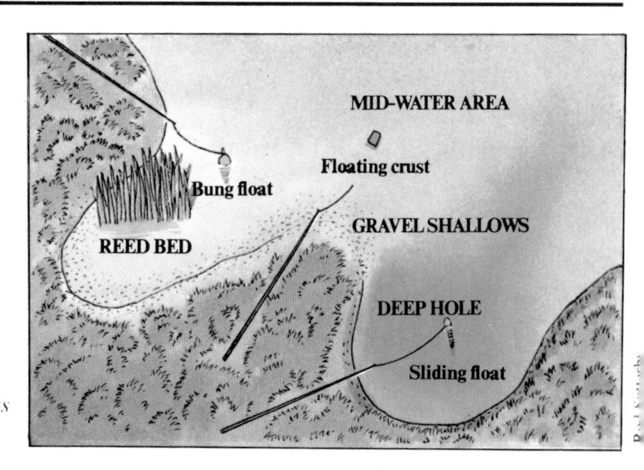

Robin Fletcher

*(Left) Flooded gravel pit at Steeple Langford, Wiltshire. An established water where the banks have been cleared and shored up with the angler in mind. A likely swim is seen at left. (Right) The irregular contours of this recently flooded Hampshire pit provide numerous vantage points for the fisherman. Trees have been cut back to give access to the water.*

important and predictable feeding periods.

How the fish will bite will depend on whether the fish are feeding boldly or just playing with the bait. Tench are notorious for plucking at the bait, causing the indicator to jerk as if a roach or rudd were nibbling. Counter this by jerking back. If the indicator moves up a little pull it back down. A little teasing of this sort often provokes a decisive take from a hesitant fish.

**Buoyant baits**

The shallows usually contain weed in plenty and large amounts of natural food, and it is in these areas that fish are found at night. Excellent catches can be made in as little as 18in of water. A light ledger or mini-swimfeeder can be used to place the bait on the bottom, but off-bottom techniques also work. For example, a buoyant bait such as a crust cube or a fat lobworm, free-lined or cast on a ledger trail long enough to enable it to float, will catch not only surface feeders like carp and rudd, but also tench, roach and bream who are normally bottom feeders.

Big carp are a popular quarry nowadays. In gravel pits, which are sometimes specially stocked with them, they often reach 20 or 30lb. Carp tackle includes a 10 or 11ft carp rod, line of 8-15lb b.s., and well-sharpened, eyed hooks.

The bait is fished on the bottom—free-lined if heavy enough to cast on its own; ledgered if it is a lightweight particle bait. All the baits so far mentioned will tempt big carp. Parboiled potatoes are another effective bait, and in recent years sweetcorn has proved very successful with carp and other species. Pastes can be concocted from pet-

Bill Howes

foods and meat products, and artificial high-protein baits can be purchased.

Carp also feed near and at the surface, and can be lured by floating crust. In breezy weather, providing the depth is not too great, a crust can be anchored in position by ledgering it on a trail equal in length to the depth fished.

During the summer and autumn months carp-strength tackle can be used for big eels— a species unjustly neglected in gravel pits, for specimens of over 4lb are often to be caught. Big eels turn up occasionally during the day, but night-time, when they are feeding in the medium depths, offers the best sport. Deadbaiting is the best method to employ for this underestimated, fighting fish.

In winter pike and perch abound. Rudd, tench and eels are less active, but bream, carp and roach can still be caught. The two predators, pike and perch, are taken in summer on various baits and with spinners and plugs, but winter fishing will produce the larger specimens.

**Ledgered lobworm**

Perch gather in deep holes in gravel pits and can be caught on a running ledger or running paternoster rig baited with a whole lobworm. Place the rod on rests, leave the bale-arm open and give a run plenty of time before striking.

For pike, a sturdy purpose-built or carp rod, 10-15lb b.s. line, and a wire trace carrying two or three treble hooks, is standard kit. Good baits are dead roach, small bream, herring and mackerel and can be free-lined on the bottom or, in breezy weather, cast out beneath a sliding float to work across water with the wind. A deadbait, cast far out and retrieved jerkily to simulate the erratic progress of a sick or injured fish, makes an effective bait when searching large areas of varying depth. Pike, like carp, regularly patrol channels and shallow bars through deep water. Such spots are always worth special attention.

**Advantage of float-fishing**

Float fishing is also widely practised in gravel pits and has some advantages. A sliding float, an antenna or, in windy conditions, a long, wide-bodied float, can be used to search deep water under the bank for tench, bream and roach during the summer months. A float is also helpful when fishing deep water beyond a shelf on which a ledger rig would snag and so reduce bite indications, especially when the fish are shy biters.

Lastly, remember that the steep banks of gravel pits and the deep water immediately beyond them are dangerous places. Watch for crumbling banks, and note them, especially when night fishing. Remember, too, that while you may be enjoying your night's fishing, others may be sleeping. Not only is it bad fishing to create noise and disturbance, it can also lead to ill-feeling between anglers and local residents.

# Trotting

Trotting, sometimes called 'swimming the stream', is a method of float fishing in flowing water where the float and bait is allowed to travel with the current. The depth at which the bait is fished depends on the species of fish being sought and at what depth it is most likely to feed. Generally, the float and bait are cast slightly upstream of the angler and allowed to travel downstream until the end of the swim is reached. The procedure is then repeated.

**When to trot**

Trotting is employed when the fish are feeding off the bottom. In summer, for example, both chub and roach feed in midwater or just below the surface and, on occasions, bream feed here as well. Trotting can be successful in winter too. Specialist dace anglers fish this way almost exclusively, while both roach and chub often prefer a moving bait to a stationary one.

Clear or fairly clear waters are more conducive to good sport than coloured waters, especially where they flow fast where the bait, because of reduced visibility, is less likely to be seen by the fish.

**Allowing the bait to rise**

The manner in which the float and bait are allowed to travel downstream is important. Usually they should move at the same speed as the current but sometimes, when fishing with a stick float and caster, for example, the float should be held back allowing the bait to rise up in the water. This may be done either at the end of the swim or, if it is a long one, several times as it passes through.

In fast shallow water, the angler sometimes wades with the rod pointing downriver. The float, depending upon the whim of the angler (or a bite from a fish), will be checked very slightly as it travels downriver, making the bait rise and fall as it travels through the swim. This method of presenting the bait is especially effective on such waters

S. L. Ward/Natural Science Photos

S. L. Ward/Natural Science Photos

*(Above) Trotting from midstream demands the landing net and bait must be carried. Peter Ward is playing a dace on the Kennet. (Left) To get a clear run downstream for the terminal tackle, a long rod is necessary when dapping from the bank.*

as the Avon and Kennet when barbel and chub are the quarry.

On the Upper Thames, many chub are taken by trotting the opposite bank. For this technique the float is cast well upstream of the angler and retrieved when some 15 yards below him. Bites can be expected at any time. Unlike trotting under one's own bank, or in the centre of the river, when the float starts its run almost opposite the angler, for trotting the far bank the float must begin well upstream of the angler.

Tackle is important and should be as light as possible. The rod should be a long one, 12ft, 13ft or 14ft with a 'tippy' action for roach and dace and an all-through action for such bigger fish as barbel, chub and bream. It should also have plenty of rings to prevent the line sticking to it in wet weather. Line strength varies, depending upon the species being sought, but should be between ½-4lb b.s. Although most present-day anglers prefer a fixed-spool reel there is no doubt that for trotting a centrepin is far superior for control of the tackle.

**Mending the line**

Sometimes, especially when fishing across river, a 'bow' will appear in the line which must be corrected to ensure that when the angler strikes the hook is driven home. This is achieved by flicking the rod back against the direction of the current thus making the line straight. This is called 'mending the line'. Because of this the line must float and although some monofilaments will float reasonably well, for perfect tackle control the line should be greased before fishing.

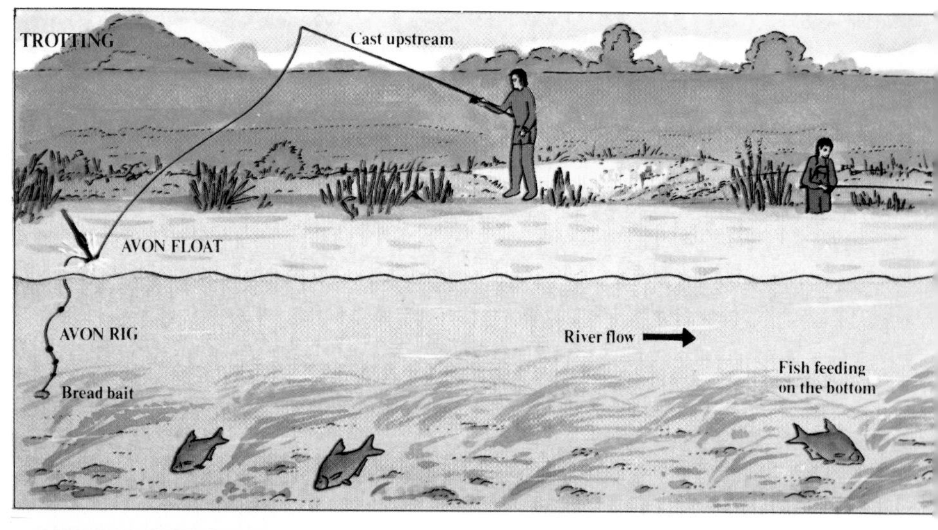

*(Above) A number of modern floats are designed for trotting. They are often variants on traditional patterns such as the Avon.*
*(Left) The centre-pin is ideal for trotting. Its drum is controlled by finger-pressure on the rim.*
*(Below) When trotting with the fixed-spool reel, the bale arm is left open. Line is controlled by a finger on the spool.*

Hooks depend upon the bait and will vary from a No.18, for caster and single-maggot fishing, to a No. 6 when using big bread-crust or flake.

The kind of float is very important. In fast-flowing waters a float carrying between one and four 'swan' (SSG) shots will be necessary and must have a fairly stout tip. This will ensure that the float remains visible even in turbulent water. The same kind of float will also be used for trotting bread against the far bank for chub, and minnows for barbel. These floats are attached to the line both top and bottom and are sometimes known as 'Chub Trotters'.

Mike Prichard

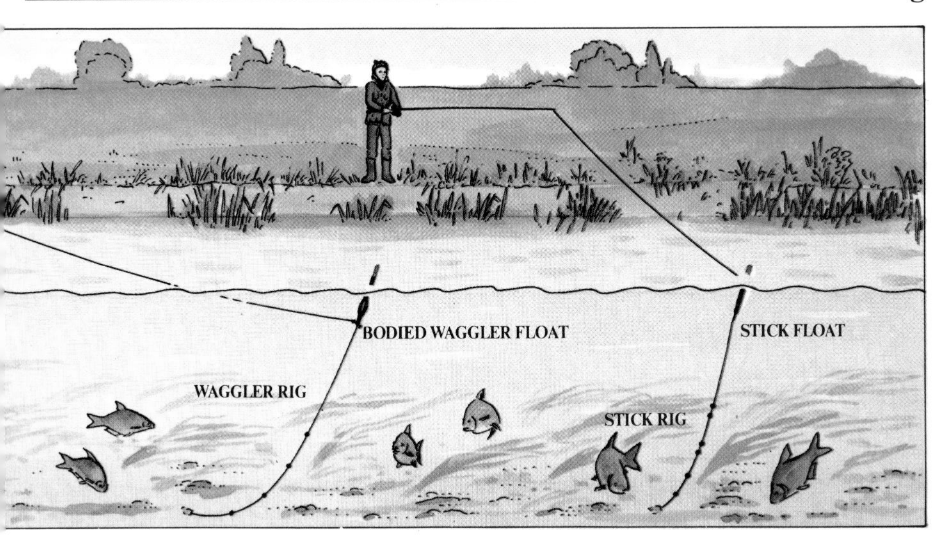


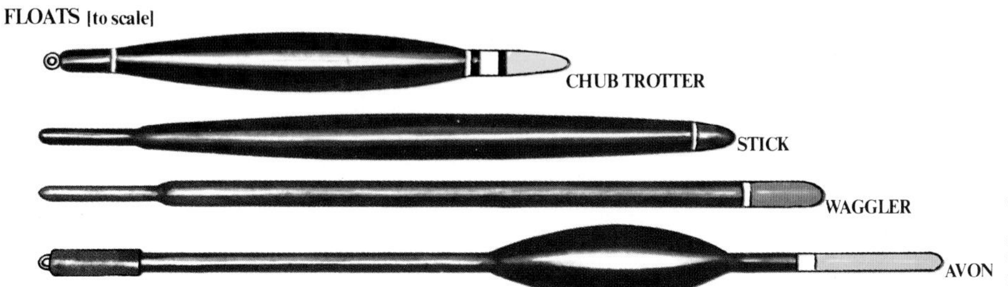


Rod Sutterby

In waters of medium flow, lighter floats can be used. For roach, dace and bream, one with a short, thin antenna will make for more sensitive fishing, although in choppy water it may be difficult to see all of the time. In this situation, a float with a slightly stouter antenna would be better. These floats are attached either bottom, top, or both.

**'Waggler' floats**

In recent years 'Wagglers' have become popular. This float has a stout body, usually made of balsa, situated at the bottom of a length of peacock quill or Sancandas reed. The 'Waggler', a heavy float even in its smallest size, takes a lot of shot and is fished by casting upstream and retrieved when below the angler. It is attached to the bottom only and fished with the line sunk.

Another popular float is the 'Stick'. Used mainly for caster fishing it consists of a tapered body made from varying proportions of cane and balsa. Best used for fishing close or fairly close in, it is shotted so that no more than $\frac{1}{8}$in of the tip shows above the surface. Like the 'Waggler', it is attached to the bottom and fished with the line sunk.

The manner in which the strike is made depends upon both the float used and the method employed. When trotting against the far bank which is more than 15 yards away, or wading with the float downstream, the strike is overhead, the rod being pulled back over the shoulder. For middle-of-the-river and close-in fishing, a sideways strike against the current is preferable. When fishing with a sunken line or with a 'Waggler' or 'Stick' float, the strike is made with the rod held low. With the 'Waggler' float, not only should the rod be kept low but the strike should be made downstream.

# Spinning

P H Ward/Natural Science Photos

Spinning is the art of casting and retrieving a lure designed to look or act like a small fish frog or mouse. Spinning is often a deadly method and most sea, game or coarse anglers find it necessary to spin at times. Using a variety of spinner-spoons, plugs, jigs or pirks, anglers use it for a number of different species on waters throughout the country.

Spinning is also one of the best methods of fishing for young anglers. Armed with one or two plugs, a closed-face fixed-spool reel and a decent spinning rod, the novice will learn to both cast and catch a sizeable fish.

**Species caught with spinners**

Most game fish take a spinner readily. Many sea fish, even flounders, fall to them, and in coarse fishing, pike, perch, zander and chub take these lures often, while other fish in the carp family (bream, carp, tench, and others), do so occasionally.

Generally speaking, spinning is a good method for the open river where there are deep pools, or for large stillwaters, gravel pits and reservoirs. One should not spin in confined spaces, as retrieval will be difficult. If the river is overhung with much vegetation, bad casting will result in lost lures.

*A pike of nearly 20lb—the fish of a lifetime for most anglers—falls to a well-used spinner. As this catch demonstrates, it is not always necessary to offer a new, shiny lure in order to take a specimen fish.*

Spinning is an active method of fishing and good to use in cold weather.

Choice of rod depends on the water more than anything else. On big rivers, gravel pits or reservoirs you may need a powerful, two-handed, stepped-up carp rod to throw biggish spoons, spinners or plugs a long way. In contrast, on small rivers, canals or ponds, short casts with a 7-8ft spinning rod of hollow glass for use with lines of 5-8lb b.s. may be adequate.

A certain amount of common sense is needed in choice of rod: big pike or salmon on a small river, for example, would need a powerful line, from 10lb to 20lb b.s.

The choice of reels is legion. It is possible, though, for the experienced angler to spin directly from a top-class centre-pin. With plugs you can pull off loops of line from the rod rings, while for sizeable plugs and heavy spinners you may use a multiplying reel.

Bill Howes

*(Left) A spinning enthusiast with a box of spinners and lures.*
*(Below) A spinning rig incorporating a Wye lead to prevent the line kinking. One swivel or a plastic vane between two swivels, both rigs leaded, will also serve as an anti-kink device.*
*(Overleaf) The single-handed overhead cast begins with the rod tip at eye level and the line held by the fore-finger. The rod is raised smoothly to almost vertical and brought forward smartly, when line is released and the forefinger applied to the spool to check the cast.*

Multipliers are accurate on short to moderate casts but difficult to cast light baits.

Other than for light spinning, closed-face reels are rarely used. For playing heavy fish they prove ineffective since the line within the housing goes through too many angles, creating considerable friction. Many open-faced fixed-spool reels are, however, superb. One with a roller pick-up and a reliable, easily reached anti-reverse switch is especially useful.

The species of fish also governs the choice of rod, reel and line. In weedy waters, like the Fenland drains, you need heavy line and a powerful rod to hold the fish. The same applies to heavy fish in small waters. On the other hand, when perch or chub fishing, a MK IV carp rod, or its lighter version, the Avon, in glass or split cane, are excellent.

**Ultra-light spinning**

Ultra-light spinning is proving to be increasingly popular. For this, a sawn-off length of fly rod, 5-6ft, with a line of 2-4lb b.s. is recommended. A tiny fixed-spool reel of high quality, like one of the small Shakespeares, Daiwas, or Ryobis, and small lures, almost down to big flies in size, but

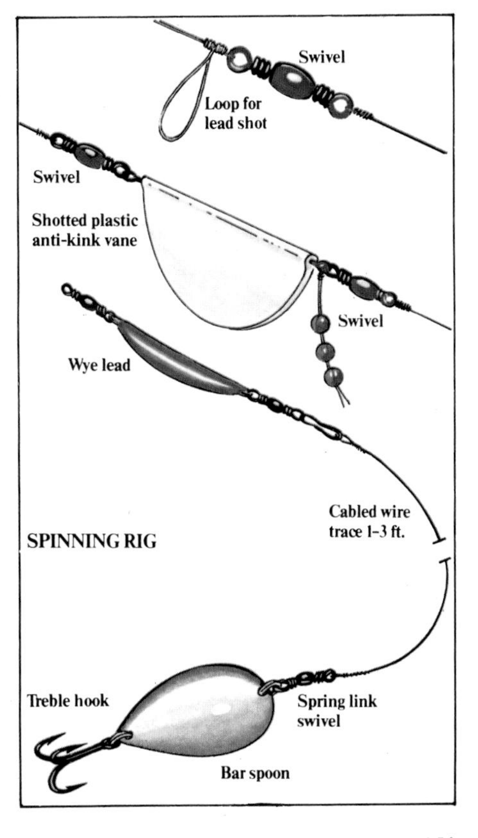

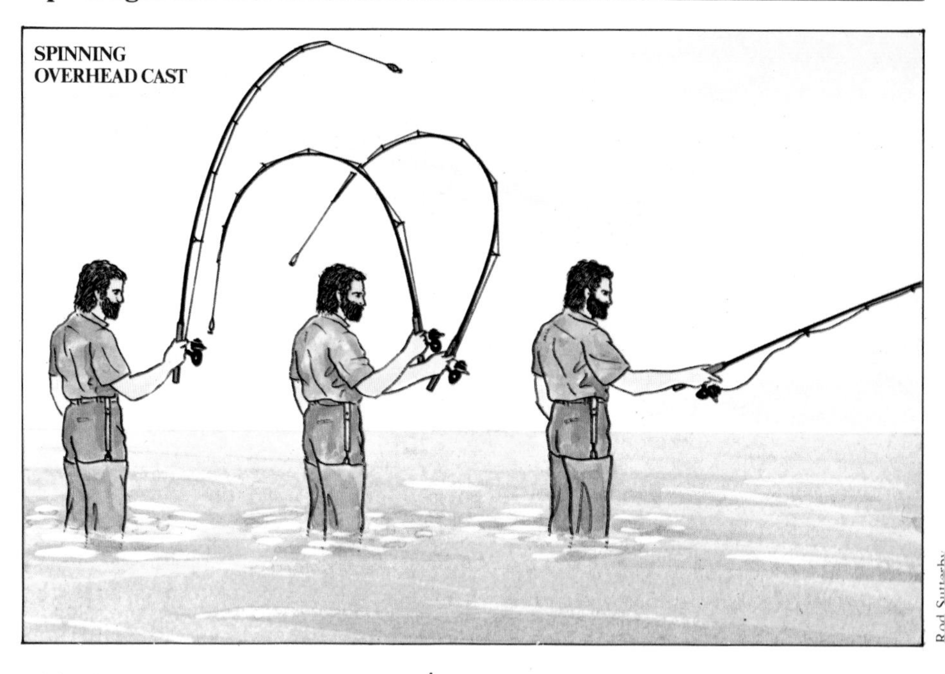


with diving vanes or propellors, are also necessary. You can, in fact, make your own lures on big single hooks, and catch more carp species with this than you would on conventional spinning gear.

The wide range of rods and reels provides great versatility of spinning. Lines are also varied, but a good standard line is a simple monofil, usually dyed dark in colour, and supple. Some anglers use plaited nylon, particularly on multiplying reels, but monofil generally has more stretch. Other spinning, such as trolling from a boat, may require special lead-cored lines, and some sea spinning is done with wire lines. Different strengths of nylon monofil together with appropriate weights to get the spinner down, usually prove adequate.

If a fish has a lot of sharp teeth you may need a wire trace on the line. This applies particularly to pike and zander and many sea fish, but not when spinning for game fish, perch or chub.

Cabled, supple, dark-coloured wire is better than made-up, plastic-coated, shiny traces. Add a swivel to one end and a safety-pin link swivel to the other by passing 2in of cable wire through the swivel eye. Laying it back parallel, twist the two parts together by hand. Crimp-on sleeves can be used to secure the join, or strong glue.

**Minimum of equipment**

At the waterside, remember that you are always on the move, so a minimum of equipment is advisable. A small rucksack on your back is best, to hold food and waterproof clothing, and an angler's waistcoat with numerous pockets for spinners, spoons and miscellaneous items of tackle such as a spring balance, forceps for removing lures from fishes' jaws, a sharpening stone for blunted hooks, scissors and other small items, will prove useful. For landing salmon a small, collapsible net or gaff is necessary.

Always take enough clothes to keep warm. If possible wear plimsoles or walking boots rather than wellingtons or waders, although weight and heat saving on footwear is not always a good thing. Clothes should be drab, and the approach to the waterside quiet. It is a good plan to fish through the spot you intend standing at, particularly on a coarse fish water where another angler's groundbait

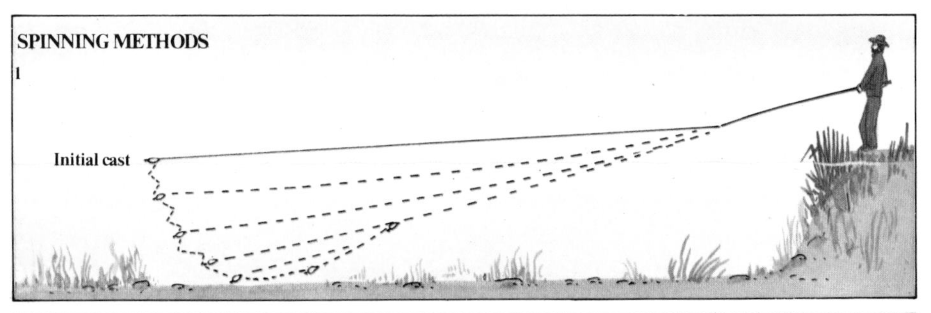


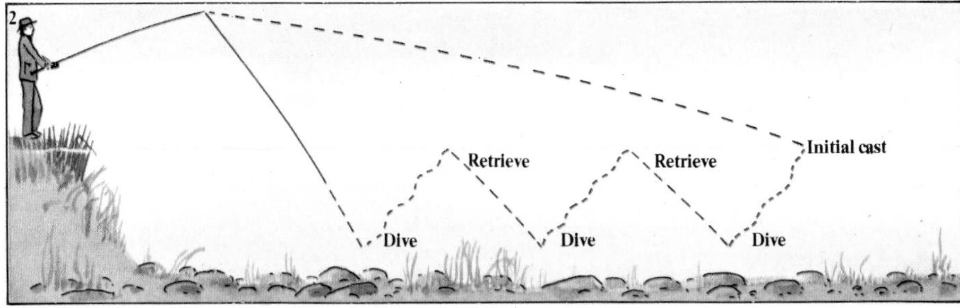


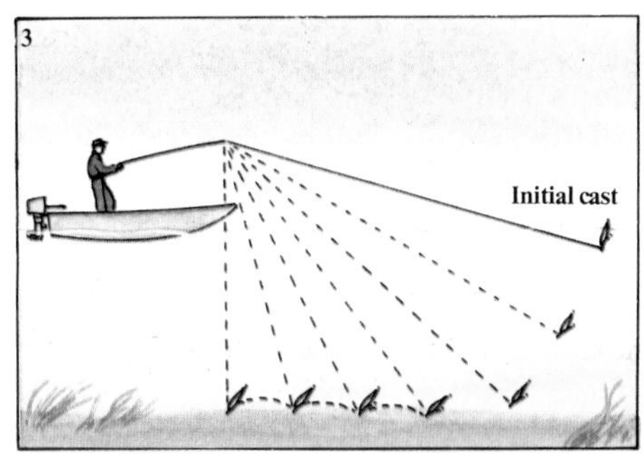


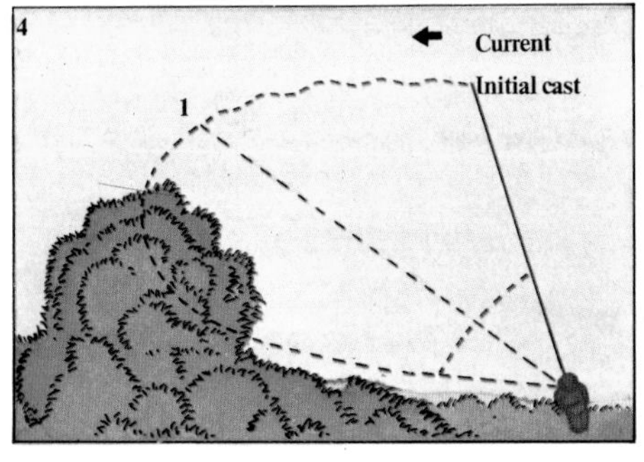


Rod Sutterby

may have attracted shoal fish and predators close to the bank.

**Where to cast**

Where to cast? First, with a sinking spinner, find out the depth of water working on the principle of retrieving slow and deep. Cast out and allow the spinner or spoon to sink with the pick-up off, and judge the time it takes the spinner to strike the bottom. As the spinner nears the bank, raise the rod top to avoid the lure running into the slope. Casting in a fan-wise fashion, each cast being some five degrees to the side of the previous cast, is also used, but this can make for boring fishing, except from an anchored boat. It is probably better to cast where you think the predator will be.

Having explored the most likely places—ledges, sunken branches, and holes behind boulders—move on and try another spot.

Some anglers have difficulty estimating how far out the lure is. To remedy this, tie a nylon stop knot, such as a Billy Lane stop knot, to the line at a fixed length above the lure, perhaps 15ft. As the knot clicks through the top ring you will know where the spinner is. This is particularly useful for night spinning—one of the most exciting forms of fishing that there is.

For night spinning you also need a shot clipped on the line just above the trace swivel, or if not using a trace, some 2ft up the line. This prevents the trace swivel being reeled into the end ring of the rod, or the

*(Previous page) (1) The rod is held low and the spoon returned a little at a time until it bounces off the bottom. (2) With the rod at an angle of 45° the minnow is allowed to dive deep and is then retrieved. (3) From a boat the Deep Diver is retrieved rapidly as it sinks to the bottom. (4) A plug is used to reach fish beneath over-hanging trees. The plug drifts downstream* [***1***] *before the rod is dipped below the water and line slowly reeled in* [**2**] *, dragging the lure in anarc beneath the tree* [***3***]*. (Right) When spinning, the angler is very visible and so should wear dull colours.*

Arthur Oglesby

spinner itself being retrieved too close to the rod tip. It should usually hang a couple of feet from the rod tip prior to a cast. Another important consideration when spinning at night is to know how far you have cast. Fortunately this is fairly easy. In daylight measure out a suitable-length cast by pulling line off the reel, then secure a rubber band round the spool before reeling the line back on to the reel. This avoids overcasting.

**Colours and sizes**

Spinners, spoons and plugs come in all colours and sizes. Simple spoons are egg-shaped and can be made from dessert spoons. Despite their simplicity they will take almost anything that swims. Drill a hole out at each end and by using a split ring, add a treble hook at one end and a swivel at the other. Elongated, concave-convex spoons with or without fins, are also useful.

Bar spoons are attached at one end to a bar forming an axis around which the blade spins. The tiny sizes will take trout, sea trout and perch, and the large sizes pike and salmon. They retrieve with greater vibration, but, unlike many spoons, retrieve in a more or less straight line unless the angler alters the position of the rod end. Fly spoons are a kind of small bar spoon, while many other spinners, like some minnows, and mackerel spinners, have a hole through them and rotate about their whole length.

Plugs can be floaters (poppers or crawlers), floaters which dive to various depths, or sinking plugs. These are available in one piece, or with two or more pieces. Some plugs dive shallow, some deep. Perhaps the most versatile, all-purpose plug is the smallest. Around an inch in length, with wool, fur and feather attached, it is almost as good as the fly-type lures, and can be fished on fly rods or with ultra-light gear.

The action of the spinner in the water is essential to a successful catch. Aim to retrieve in short bursts, swinging the rod from side to side. This will vary the direction and add a lifelike flutter to your spinner. When retrieving try not to be too quick, as the lure will rise high in the water; on the other hand, one should not retrieve too cautiously for fear of snagging your lure.

Plugs and spinners lend themselves to home-making—adding, in many ways, to one of the most enjoyable aspects of fishing.

# Playing and landing

Despite thousands of words of sound advice from fishing writers on the subject of playing and landing, many fish are nevertheless lost by anglers who lack this basic skill. The most common weak spots are: little or no understanding of the slipping clutch on the frequently used fixed-spool reel and not knowing how to coax out a fish that has run into weed (which can happen to the most experienced angler).

First, then, the slipping clutch. Before making the first cast, hold the rod in one hand and place one finger lightly on the edge of the spool. With the other hand take hold of the end of the line and pull as hard as possible. The clutch should now slip. If it does so before reaching maximum pressure the clutch is set too loose, while if the line breaks the clutch is too tight. With the spool set correctly it is impossible for a running fish to break the line, providing, that is, that everything else is done properly.

When a fish is hooked, immediately apply one finger of the rod hand to the rim of the

*(Above) This angler has hooked a barbel while fishing the River Kennet, a tributary of the Thames, in Berkshire. He is applying vertical pressure to the fish to prevent it from taking refuge in the weeds.*
*(Left) Netting another Kennet barbel. The landing net is ready under the fish, which, played out and rolling on the surface, is drawn gently over it. The rod is held high to avoid tangling with the fish.*

spool. In this way, when the rod is held at an angle of between 15 and 30 degrees to the vertical, maximum pressure is brought to bear on the running fish. The line will be almost at breaking point but, if the spool is set right, will not actually break.

**Pumping and netting**

When the fish stops its run, line is recovered by the process known as 'pumping'. For this, assuming the fish is stationary or nearly so, turn the reel handle, at the same time lowering the rod until the tip is at waist level. Then increase finger pressure on the spool rim and bring up the rod to its former position. Repeat the process until the fish runs again or is ready for the net.

It is now—at the point of netting—that most mistakes occur. When the fish is played out, the net is placed in the water, ready for use. With the fish wallowing or lying on the surface, bring the rod tip down to waist level once more, and, with the other hand holding the net, draw the rod back over the shoulder, maintaining strong pressure on the spool all the time. Steady the net about 12in below the surface and draw the fish towards and over it. Do not lift until the fish is over the net.

Sometimes, as the fish is drawn to the net, it will suddenly find new strength and either swim off or change direction. Let it do so for it is unlikely to take line. Keep the finger on the spool and allow the rod to take the strain. Two important points must be remembered: first, as the fish comes over the net make sure that the rod is no farther back than 30 degrees to the vertical. If it is, you will not have complete control over the fish. Secondly, never move the net towards the fish but keep it still and pull the fish over it.

The problem of the fish that runs into weed is one that requires swift action. Some fish, especially roach and chub, however quick one's reflexes are, will manage to transfer the hook to the weed and escape. Other species, barbel and tench in particular, are not so clever and must be extracted from the weed by 'pumping'. As soon as the fish reaches the weed, use the technique de-

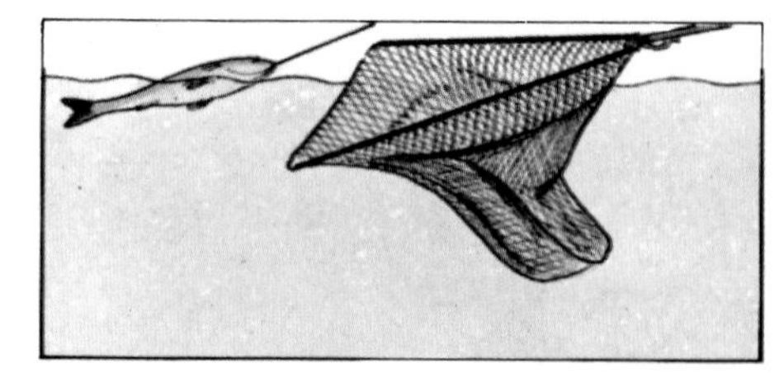

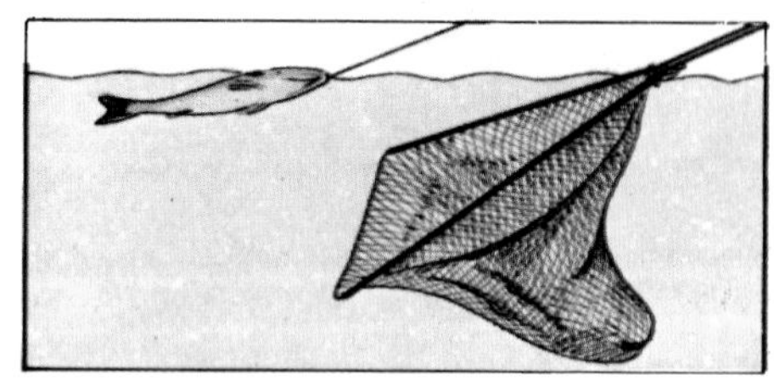

P. H. Ward/Natural Science Photos

*(Top) A common mistake made in netting a fish. The net is held too high and is used to scoop at the fish. (Above) The net should be sunk beneath the fish and ready to receive it as it is drawn in exhausted. (Left) Peter Stone unhooks a 5¼lb tench. He leaves it in the landing net to avoid unnecessary handling. If the fish is to be set free at once the landing net can simply be lowered into the water again.*

P. H. Ward· Natural Science Photos

*(Left) When a fish heads strongly away to the right or the left, opposite side-strain must be applied. This will give the rod a chance to work most efficiently. (Below) Holding his rod high to bring the fish close, a Southern matchman prepares to net it. It is important to put the net carefully into the water well before the fish is drawn near.*

scribed earlier, repeating the process without stopping and keeping the finger down hard on the spool. Once the fish starts to move, keep control of the situation with continual pumping, as this will, in the majority of cases, get the fish out of the weed. This technique relies on knowing how much pressure your line will take—something that only comes with experience, and not normally before the loss of a fish.

**Coaxing a fish through weed**

When a fish runs into streamer weed *(Ranunculus)*, you must get downstream of it in order to extract it. Trying to coax a fish through this weed from upstream only worsens the situation. Although fish of all sorts can be forced out of 'cabbages' (underwater lilies) or various types of weedy growth, it is extremely difficult to move a fish from a cultivated lily patch by 'pumping' and many battles have been lost here.

Playing a fish on a centrepin reel is much easier than on a fixed-spool. Immediately the fish is hooked, turn the handle slowly, keeping the line tight. If the fish runs let it take line, but rest the palm of the hand lightly against the rim of the reel, facing upwards. In this way, by applying a light but insistent pressure, the fish has to fight for every inch of line but will not break it.

To sum up, when playing a big fish the important thing is not to allow the fish to take control. If this happens then it is likely to be lost. Do not hurry the playing—a sure

Bill Howes

way of losing the fish—yet do not drag it out longer than necessary, for the object, it must be remembered, is to get the catch on the bank. Maintain a steady pressure and give line only when you have to. When the fish tires or stops, even if only momentarily, take advantage and retrieve line.

Normally, one holds the rod pointing upwards, as described, but remember that fish do turn sideways and, when they do, sideways pressure must be applied. Bring the rod down to the horizontal position and keep it there while playing the fish running to the side.

# Conservation

There are two ways in which coarse fishing enthusiasts commonly approach the problem of conservation: the first is by insisting that all fish they catch should be returned to the water unharmed; the second is by encouraging restocking. Yet while the sentiments are praiseworthy, neither of these practices is necessarily the best way for anglers to conserve their fishing.

**Problem for the experts**

The first difficulty is that most fishing waters in this country are vastly overstocked, rather than being short of fish. Adding fish to already crowded waters will only lead to stunted adults, mature fish which have stopped growing due to overcrowding and shortage of food, while only a few inches in length instead of a healthy 7in or 8in. Assessing the correct fish population for a fishing water is a problem for the experts. Fish will be examined, weighed, their age determined by 'reading' the scales, to decide whether the fish is healthy and of average weight and size for its age. It is vital not to attempt restocking indiscriminately.

The second difficulty for the angler lies in deciding when a fish should be returned to the water. Many anglers will at some time have returned a damaged or exhausted fish to the water knowing that its chances of survival were slim. So it is important to know how fish are affected by being caught and how they can best be saved from unnecessary harm.

If fish are returned to the water immediately after they have been unhooked they will have a far better chance of survival than if they are given the usual treatment meted out to them by anglers. During a match, and when 'pleasure' fishing also, a large fish is played out after being hooked until it can be brought to the landing net. By then it is weakened to the point of exhaustion.

Smaller fish are held in the hand while the hook is removed. They are then thrown or dropped into the mouth of the keepnet. Their suffering continues, for every time another fish is dropped in they receive a further shock and their resistance is lowered a little more. Finally they are in a very poor condition and would die in a few hours if not soon released.

At the end of the fishing period the keepnet is hauled out of the water and dumped on the bank. If it is a match the fish

will be put in a metal basket to be weighed, and finally released back into the water.

By this time they have probably lost several scales and are in a state of neurosis. If they survive, it will take all of the ensuing year's growth to replace the lost scales, and if the fishery is overstocked, survival will be very doubtful. It would be better to kill them and take them away from the water.

Anglers can help in other ways: for example, if they were to bring in their fish on tackle of adequate strength in the shortest possible time, unhook them in the landing net and return them immediately to the water, little harm would be done to the fish,

*Match fishermen cause fish suffering by throwing them into the keepnet. All too often this is overcrowded and shock increases each time a fish is added. In this condition they could die within hours but before being freed, with many fish irreparably harmed, the catch is weighed in a harsh metal basket.*

Bill Howes

P H Ward/Natural Science Photos

*Rough handling during a fishing match has damaged the dorsal and caudal fins of this common bream.*

particularly if barbless hooks were used.

On the Continent, matches are decided by length and not weight. As it is caught, each fish is measured and noted, then returned immediately to the water. A statutory size limit is observed and the events are closely supervised by stewards. The advantages of this system are that the fish are only handled momentarily while being measured, and that they do not spend hours confined in a keepnet with many other struggling fish. A further advantage is the avoidance of the fishes' breathing in of harmful mud stirred up by their struggles in a keepnet left in muddy water close to the bank.

**Needed—a balanced population**

Conservation is best achieved by maintaining a fish population at the correct level for the water. Expert advice will provide this figure. A balanced fish population will allow the fish to grow to their proper size and provide good sport for the angler.

Another way of maintaining stocks is to ensure that they have everything they need for their well-being. Fish need an adequate and continuous food supply, both when they are small and when adult. They need cover into which they can dive when danger threatens, and they require spawning facilities.

Weedbeds provide all of these requirements and on all fisheries there should be plenty of weeds because this is where the fish's food lives. Fish need them for cover and in which to shed their spawn.

**Reason for the close season**

Weeds should never be cut until the fish have finished spawning, otherwise much of their food and a great many of their offspring will perish. Spawning is the most important stage in the yearly cycle and fish should be protected by a close season which covers not only their spawning time, but a period before and afterwards. The period before spawning is the most important. If handled in any way at this critical time, fish will shed scales. Their need for protection from disturbance at this time should be impressed on the young or inexperienced angler.

During the actual spawning period, fish seldom feed, being interested only in procreation. Afterwards they clean themselves and begin to feed in order to regain condition and start growing again. They can be handled at this time, but should be treated with care because they are in a weakened condition and any severe shocks will prolong recovery and reduce growth.